Freud and the Ludic Mind

Freud and the Ludic Mind

New Ideas in Psychoanalysis

Francisco Lafaiete Lopes

It turns out that bliss—second-by-second joy and gratitude at the gift of being alive, conscious—lies on the other side of crushing, crushing boredom.

DAVID FOSTER WALLACE, *The Pale King*

Boredom is not the disease of having nothing to do, but the worse disease of feeling that nothing is worth doing.

FERNANDO PESSOA, *The Book of Disquiet*

IPBOOKS.net
International Psychoanalytic Books

International Psychoanalytic Books (IPBooks)
New York • http://www.IPBooks.net

Freud and the Ludic Mind: New Ideas in Psychoanalysis

Published by IPBooks, Queens, NY
Online at: www.IPBooks.net

ISBN: 978-1-956864-30-4

Contents

Preface

What might have happened to psychoanalytic theory if, instead of shifting his research towards the death-instinct hypothesis, Freud had decided to explore the alternative of a *Spieltrieb*, which he mentioned in his 1915 paper on instincts and their vicissitudes?

I understand the *Spieltrieb* idea as a "ludic drive," an impulse for living an active life, in which I am all the time doing, feeling, talking, listening, or imagining something. The hypothesis is that this drive results from an innate intolerance to inactivity. This assumption produces a new theory of the mind that, in a peaceful and non-exclusive way, incorporates many recent developments of psychoanalysis into the classical Freudian construction, opening up a wide range of new possibilities for clinical activity.

I wrote this book thinking of readers with a psychoanalytic background. But since other readers might also be interested, I summarize some of its main conclusions here, trying to avoid academic technicalities.

1) Since we may find a ludic drive impulse in man and in some other animal species, we may conclude it must have some survival value for those species in which it is present.
2) In these species, the young play, producing an adult that is smarter and better equipped to survive and perpetuate the species.
3) Since this intolerance of lack of activity is extreme in young human children, they want to dedicate themselves all the time to playful activities (of a predominantly motor nature).

4) An overwhelming sense of boredom arises if this craving for activity and stimulation cannot be satisfied.

5) Species in which we find this ludic impulse are only a tiny part of the total of more than one million animal species currently in existence. Prolonged confinement produces observable signs of boredom in these ludic animals, such as agitation, anger, depression, and apathy.

6) The intensity of suffering in human individuals in solitary confinement is known, resulting from lack of stimuli, darkness, total silence, lack of perceptions, and absence of associative activities: in other words, from a significant restriction of the ludic impulse.

7) From the sixth month of life, the human child is motivated by the ludic impulse to explore a world of infinite possibilities that become accessible as their physical capabilities increase. But reality soon demonstrates its danger as well. Minor accidents and falls are greatly amplified in the child's mind, teaching it that it needs the help of adults to feel safe in these new endeavors. Typically, the mother or other caregivers begin to function as "support objects" for the child's ludic motivation.

8) Over time, children learn to use adults not just as sources of security for their ludic motivations, but also as an exclusive audience for encouragement, applause, and approval. This becomes evident when children dress up as princesses or superheroes in their play. At this point, adults become objects of support not only for ludic motivations (*i.e.*, for the urge to be active) but also for "narcissistic ludic motivations" (*i.e.*, for the urge to be active while being admired and approved by relevant adults). A combination of these two types of support will be essential for healthy mental development.

9) Sometimes adults do not function well as support objects and become "objects of frustration." This frustration sometimes results not from actual support failures, but from unconscious fantasies that can also

produce ambiguous, love-hate relationships with significant adults. Consequently, mental development can be affected by the emergence of significant pathologies.

10) Eventually, young people unconsciously discover that a "ludic identification" increases their chances of getting an adequate amount of support. By imitating relevant adults in different dimensions of behavior, these young people manage to generate attention and sympathy, resulting in greater availability and interest in those adults in supporting their ludic activities.

11) Ultimately, however, neither support objects nor ludic identifications are sufficient to build a properly structured adult. If personality development is interrupted at this point, the consequences can be traumatic, with potent inhibition of the ludic impulse and the development of a personality chronically deficient in its capacity for healthy living. The individual remains indefinitely dependent on the unsatisfactory support mechanisms that characterized his childhood, even when he has reached maturity. Symptoms such as low self-confidence, vague depression, lack of initiative and enthusiasm for work, hypochondria, shyness, and significant vulnerability to shameful situations may arise.

12) To avoid this, a delicate process of mental transformation must take place, whereby the individual begins to produce on his own the same results previously obtained through ludic support objects and ludic identifications. When this works well, the mental apparatus will have incorporated a "support superego," which is a precondition for a satisfactory life in maturity, a life full of joy and self-confidence.

13) The support superego should not be confused with the traditional Freudian superego. The Freudian superego represses or controls sexual and aggressive impulses; the support superego sustains ludic impulses.

14) The hypothesis of an innate aggressive drive, which Freud saw as resulting from a mysterious death instinct, is unnecessary. More relevant is to note that there are different types of aggressive behavior, as we can see in the study of animal behavior. When a predator tries to kill its prey, we have "assertive aggression." The hunter's activity is not driven by anger and clearly has a ludic element, a pleasure to perform a task well. I see here just the action of a ludic impulse combined with the self-preservative motivation to obtain food.

15) The case is different when the predator encounters a resistant prey that desperately fights to defend itself, counter-attacking its hunter. This reaction of the prey under attack, driven by a combination of anger, panic, and rage is what we call "impulsive aggression."

16) This aggressiveness, however, is not an impulse similar in nature to the sexual or ludic impulses that result from specific drives. It is just a reflex triggered by an excessively high level of discomfort/stress resulting from the approach of some potentially threatening animal.

17) We can easily carry these observations about animal aggression over to human aggression. Assertive aggression results only from a ludic impulse, as when a fighter pilot seeks to shoot down an enemy in aerial combat. On the other hand, impulsive aggression results from an aggressive mobilization produced by an excessively high level of discomfort/stress. It is a reflex triggered when the discomfort reaches an intensity above a critical value.

18) Aggressive mobilization may result from a perception of fear. It can also result from irritation or rancor produced by the unwelcome presence of a stranger or from the action of someone or something that harms the satisfaction of some instinctive impulse, be it self-preservative, sexual, or even ludic. Internal conditions can also act to produce discomfort and aggression. The angry cry of the human baby is the first manifestation of impulsive aggression in our lives.

19) The final conclusion is that human behavior results from the interaction between self-preservative impulses (such as the desire to satisfy hunger or urinate), sexual impulses, ludic impulses, and reflexes, such as impulsive aggression. Psychoanalytic therapy must consider all these different dimensions of human motivation.

20) By following the Freudian tradition of stressing the role of drives in human motivation, I may give the impression of contesting the current tendency in psychoanalytic literature to emphasize the role of relationships. I believe, however, that this is a false dichotomy, as we can easily integrate these two aspects of the human condition into a single theoretical framework.

Since the production of this book has occupied me for more than a decade, I want to thank family and friends for their enormous tolerance towards my obsessive dedication to this project. I am also grateful for the generous attention of psychoanalysts Osmar Salles, Renato Barauna, and Jurandir Freire Costa, and for the valuable editorial support of Cynthia Azevedo, Claudio Rothmuller, and Sergio Pugliese.

Introduction

In his essay "On Being Bored," Adam Phillips (1993) pointed out that children ask the following question with persistent regularity: "What are we going to do now?" Breuer, in the book on hysteria with Freud (1895), argued that man is intrinsically intolerant to inactivity and the absence of sensory stimuli. In a paper on the psychology of boredom, Fenichel (1934) also mentions this phenomenon of a craving for stimulation. These are just some examples, among many others, that corroborate the central thesis of this book: humans are motivated by a ludic drive, a biological urge to be active that produces intolerance to inactivity and boredom. It can explain why people engage in ludic activities not motivated by sex, aggression, or self-preservative needs.

Freud did mention the possibility of this drive. Still, he did not pursue it, sticking to his "mythology" of Eros and Thanatos, which assumed both a loosely defined sexual drive, the libido, and an aggressive-destructive drive fueled by a death instinct. In this book, I want to go back to Freud's drive approach and pursue the instigating idea of a ludic drive. We will see it allows the construction of a modernized version of Freudian metapsychology that, by borrowing some developments from more recent schools of psychoanalysis, produces new theoretical ideas and exciting clinical insights.

James Strachey, Freud's English editor, translated *Spieltrieb* as "instinct of play." Indeed, children's play is an example of ludic activity, yet I do not use the term "play drive" because I have in mind a broader concept. As pointed out by historian Johan Huizinga in his *Homo Ludens* (1944, ch. II), the word

1

"play" is full of meaning nuances in different languages. He even created a new Dutch adjective, *ludiek*, similar to the English "ludic." Mielicka-Pawowska (2016) notes it has now become a vogue word in Netherland's politics, usually understood as playful in form, but also relating to serious matters or serious intents.

There is a natural tendency to associate the term "ludic activities" with children's play. Take, for example, my copy of Winnicott's influential *Playing and Reality* (1971). It has a front cover full of toys and baby pictures. It seems to suggest that the book deals with children's play and games, but there is much more there. For example, it argues there is as much of a creative ludic impulse when an artist produces his masterpiece as when anyone—baby, child, adolescent, or adult—does anything deliberately in a healthy way. It is present in the moment-by-moment living of a paralyzed backward child who still enjoys daydreaming, and also in the inspiration of a brilliant architect who suddenly finds what he wants to construct. It is clear Winnicott was not just discussing children's play activities. He was thinking on the much broader notion of ludic activities. This book argues that these activities are motivated by the ludic drive, a key element in human mental processing.

PART I. REVISITING FREUD

1. On the Fragmentation of Psychoanalysis

Freud presented a final version of his theory of mind in *An Outline of Psychoanalysis* (1940a). It had a tripartite mental apparatus (id, ego, and superego) processing psychic energy, the notion of instinctual impulses or drives as fundamental determinants of human motivation and behavior, and a concept of psychic qualities, identifying mental processes and memory content as conscious or unconscious. At this final stage of his long career, after some trial and error, his thought had evolved to the assumption of two basic (or primal) drives, a broadly defined sexual libido, and a destructive impulse.

Eight decades later, a wide diversity of schools has replaced this basic Freudian model. Greenberg (2012) wrote that contemporary psychoanalysis has come to a new "era of pluralism" in which there is neither a single dominant theoretical perspective nor a "mainstream" organizational structure. But Goldberg (2012) sees a sectarian atmosphere and a terrain fraught of competing theories, in which no school has proved itself superior to the others. There is also a substantial shift of interest towards clinical models with very modest pretensions of theoretical certainty and technical efficacy.

The existence of alternative explanatory systems is now a reality taken for granted. Diversity may, of course, be beneficial when it reflects a rapid movement of intellectual progress, but excessive fragmentation may also be a problematic symptom when it constrains communication channels between increasingly isolated schools. It has obvious negative consequences for clinical work. Today, the typical analyst is either a faithful adherent to one of the schools, drastically rejecting all others, or he may do as proposed by Alexis Johnson (2019, p. 1). After seeing that the big thinkers disagree profoundly and often, he decided to take the fragmentation lightly and use some personal *ad-hoc* criteria for finding a better fit for some clients in one school and some in another.

We may see that these competing schools are of two different types. A few older ones preserve the original Freudian drive model and just add some new features. For example, ego psychology adds a new conflict-free area to the psychic apparatus. Melanie Klein and some of her disciples add a new inner world of good and bad objects and the notions of paranoid-schizoid and depressive positions. However, some new schools make a more decisive rupture by moving away from the Freudian notion of instinctual impulses or drives as the foundation of human motivation.

For Freud, there was never any doubt about the role of drives. The mind results from something innate that emerges from within the organism. But for the new relational theories, the mind results from social interactions. They point to clinical activity showing the critical role of human relations in both adults' and children's psychic lives. Hence, the solution is to shift from the Freudian emphasis on impulse repression into a new focus on these relationships that sustain mental health.

But what strikes most is that none of the new relational schools attempted to preserve the core Freudian model while simultaneously changing and modernizing it. I suspect this may have resulted from some sort of totem phenomenon. The founder of the discipline has achieved a totem-like status, and its members seem more willing to get away from him than to commit the blasphemy of changing his work. Wallerstein (2006, p. 702) points to this historic mythic relationship as a fantasied continuing process. Kohut (1985, p. 178) notes how difficult it is for the psychoanalytic community to overcome its idealization of Freud's work.

Hence, new theoretical elaborations should never attempt to correct or improve the original Freudian construction. Psychoanalysis still renders ceremonial worship, despite no longer believing in its usefulness for theory development or clinical work. Nowadays, young analysts graduate first in Freudian theory only to "unlearn" it later. Freud himself was concerned with avoiding any idealization of his work. He claimed to be ready "to admit the imperfections of his understanding, to learn new things, and to alter his methods in any way to improve them." (Freud, 1919, p. 105) However, we know that a totem does not depend on the will of its originator, as it is a cultural construction of its descendants.

This book follows a different, uncharted path. It takes the psychoanalytic theory of mind back to where Freud left it in 1940, and from there, tries to build an improved and modernized version with the introduction of the ludic drive. The result is a metapsychology that merges ideas from Freud and modern authors to produce unexpected and exciting results. This new model of the mind will perhaps help attenuate the present state of widespread fragmentation in psychoanalysis.

2. A New Path

This book proposes two main innovations to the classic Freudian model. First, it explains the mind's functioning as a result not of energy flows, but of information processing. Second, it makes a profound overhaul of drive theory, assuming a new ludic drive complementary to the traditional set of drives. It also posits there is a direct connection between drives and homeostasis, and it disavows the aggressive drive, showing it is always a case of either a ludic drive or a reflex.

The first main innovation is to use the concept of information to understand the working of the mental apparatus. For Freud, the mind was an energy processor, but this notion produced enormous conceptual difficulties. It forced psychoanalysis to carry out what Sandler (1981) saw as intellectual contortions. In Freud's energetic model, it was difficult to find satisfactory explanations for concepts such as memory or repression, to name a few. If the mind processes energy, the basic principle of energy conservation engenders significant complications. Indeed, hostility toward Freudian metapsychology in the early 1970s may have resulted less from the notion of "drive" than from the notion of "psychic energy."

I propose to replace psychic energy with information.[1] The mind is conceived as an information processor, not an energy processor, although

---

1 Gleick (2001) has a good survey of the historical development of the concept of information. Nobel Prize Winner Paul Nurse (2020) argues that "information processing permeates all aspects of life" (p.85) and that "concepts based on information processing are essential to understanding how life works" (p.89).

brain functioning will still require some metabolic energy. This notion has been adopted by cognitive psychology and neuroscience in the last sixty years, and there is no reason why it should not be used in psychoanalysis.[2] With an information approach, many ideas become more straightforward and precise.

The second main innovation of the book is a profound overhaul of drive theory. That may seem strange, as psychoanalysis has almost utterly forsaken this concept, moving towards relational approaches. This migration is happening at the same time when neuroscience seems to be rediscovering the drive. For example, in *The Age of Insight* (2012, p. 47), Eric Kandel states that Freud's fundamental ideas have held up well and are now central to modern neuroscience. One is that most of our mental life occurs unconsciously. Another is that mental illness often consists only of extreme and exaggerated forms of normal mental processes. And the third is that sexual and aggressive behavior results from drives of biological origin that are already evident early in life.

Another example of how neuroscience is rediscovering the drive is the 1999 book by Donald Pfaff with the suggestive title *Drive: Neurobiological and Molecular Mechanisms of Sexual Motivation*. Pfaff examines in-depth the biological mechanisms of the sexual drive, showing that many of Freud's hypotheses (such as the concept of erotogenic zones) have sound biological foundations.

For Freud, the concept of drive has always been the foundation of the theory of mind. Freudian tradition teaches that, at a level close to experience, human behavior results from three kinds of instinctual impulses: the sexual drive, the aggressive drive, and the set of self-preservative drives, namely hunger, thirst, and others. I will follow Franz Alexander's (1951) understanding that the pleasure principle concerns the organism's homeostatic balance. Hence,

---

2 See, for example, Gardner (1985) on cognitive psychology and Pfaff (2006) or Kandel (2006) on neuroscience.

drives result from homeostasis, which is the primary regulatory principle of animal behavior. It is a hypothesis of fundamental importance as it provides a solid biological foundation for the drive concept. The notion of homeostatic design, advanced by Antonio Damasio (2010), explains the differences in drive repertoire between animal species.

I propose the hypothesis of a ludic drive, which motivates people to engage in ludic activities, that is, activities that do not result from sexual, aggressive, or self-preservative motivations. Children's play is a ludic activity, but not all ludic activities are children's play. All ludic activities aim to produce a particular kind of pleasure that has been described, in a not accurate way, as high self-esteem, or just joy.

This notion of a ludic drive has been latent in much of psychoanalytic literature, sometimes almost explicit, as in Hendrick's pioneering work, and sometimes implicit, as in Winnicott and Kohut. One could say that even Hartmann toyed with the idea when he emphasized the role of Bühler's pleasure in functioning (*Funktionslust*) in the process of adaptation. Freud's contemporary Karl Groos advanced the notion of an instinctive ludic impulse in both animals and man. His work gave rise to a field in biology dedicated to animal play, with substantial research output.

Freud even quoted Groos, but eventually dismissed the idea of a "play drive" (*Spieltrieb*) as superficial, preferring to stick to more fundamental primal impulses (Ürtriebe). Around 1915 he was arguing these were the sexual and self-preservative drives, but by 1920 he had accepted Jung's suggestion of merging sexual and self-preservative motivations into a single drive. From then on, he assumed an expanded libido as operating in conjunction with a new aggressive drive that results from a death instinct. I wonder what would have happened to the evolution of psychoanalysis if Freud had taken the possibility of the ludic drive more seriously.

This book is organized in seven parts. After this initial introductory part, Part II introduces a new Ludic Drive Psychology. Starting from Breuer's (1895) observation about our intrinsic intolerance to inactivity and discussions about boredom in psychoanalysis and in the literature in general, one can demonstrate the biological plausibility of the ludic drive, which results from the hypothesis that a desire for stimulation and activity is part of man's homeostatic design. The analysis of the vicissitudes (or destinies, "*Schicksale*") of the ludic drive leads to the fundamental new concepts of support object, ludic identification, and support superego. The support superego is not the same thing as the Freudian superego and results from a Kohutian process of transmuting internalization. Its satisfactory structuring is an essential requirement for a healthy and joyful life.

There follows a discussion of how ludic drive psychology relates to Kohut's self psychology and to some of Winnicott's ideas, including what I consider a more accurate interpretation of the Kohutian notion of the self as a superordinate configuration. A final chapter in this part shows that the apparent conflict between drive and relational approaches to psychoanalysis is a false dichotomy, for I have shown in this book how to bring together these two aspects of human behavior into a single theoretical framework. The chapter also discusses Bowlby's contributions, showing that his attachment theory can be considered as complementary to the drive formulation of the Freudian model. Nevertheless, Bowlby had the great merit of showing that psychoanalysis needs to consider both reflex (Freud's *Reiz*) and drive in a complete explanation of the human mind.

Part III deals with the riddle of aggression, one of the most complex problems in psychoanalysis, also analyzing the work of Melanie Klein. It shows how Freud's thought evolved into the "mythology" of Eros and Thanatos, which was never fully accepted by the psychoanalytic community. Konrad Lorenz's study of animal aggression suggests alternative paths. In the typical fight between predator and resistant prey, the first is motivated by assertive aggression, which is not a drive and results only from hunger and the ludic drive. On the other hand, there is a critical reaction reflex when a resistant prey desperately fights for survival. It is a combination of fear, despair and anger that produces impulsive aggressive behavior. We must always keep in mind the difference between assertive aggression and impulsive aggression. There is also an essential difference between destructive and non-destructive aggression.

These ideas can be transposed to humans without the need for the death instinct hypothesis. There is assertive aggression, resulting from the ludic drive, and impulsive aggression, which is a reflex, not a drive. Therefore, there is no aggressive drive. An aggressive mobilization is triggered when an indicator of discomfort or stress reaches an intensity above some critical threshold value. The first manifestation of this in humans is the fierce crying of newborn babies. Destructive aggression is not innate, as only relatively grown children can acquire it through ludic activities. This part of the book also discusses what becomes of Melanie Klein's work when we substitute psychic energy for information and deny the existence of an innate aggressive-destructive drive.

Part IV is a survey of psychoanalytic literature showing that the notion of a ludic drive was already present, although sometimes implicitly, in the works of Freud, Hendrick, Groos, Piaget, Winnicott, and Kohut. The first mention of a *Spieltrieb* occurred in Schiller (1795), who seems to have been an author with a strong influence on both Freud and Groos. This part of the book also discusses some criticisms of psychoanalytic literature that have tried to reduce the ludic drive to a phenomenon of sublimation.

Part V shows how we must reformulate the Freudian mental apparatus when we use information instead of energy. The concepts of homeostasis and homeostatic design are used to explain drives as homeostatic impulses. Other important ideas, such as pfunctions, memory organization, associative keys, repression, object, and self-representation, are also dealt with.

Part VI discusses some other themes of the Freudian tradition. It deals first with the Freudian superego and the notions of reality testing and fantasy.

Then it discusses automatism, a concept that has virtually disappeared in modern psychoanalysis, despite being fundamental for understanding the repression of mental processes and the formation of neurotic symptoms. It closes with a discussion of the role of the elaboration process in the therapy of neuroses and the complex problem of achieving complete elimination of automated symptoms.

Part VII has a short chapter on "the practical task," a title I borrowed from Freud's posthumous *Outline of Psychoanalysis*. It deals only briefly with clinical applications. The book ends with two appendices. Appendix A discusses Freud's dream theory, a construction of striking ingenuity that still seems to be the best explanation for some phenomena in the deepest, unconscious layers of mind. Appendix B deals with the scientific status of psychoanalysis. Can a psychoanalytic theory of the mind be scientific? The answer is that it can be a non-experimental science, just like economics, astronomy, meteorology, and others. But in the case of any science with a weak experimental side, it is essential to have a solid theoretical basis with well-defined concepts in logically consistent structures.

PART II. LUDIC DRIVE PSYCHOLOGY

3. Biological Foundations

Freud used to say that psychoanalysis need not understand the biological process that gives rise to any drive. Still, he reminded us that "all our provisional ideas in psychology will presumably someday be based on an organic substructure" (1915a, I p.71). Indeed, he always sought to demonstrate, albeit in broad sketches, the "biological plausibility" of the libido and the death instinct. Our challenge is to do the same for the ludic drive.

It is easy to understand the phylogenetic foundation of this drive. As emphasized by several authors, the prevalence of ludic behavior in nature suggests that this type of activity should have some survival value for the species in which it is present. Otherwise, natural selection would have eliminated it. Typically, an animal does not have resources available to spend on useless behavior, as it must survive in hostile environments, avoiding predators and natural hazards and competing with other animals for food and mating. But from Groos' pioneering work we have learned that early-life play produces a smarter adult, better equipped to survive and perpetuate his species. Yet we still need to explain the ontogenetic basis for ludic behavior: what motivates this type of activity in the case of any individual of the species.

Chapter 23 of Part V explains in detail how drives result from homeostatic demands. At this point, it is sufficient to note some examples. A nutrient's deficiency produces the sensation of hunger and the urge to eat. Similarly, a lack of fluids in the body creates the feeling of thirst and the urge to drink. Something analogous occurs with all self-preservative drives. In the case of sex, hormonal changes produce appetite and predisposition for this type of activity, and the consequence is the sexual drive (Pfaff, 1999). But what kind of homeostatic demand may underlie the motivation for ludic activities? In other words, what features of the homeostatic design of some species (including humans) are responsible for the emergence of a ludic impulse?

Breuer in 1895 provided a clue in his instigating theoretical chapter in the joint book with Freud on hysteria:

> When the waking brain has been quiescent for a considerable time... there arises a need and an urge for activity. Long motor quiescence creates a need for movement (compare the aimless running round of a caged animal) and if this need cannot be satisfied a distressing feeling sets in. Lack of sensory stimuli, darkness and complete silence become a torture; mental repose, lack of perceptions, ideas and associative activity produce the torment of boredom (Breuer & Freud, 1974, p. 272).

Breuer suggests that man has an intrinsic intolerance to inactivity and the absence of sensory stimuli. In the non-sleeping brain, prolonged rest creates a yearning for activity and stimulation. If this need cannot be satisfied, there arises a distressing feeling of discomfort, which may be associated with the "torment of boredom."

The same idea was brilliantly summarized by Adam Phillips when he noted that "children are not oracles, but they ask with persistent regularity the great existential question: what shall we do now"? (Phillips, 1993, p. 68). Look at a small child, say about three to five years old, being forced by parents to behave while sitting inactive at a restaurant table. It is inevitable the appearance of a diffuse restlessness that quickly turns into an active manifestation of irritation and rebellion, demonstrating unequivocally the torment of boredom mentioned by Breuer. Intolerance to inactivity is particularly strong in young children, and for this very reason, they wish to engage in ludic activities (predominantly sensorimotor) all the time. Adam

Phillips adds that every adult can undoubtedly remember the feeling of boredom at some points in childhood, as boredom punctuates any child's life.

Gordon Burghardt (2005), one of the leading researchers on animal play, suggests that the same argument holds for many animal species. His review of a large body of research in the area, particularly in Chapter 6, shows that play only happens in animals not subjected to severe stress and without food deficiency. It results from the combination of an adequate amount of metabolic energy (which should not be confused with Freud's mysterious mental energy) with an intrinsic demand for stimulation. This last factor, the inherent need for activity, is of crucial importance. It is what arouses the neurological behavior systems typical of each species, creating a susceptibility to boredom if left unattended.

Play activity occurs in only a small minority of the total of more than one million animal species existing on earth (Fagen, 1995). It can be found in many species of mammals, such as dogs, monkeys, cats or horses. It appears to be more frequent in animals with large brains in relation to total body mass (Fagen, 1981). It is not very clear whether it also occurs in some bird species, such as crows (Heinrich & Smolker, 1998), or reptiles, such as the turtle (Burghardt, 1998).

If Breuer and Burghardt are correct—as we want to assume—the homeostatic design of each of these species in which we observe ludic activities must include some degree of intrinsic intolerance to inactivity or absence of stimuli. Of course, intolerance can appear with differing intensities. For example, in the casual observation of domestic animals, we see that dogs seem far more intolerant to inactivity than cats. We could order species along a continuum, depending on their degree of intolerance to inactivity.

Take, for example, the comparison between homeostatic designs of a human and a reptile, say a lizard. The lizard, when it gets out of the egg, already looks and behaves like an adult. It does not need special care from other individuals of the same species, or a childhood phase to develop intelligence and acquire skills useful for survival. The resources it will successfully use throughout life are already there at birth. Indeed, its homeostatic design need not incorporate any inactivity intolerance. For it, any ludic activity would be just a waste of time and energy. If the lizard is not eating, sunning, having sex, or defending itself from outside threats, the best it can do is stay inert and sleep, saving energy.

On the other hand, the human baby is born too early with enormous fragility and is entirely dependent on maternal care. It is far from ready and needs a long time dedicated to ludic activities that will allow the development of his intelligence and the acquisition of skills useful for survival. The human-animal would not be viable without a ludic childhood. Therefore, his homeostatic design must include an active intolerance to inactivity, which reveals itself as a longing for stimuli and a great aversion to boredom.

Françoise Wemelsfelder (2003) and Marc Bekoff (2007) showed that prolonged confinement of animals of species with ludic activities produces observable signs of boredom. Drastically reducing opportunities for voluntary interaction with the environment produces agitation, anger, and ultimately, depression and apathy. A caged animal may react maniacally to the point of self-mutilation but eventually fails to look for things to do and falls into permanent lethargy. It is difficult to visit a zoo without realizing the chronic state of boredom in ludic animals kept in confined spaces.

In the human animal, as noted by Breuer, craving for stimulation and intolerance to inactivity are permanent throughout life. In an interesting article on the psychology of boredom (1934), Otto Fenichel also mentions the phenomenon of craving for stimulus. His starting point is the definition, attributed to Theodor Lipps (1903): boredom is a feeling of displeasure that results from the conflict between a need for intense mental activity and discontent with available stimuli or with an inability to be stimulated by them. However, his analysis is somewhat confusing, perhaps because there was no way to explain how yearning for stimulation arises in the context of the classic drive model, based solely on sex and aggression. The introduction of the ludic drive as consequence of the need for stimulation makes these facts much clearer. As indicated by Breuer, the torment of boredom is a consequence of an inhibition of the urge for activity, that is, inhibition of the ludic impulse. Boredom may result from absence or insufficiency of ludic activity.[3]

Adam Phillips (1993) notes that any child can explain that boredom results from having nothing to do. Stuart Grassian (1983; 2006) clearly shows the intensity of suffering in individuals in solitary confinement. Breuer explains that it results from a lack of stimulation, darkness, total silence, lack of perceptions, and associative activities: in other words, from the inhibition of any ludic activity.

Throughout history, many thinkers and philosophers have also noted the association between boredom and inactivity. In the Middle Ages, Church Fathers had already identified *acedia*, a Greek term meaning something like apathy or indifference, one of the worst sins. The acedia demon attacked the monks in the middle of the day, between the fourth and the eighth hour, producing the vice of annoyance. As the hermit Evagrius Ponticus wrote, the noon demon (*daemon meridianus*) first makes the day seem to pass very slowly, encouraging the monk to look out at the window continually. It makes him leave his cell for the sun, curious if any brothers are around. Next, he makes the monk dislike his life in that place and even the work of his hands. It brings to his mind the memory of his family and his old way of life, and uses all his evil to make him leave his cell and abandon his vocation.[4]

Blaise Pascal (*Pensées* & 201, *Ennui*) wrote that man finds nothing as intolerable as a state of complete rest without passion, occupation,

---

3 Alternative explanations for boredom by Svendsen (2005), Toohey (2011), or Eastwood *et al.* (2012) do not invalidate Breuer's thesis.

4 For more on this, see Wensel (2003), Sinkewicz (2003), or Toohey (2011).

amusement, or effort. He then feels his nullity, his loneliness, his emptiness. Soon he sees boredom, depression, resentment, and despair emerge from the depths of his soul. Nietzsche believed that boredom is the unpleasant calm of the soul that precedes creative acts. To escape boredom, man either work harder than necessary or invent play (Svendsen, 2005, pp. 58–59).

It seems clear that in man the ludic drive is the result of intolerance to inactivity that produces a yearning for stimulation. A deeper reflection, however, shows that we have two difficulties here. First, there is no doubt that children's play can satisfy this intolerance, since it is predominantly a sensorimotor activity, but what can we say about symbolic play? It is the most common ludic activity among adults and does not necessarily require physical exertion. We must admit that there is in man (and particularly in adult man) an intolerance to the absence of motor activity, but also, and perhaps predominantly, an intolerance to the lack of mental activity.

Hendrick (1942) noted that a young child, who is still primarily engaged in sensory-motor activity, could compulsively engage in the same pattern of physical movement without boredom. This behavior led some authors, including Freud himself, to think of a compulsion to repeat. In this case, the child loses interest in the activity only after becoming proficient in it, when it is incorporated into a repertoire of functional abilities. But this behavior is less common in a child who has already entered the symbolic phase, or in an adult. In this case, a repetitive game tends to become tedious if it does not introduce some variation or challenge or competition. The interest here is more in mental stimulation than in physical activity. Eventually, a more mature adult can fully satisfy his ludic needs by engaging in intellectual activities without any physical effort. These facts show that the ludic drive results from a desire for stimulation that can be achieved by physical and mental activities, with the latter becoming more present with the maturation of the individual.

Daniel N. Stern (2010, p. 21) mentions this phenomenon of "mental movement" as equivalent to physical activity. A thought process typically has a beginning, middle, and end, as if it were a "little journey" that develops over time. Often thought includes imaginary movements as when the individual prepares to perform a particular activity. Imagining a particular action's performance generates a pattern of brain activity that is close to that generated when the activity is performed. Jeannerod and Frak (1999) have proven this phenomenon of virtual movement experimentally.

A second difficulty with the notion of intolerance to inactivity is that yearning for stimulation does not necessarily lead only to ludic activity. Stimulation can also result, for example, from self-preservation activities (such as eating, running from dangers, or attacking enemies) or sexual activities. The solution to this difficulty is to assume that the ludic drive arises when the yearning for stimulation finds no discharge in other types of drives or reflexes.

In other words, an essential feature of human mental processing is intolerance to inactivity, broadly understood to include the absence of both motor and mental activity. This intolerance is also present, with different intensities, in other animal species in which we find ludic activities. Inactivity produces the discomfort of boredom. Of course, the individual can avoid this discomfort by engaging in various types of non-ludic activities, with different motivations arising from different homeostatic demands. But when these other demands are not present, ludic activity is the only alternative to avoid the discomfort of inactivity.

Freud mentions this phenomenon in his book on jokes. He notes that when we do not need our mental apparatus to obtain one of our "indispensable gratifications," we allow it to function to derive pleasure exclusively from its activity (Freud, 1905b, p. 113). When the mind is not busy attending to self-preservative, sexual, or aggressive impulses, it can still avoid boredom by enjoying its activity. Mental activity, by itself, can be a type of ludic activity. Interestingly, Freud added that he suspects that "in general, this is the condition that governs all aesthetic ideation." It is reminiscent of Groos' conclusions at the end of *The Play of Animals* (1896), but Freud acknowledged that he understood too little of aesthetics to try to expand this observation. It was Otto Rank (1932) who sought to analyze in-depth the possible connections between ludic activity, a creative impulse, and the arts.

In animals where ludic activities do not occur, the situation is different. Since inactivity intolerance is not present, the animal stays inactive if those other homeostatic demands are absent. It is the presence of the intolerance that gives rise to ludic activity, one that is neither motivated by self-preservation nor sexual interest nor any reflex. This analysis suggests that in activities motivated by self-preservation or sex, there may be a specific component of motivation and a generic component that results from intolerance to inactivity. Perhaps that is why it is often possible to observe in man what appears to be a fusion of ludic and non-ludic activities. For example, it happens in the erotic practices preliminary to regular intercourse, as well as in fetishes and sexual fantasies. Other examples are the rituals and artistic manifestations at meals, which should ultimately serve only to satisfy hunger. We also find it in pleasurable fantasies anticipating activities that effectively meet self-preservative or sexual needs. These fantasies produce a joy-type pleasure, which is characteristic of the ludic drive even before the ultimate pleasure resulting from the satisfaction of the specific motivation of the activity.

Here, one can note a similarity with Pfaff's (2006) notion that drive is the name given to a neural state that energizes and commands behavior and always consists of two components. There is a generic component of arousal common to all types of drives and a specific component, driven by motivations such as hunger, thirst, need for warmth, sex, or even play. Stern (2010) argues that this generic component is the fundamental force for all bodily or mental activities. Without the support of an arousal system, the individual cannot think, feel, perceive, or move voluntarily. However, our conception is that arousal is not an autonomous fundamental force and must always be activated by some drive resulting from homeostatic imbalance or by a reflex. Without it, there is no arousal, and the mind remains at rest.

4. Ludic Objects

Throughout life, the ludic drive interacts with the mental apparatus, and, as a result, essential transformations occur on both sides. By examining this process in detail, we can identify a typical trajectory for the development of ludic activities, which allows us to understand the mechanics of some pathologies. The aim (*Ziel*) of the ludic drive is to meet an internal demand for stimulus by producing a specific type of pleasure that we call joy. For this, it needs an object that Freud defines as "the thing in regard to which or through which the instinctual drive is able to achieve its aim." Our goal here is to understand the objects of the ludic drive and how they evolve throughout life.

Several authors noted the presence of the ludic impulse in the baby's behavior early in life. For Hendrick (1942), for example, the baby's sucking is not only an innate reflex but also an activity learned in practice, and this learning always has a ludic component. Melanie Klein (1952) drew attention to research by Merrill Middlemore (1941) on a set of "satisfied and sleepy infants," showing that by the fourth day of life, babies seemed to enjoy licking the nipple and rubbing it with lips as much as breastfeeding. One of these sleepy children started each feeding by playing with the nipple before sucking.

Winnicott (1988, p. 105), with the authority of his experience as a pediatrician, argued that the initial contact between the baby and the mother is a ludic activity. The baby, who discovered the nipple and who experienced a mother who always seems ready to offer her breast at the right time, does not seem to be in a hurry to start breastfeeding. There can be a period of playing and chewing the nipple. From the beginning, each baby has its mannerisms in this activity.

From the second or third month of life up to around six months, there is a phase in the baby's life called symbiotic by Margaret Mahler (this comes after a previous autistic phase). At this stage, child and mother seem to function as an integrated duo, with the child's rudimentary and not yet fully functional ego being complemented by the mother's synchronized care (rapport), in a kind of emotional symbiosis. At this stage, the baby's repertoire begins to include vocalizations and facial expressions in response to adult caregivers' behavior. From then on, mutual interactions emerge that acquire a face-to-face game' character and become the dominant play activity at the beginning of life.

Daniel N. Stern describes the phenomenon precisely and expressively, noting that the stimulus for the baby in this ludic activity comes from the mother's eyes, face, body, and voice. For the child, the adult represents a real sound-light show (2010, p. 107). In a typical situation, this ludic pleasure in the form of joy emerges from many sequences of mutual smiles, from many delightful exchanges and exciting games and rituals that punctuate the day (1990, p. 15). Often in routine breastfeeding activity, when a third or half of the bottle has already been drunk and hunger becomes less acute, the baby seems to prefer to seek a ludic stimulus rather than continuing to satisfy a less critical self-preservative drive. Many mothers must be careful during feedings, so as not to present a subtle invitation for this ludic and cheerful interaction. Even a small raise of the eyebrow or the suggestion of a smile can make the child want to stop eating and start a ludic interaction with her.

In the first six months of life, the ludic drive's main object is this "delicious interaction" with the mother. Some less exciting secondary objects result from solitary ludic activities, typically of a sensorimotor nature. Examples are the intense "exercises" for the development of motor coordination of arms and the grasping of the hands or the efforts to develop and control vocalization (babies' cries) or the activity of developing eye perception and synchronized head movements. Hendrick (1942, p. 42) recalls that the adaptation of hearing, sight, and touch organs to changing external conditions and the development of motor skills such as grasping, reaching, manipulating, turning, and sitting result from long periods of focused training. The memory registers of these experiences are objects in the Freudian sense because they are invested (or cathected) with ludic drive: associated with pleasant memories of moments of joy, which is the type of pleasure produced by this drive.

In Mahler's developmental scheme after the symbiotic phase, the child enters a period of separation-individuation in which his interest in solo ludic activities grows. She discovers that there is a world of infinite possibilities to be explored and realizes that her physical capacity only increases. Sensorimotor ludic activities dominate this phase, but now a phenomenon of the highest importance happens. The child also finds that this new world is as fascinating as it is dangerous. In his developing mind, small accidents and falls get colossal amplification. He immediately goes into open crying and searches for refuge in his mother's lap.

The child is surprised when realizing that the world always seems to be inventing new ways to hurt him and produce discomfort, every time frustrating his ambitions for magical control over the environment. The reality principle shows its hard face. The world is a permanent invitation for exploratory activities that satisfy the impulse of mastery, as put by Hendrick, but also threatening. This organism that tries to emerge into an active life is now in a situation of conflict. On one hand, the ludic drive pushes him towards the fascinating and pleasurable endeavor to explore and know the world. On the other hand, day-by-day experience quickly teaches him that reality can hurt and produce pain, something that the child has difficulty enduring. Intolerance to discomfort is a hallmark of early life. Every small child opens into screaming when suffering any setback. Consequently, the ego learns that it is necessary to repress manifestations of the ludic drive that can cause accidents and discomfort. It is as if it learns to suppress independent activities with a command such as *"never explore the world on your own."*

One must avoid the assumption that these small accidents and falls are not significant enough to produce permanent changes in the structure of the ego. Psychoanalysis has already taught us how the experiences of the first years of life are fundamental determinants of the adult personality. Melanie Klein convincingly showed how the child's mind seems to be populated by primitive fantasies, ghostly images, and anxiety-generating terrors. For the little boy of just more than two years old who starts to walk in an insecure way, but soon gets excited, gains speed, and ends up hitting his forehead against the wall, this little accident looks like purposeful strong aggression. For him, that wall had the intention of hurting him, and we do not know what other fantasies go through his little head at the time of pain.

Regardless of fantasies, however, there are also real risks in childhood. There is a large literature documenting the threats to survival that result from children's or young 'animals' play[5]. Ludic activities of young animals can easily result in broken bones, stretched muscles, ugly bites, and even natural death. Predators are known to have youngsters as their preferred targets. Harcourt (1991) reports that eighty-five percent of a seal-pup population was killed by sea lions while playing in shallow water. Serious and often fatal accidents with human children are also common, owing to lack of adequate care on the part of adults responsible for them.

But these risks do not completely inhibit the ludic impulse, and the child soon finds a compromise solution such as: *"Okay, it is dangerous to explore the world on my own, but there is no problem; my mom will be with me."* It is as if the rapport of the symbiotic period has extended into the next phase of separation and exploration. Mahler describes how this is visible at the beginning of this phase, around seven to eight months of life:

---

5 See references, for example, in Fagen (1981 and 1995) or Byers (1998).

All infants like to venture and stay just a bit of a distance away from the enveloping arms of the mother; as soon as they are motorically able to, they like to slide down from mother's lap, but they tend to remain or to crawl back and play as close as possible to mother's feet (Mahler, 1975, p. 55).

This checking-back-to-mother pattern becomes a hallmark of childhood. With the development of motor and cognitive abilities, it becomes possible to explore a much broader environment than the familiar world of the symbiotic phase. There is so much more to see, hear, or touch. The behavior of the mother will determine subtly how the young individual will conquer this new world. She remains at the center of the infantile universe, from which the child only gradually moves in search of a constantly expanding area of activity. Mahler describes the behavior of a seven-month-old baby:

He began to crawl and to pull himself up to a standing position. These new acquisitions of skill, however, brought him pain rather than pleasure. He fell frequently and cried hard after every fall. . . . With mother as an anchor, a center to his world, the frustrating part of the new experiences and explorations become once again manageable, and the pleasure part of exploring predominated (Mahler, 1975, p. 67).

With exploratory activities, children learn to perceive and recognize their mothers from a greater distance. The development of a distance contact capability is a crucial factor in this development phase:

For long periods of time, they happily occupied themselves with exploring the physical environment on their own, showing what Hendrick (1951) has described as pleasure in mastery (*Funktionslust* of K. Bühler). They returned to their mothers from time to time for emotional refueling. Both mothers accepted the gradual disengagement of their infant-toddlers and fostered their interest in practicing. They were emotionally available, according to the child's needs, and provided the kind of maternal sustenance necessary for optimal unfolding of the autonomous functions of the ego (Mahler, 1975, p. 68).

It is important to note that, unlike what happens in the symbiotic phase, the mother here does not participate directly in the ludic activity. Most of the time, her role is just that of an observer, but she can also cheer and stimulate, showing interest in the event. A good mother responds to the child's persistent urges by celebrating her small achievements in the ludic effort, and this mirroring, to use Kohut's term, seems to be of the utmost importance. The child has the feeling that he is being taken care of even when he is really on his own, as falls and occasional accidents do not let him forget. Even at these moments, however, the attention and quick help from adults in response to his crying reinforce his self-confidence, and the ludic activity is immediately resumed.

Mahler presents an inspiring quote from Kierkegaard (1846) that masterfully captures this everyday moment of human development:

The loving mother teaches her child to walk alone. She is far enough from him so that she cannot actually support him, but she holds out her arms to him. She imitates his movement, and if he totters, she swiftly bends as if to seize him, so that the child might believe that he is not walking alone... Her face beckons like a reward, an encouragement. Thus, the child walks alone, with his eyes fixed on this mother's face, not on the difficulties in his way. He... constantly strives towards the refuge in his mother's embrace, little suspecting that in the very same moment that he is emphasizing his need of her, he is proving that he can do without her, because he is walking alone (Mahler, 1975, pp. 72–73).

Winnicott (1958) also emphasizes the importance of this crucial experience of childhood, which is feeling alone in the mother's presence. It happens when a child in a ludic activity on his own is nevertheless sure he is being watched and taken care of by a trusted adult. In this case, "ego immaturity is naturally balanced by ego-support from the mother" (Winnicott, 1958, p. 32).

At this point, I must introduce the new concept of *support object*. In psychoanalysis, the notion of an object has to do with a property of a set of memory registers. Arlow (1980) wrote it is a set of sensory impressions, accompanied by a pleasurable feeling tone resulting from a specific instinctual impulse. They produce the mental representation of something associated with the gratification of a drive. I will examine this concept in-depth in Chapter 25 of Part V. Here, it is sufficient to fix the understanding of the object concept as a set of memory registers associated with the realization of some drive.

I also want to argue it is useful to differentiate between two related concepts: primary object and support object. Freud (1915) defined the object of a drive as the thing in regard to which, or through which, it is able to achieve its aim. The aim is always the satisfaction of the drive. We may define the primary object as the thing (or person) with which, or in which, the aim is achieved. On the other hand, the support object is something else through which this occurs; that is, something that participates in helping and making possible the accomplishment of the aim. The support object has the role of facilitating, reinforcing, or upholding the instinctual impulse. For example, in the case of playing alone mentioned by Winnicott, the mother functions as a support object for the child's ludic drive.

Take the case of the small child who needs the help of an adult to feed himself. The self-preservative impulse to eat aims to satisfy hunger; the primary object is food, but the adult functions as a support object. Or in the case of the newborn, the mother's breast functions as a support object for the self-preservative impulse to drink milk. Another example is the case of men who have sex with a woman only when stimulated by the visualization or handling of a fetish. The fetish can be, for example, a particular piece of woman's clothing. In this case, the sexual drive finds satisfaction in the sexual relationship with a woman, its primary object. But this occurs only if the fetish, the support object, is also present.

Interestingly, Freud (1927) explains fetishism with the notion of fear (or even horror) of castration. The fetish develops as a compensation for the child's fantasy that his father removed her mother's penis. This theory is quite controversial, since it considers neither the possibility of seduction by an adult nor a possible ludic dimension. However, Freud recognizes the fetish as something that supports the sexual drive, when he notes that fetishists rarely see this as a symptom of illness. On the contrary, they are quite happy with the way the fetish facilitates their erotic lives.

In the case of the ludic drive, a mother is a primary object in the symbiotic phase that becomes a support object in the separation-individuation phase. She ceases to be the exclusive focus of the "delicious interactions" and "exciting games and rituals" mentioned by Daniel N. Stern to become a kind of partner, helper, or source of support in the new adventure of exploring the world. Strictly speaking, the girl child does not want the adult to directly assume the exploratory activity, since this is the source of her ludic pleasure. What she wants and demands insistently, even with exhibitionist behavior, is an excited fan crowd and the validation of her competence in the face of new challenges. So, she is implicitly saying something like:

—*See mom, how I can do this now! See also this trick! See how I can somersault at the same time!*

From this exclusive attention and dedicated "support," the child will obtain the feeling of security and self-confidence needed to neutralize the repressive activity of the ego, allowing the impulse to flow unrestricted to new ludic activities.

Note that the term "mother" is being used here in a generic sense to designate any adult caregiver who can assume the role of support and mirroring. In traditional societies, grandparents, aunts, and people close to the family widely shared this role. Anthropologist Sara Hrdy (2009) goes so far as to claim that the remarkable development of humans, compared to other primates, has been a consequence of the introduction of this culture of sharing in the care of children. It is quite different from what happens to mothers among the great apes, such as chimpanzees, orangutans, or gorillas, who take care of their offspring alone and inseparably for long periods of months or years. For Hrdy, humans are different from other mammals in their ability to produce offspring that take a long time to mature, in a process where there is significant participation of other women in the group.

In contemporary human societies, we increasingly have the participation of daycare professionals. In these societies, there is also high pressure now for the father to actively participate in children's play. However, the most common are still short and intense episodes of dynamic interactions, such as when children are picked up and lifted upwards, experiencing a pleasant and exciting sensation of flying. The pioneering work of Michael Lamb (1981) found that typically in the United States, direct face-to-face contact between men and their babies occurs on average only for about an hour a day.

The father may not be very present in the child's daily life, but his presence, when it occurs, produces a strong impression of strength, competence, and wisdom, mixed with a calm and firm way of dealing with life. This sense of security and power radiated by the father figure is also sufficient to neutralize the ego's repressive tendency towards children's ludic activities. The child finds here another solution for compromising his ego, such as: "*Okay, it's dangerous to explore the world on my own, but that's okay; my father is strong and powerful and will help me if I need him."* In this way, the idealized image of the father as a powerful source of strength and security may also become a support object for the ludic impulse, at least as long as he is perceived as a reliable and reasonably available ally.

Therefore, the child can count on two different types of objects to support his ludic drive: on the one hand, the mother's cheering and mirroring and, on the other hand, the feeling of strength and security emanating from the idealized image of the father. Naturally, when we speak of mother and father in this context, we are only describing the most obvious situations. Strictly speaking, any adult trusted by the child can provide support via mirroring and idealization. The support by the mother or another female adult can mix moments of cheering and mirroring with alternative moments of infusion of calm, confidence, and security. The support of the father or another adult male can combine moments of infusion of calm, confidence, and protection with cheering and mirroring moments.

It is interesting to note that Freud himself, in an annex to his *Inhibitions, Symptoms, and Anxiety* of 1926, mentions a "protecting object" that has some resemblance with our support-object notion:

> Man seems not to have been endowed, or to have been endowed
> to only a very small degree, with an instinctive recognition of the
> dangers that threaten him from without. Small children are constantly
> doing things which endanger their lives, and that is precisely why they
> cannot afford to be without a protecting object (p. 104).

The attentive reader will notice a significant similarity between what I am proposing and some notions that we find in Kohut's work, such as *selfobject* or the bipolar configuration of the self. I confess I was tempted to adopt the name "selfobject" for this new concept of support object. I can also propose a third type of ludic support object, which occupies, as it were, an intermediate position in the "tension arc" between the extreme cases of support by mirroring and by idealization, or, as Kokut would say, between ambitions and ideals. It may be called twinship or alter-ego support, a kind of combination of the two other types. A support object of this type could result from the memory of interactions with someone in a similar phase in the life cycle that provides valuable support and encouragement. He works, so to say, as an engaged-fan crowd and allows for some idealization owing to his more considerable experience and the skills he already developed in ludic activities. He may be an older brother or a friend with similar interests or talents. He creates the feeling that a competent and reliable partner understands you. Kohut would say that each individual's specific configuration results from the dosages of the three types of ludic support he experienced in the formation of his personality. The result is a personal combination of ambitions, ideals, and skills.

5. Pfunctions and Ludic Identification

I introduce here briefly the idea of an information-processing function or pfunction. This concept will become more precise as it is used throughout the book, with a more in-depth discussion in Chapter 22 of Part V. It is not supposed to be a realistic idea, inspired by neuroscience. It's just a simplistic theoretical device, like what physicists call a toy model. It is just useful for understanding how human minds work.

A pfunction is a mental resource that allows the transformation of an information input into an information output. I assume the mental process has a set of pfunctions with different purposes at its disposal, as if it had access to a kind of catalogue or library.

For example, the pfunction "add two numbers and tell the result" transforms the information input represented by two numbers written on a sheet of paper, such as "3" and "5," into the information output produced by the oral statement: "the sum is eight." Or the biological information generated by your body that you have a deficiency of nutrients can be transformed by some of your pfunctions into the information output of a desire to eat. On the other hand, the information input, "I'm hungry" can be transformed by another pfunction or, more precisely, by a sequence of pfunctions, into the information output represented by a set of instructions to be executed by your body: get up from the computer, walk to the refrigerator, get an apple and eat. In this case, we can think that the final information output is the sequence of motor commands that allow you to eat the apple to eliminate your hunger.

In the set of pfunctions available to the mental process at any given moment, some are innate, and others resulted from life experience. The id pfunctions transform biological information into psychic information, in the form of sensations, drives, or emotions. The ego pfunctions transform psychic information into other psychic information. They have the challenging task of ensuring the organism's survival. They manage its social relationships and achieve the aims of the most pressing drives at any given moment. There are also superego pfunctions resulting from complex social and cultural processes.

Freud (1923b, II, p. 357) understood mental processing as a "displacement of mental energy that occurs somewhere within the apparatus as this energy proceeds on its path toward action." In my formulation, mental processing consists of the activation of a sequence of pfunctions. It transforms an information input from within the organism or its external environment into an information output that can be used, for example, for further processing or as a motor command.

Going back now to the discussion of ludic drive's vicissitudes, I note that the fact that the child needs to get his ludic drive supported from the beginning of life creates some problems. Without an adequate dose of support, the ludic impulse will be impaired or even aborted. If this happens, there will be potentially severe mental development consequences, producing pathologies such as chronic depression, low self-esteem, shyness, a propensity to shame, and hypochondria. A central existential problem of childhood is how to develop mechanisms that prevent excessive restraint of the ludic drive by the ego.

Beyond support objects, another solution is identification. Otto Rank (1924) wrote that human beings have an "enigmatic inclination to identification," which Freud (1933) described as the assimilation of one ego by another, with the result that the first behaves like the second in some ways and imitates it.[6] It can be seen frequently in everyday life. The boy has a particular interest in his father, indicates that he wants to be like him when he grows up, and follows him everywhere. If the father likes fishing and is a supporter of the X football team and loves walking with a specific type of sandals at home, the boy will be interested in fishing, support the same team, and wear the same type of sandals.

Freud never provided a satisfactory explanation for this phenomenon, and at one time even acknowledged that *"I myself am far from satisfied with these observations about identification"* (1933, p. 79). Identification requires incorporating a set of pfunctions into the ego, so that the desired parallelism with the father's behavior can occur, and this must necessarily be under the control of the pleasure principle. It is a particular case of the process of ego development that I discuss in detail later. Here, it is sufficient to acknowledge that the ego will incorporate a new pfunction only if it provides a pleasure gain (or a displeasure reduction) now or in the future. Hence it must ultimately contribute to the preservation of homeostatic balance. But what could be this pleasure gain resulting from identification?

One answer is that identification may be a process that helps support the ludic drive. As we saw above, even a good father usually has small participation in his child's day-to-day life. However, when it occurs, his presence can produce remarkable moments of wonder, with that natural demonstration of strength, skill, and wisdom. But the father's attention is deflected by and distributed among other family members, such as mother, siblings, other relatives, and friends. For the father's idealization to work effectively in supporting ludic activities, the child needs the maximum possible attention on his part. Identification is a logical way of trying to achieve this. It is as if the child wanted to say to the father, *"Look at me, you would like to see that I*

---

6   Other examples of perplexity with the concept are Widlocker (1985) and Etchegoyen (1985).

41

am like you, we like the same things, my ludic activities even remind you of your adult activities, I am a fan of the same football team, so please pay attention to me." We forget it, but a child's life is not easy when he/she is dramatically dependent on the supportive attention of relevant adults to access a tempting set of new ludic activities.

It is interesting to note that it is often the adult who first, unconsciously, induces ludic identification behaviors from his children, something that may occur in this and in all kinds of identification that we discuss next. It may result from subtle hints that somehow show that he or she also derives pleasure from being imitated by them. Of course, this may not be the case with an estranged, unresponsive adult, and it may explain why, in some cases, ludic identification does not arise or only arises in a rather feeble and distorted fashion. Scarce or deficient identifications may severely compromise the development of ludic support mechanisms.

Note that an alternative hypothesis, perhaps closer to the Freudian tradition, is that identification is the result of sexual motivation. The child identifies with the adult of the same sex in his family environment to capture the sexual interest of the adult of the opposite sex. The boy tries to look like his father to seduce his mother. This case, which could be called libidinal identification, is different from the ludic identification we are discussing here. In this book, when the term "identification" appears without a qualifier, it always means ludic identification.

Ludic identification by idealization is not limited to the father-son relationship. It can also happen with the girl who wants to study ballet because she knows that her mother, when young, dreamed of becoming a dancer. There is also the possibility of a type of identification that aims to get ludic support through mirroring. For example, a boy may be interested in card games because he realizes that the relevant adult also likes it. In general, adult games, such as sports games, are an excellent means of identification. They ensure that support of children's ludic drive will naturally result from adults' interest in the same type of activity. This is the case, for example, in a father who likes football, takes pleasure in watching his son's games, and participates with him in conversations about his performance, achievements, and difficulties.

Freud (1921) mentions another type of identification we can also associate with ludic drive support. It is what occurs as compensation for the loss of an object, as in mourning. Freud mentions the girl who lost her pet kitten and started to behave as if she were a cat herself. However, this does not seem to us to be a case of libidinal identification if the term is understood as related only to sexual interest. I do not believe that identification necessarily occurs in the case of the loss of a sexual object, but it can occur in the case of the loss of a ludic support object. It occurred in the case of the pet kitten mentioned by Freud and must also occur in most mourning situations. The loss of loved ones does not necessarily mean losing a sexual partner, since we also love our ludic support objects.

There are still two relevant types of ludic identification, which we could call perverse. One is the "false self" identification proposed by Winnicott (1960). It happens when the mother is not very receptive to a child's demands for mirroring and provides a very deficient volume of support. She is easily irritated by the chaotic spontaneity of the child's play and demands an early adaptation to her own needs and quirks. Typically, the mother requires that the child "behave" and develop his ludic activities within specific standards that she considers appropriate. The child realizes this, and his/her solution to obtain some supply of ludic support is full compliance with maternal demands. In other words, there is an identification with those "adequate" patterns of behavior. So *the child may grow to be just like a mother, nurse, aunt, brother, or whoever at the time dominates the scene*" (p. 146). This set of pfunctions, incorporated in a defensive way to guarantee the supply of ludic support, gradually builds a false self that can be rather different from the real self that would arise in an adequate support environment. In the false self, an essential element of creative originality will be absent.

Winnicott speculates on the possibility of simultaneously incorporating pfunctions characteristic of both the true and the false self. In this case, the defense of the false self can occur with low or high intensity. The false self, based on conformity, protects the true self from the restrictive demands of some relevant adults. Often the true self, although protected, still has a life of its own, but it is the false self that defines the social attitude perceived by adults. When there is a high degree of separation (split) between the two selves, the result can be an insufficient capacity for symbolic thinking and poverty of cultural living. In these cases, instead of cultural interests, we have extreme restlessness, and lack of ability to concentrate.

There is another type of perverse identification we could call "fanciful identification," to introduce a new term in psychoanalysis. Usually, in the idealized identification, the child seeks to mimic his father, or another relevant adult admired for his strength, potency, and wisdom. However, this identification may not be sufficient to provide adequate support, perhaps because the father is often absent or shows signs of insecurity or weakness. In this case, identification may occur not with the actual father, but with a fanciful image of the father that the child would like to have. That is, there is identification with the fantasy of a perfect father. Of course, the counterpart is that trying to match this fantasy produces unrealistic demands for perfection that the child will strive to fulfill without much chance of success. In this way, fanciful identification may be a restraining factor instead of a factor of ludic drive support.

Fanciful identification seems to have some relation to the confused notion of the ego ideal, presented by Freud in different versions and without much detail throughout his work. That lack of precision becomes clear when we consider the way he initially introduced the concept in his 1915 article on narcissism. He stated that the ego ideal *"finds itself possessed of every perfection,"* being *"the most powerful factor favoring repression."* Later, Freud (1923b) uses the term "ego ideal" as a synonym for the superego. Later still, Freud (1933) states that the superego is the vehicle of the ego ideal. Hence, it regularly evaluates the ego, making it strive to comply with a demand for ever-greater perfection. The ego-ideal would reflect the admiration for the perfection that the child initially saw in his parents. Hendrick (1964, p. 524) noted that it is a mistake to confuse the Freudian superego with the ego ideal. The first results from identification with those who forbid or allow behaviors; the second is just an intrapsychic representation of what one wants to be. Therefore, the superego is a set of pfunctions (or in other words, a mental structure), while the ego ideal is a set of memory registers.

Freud (1921) mentions how a charismatic leader (usually a psychopath) may get other people to develop a fanciful identification with his self-image, often built up mostly by propaganda resources. In this way, a group of passionate and faithful followers arises, as we have several sad examples in history, including Nazism. These people are often able to establish twin identification relationships with other members of the group, providing some additional support for each one's ludic drive. In this case, the group of followers can build supportive relationships mirroring each other, based on the degree of fanaticism and loyalty to the movement. The charismatic leader, who has become an essential source of support for the entire group, needs a permanent propaganda effort to maintain this status.

6. The Support Superego

Identification processes are generally not sufficient for a satisfactory solution to the problem of how to get an adequate amount of ludic support. Hence, a state of frustration may arise. If high-intensity frustrations occur in childhood, the effects can be traumatic, with strong inhibition of the ludic drive and the development of a personality with chronic deficiency in the capacity for ludic activities. The individual remains indefinitely dependent on the unsatisfactory support mechanisms that characterized his childhood, even when he has reached maturity (something like Kohut's archaic selfobjects). Symptoms such as low self-confidence, vague depression, a lack of initiative and enthusiasm for work, hypochondria, shyness, and high vulnerability to situations of shame can arise. Kohut (1971) would say that, in this case, we have a narcissistic personality disorder. Winnicott (1971) would say that the potential space was severely limited, reducing the readiness for ludic activities and producing an impoverishment of the individual's creative life. Hendrick (1951), a widely ignored precursor, would say that we have an ego-defect neurosis. He would point out that the failure of specific forms of identification bears a teleological relationship to the defective functioning of some adult personalities.

The most interesting case occurs when frustrations are frequent, but of low intensity. In this case, what Kohut called transmuting internalization may occur. Optimal frustration produces a tolerable amount of disappointment that leads to the establishment of an internal self-soothing or self-support capacity. This ability starts to have the same role of facilitating, reinforcing, and supporting the ludic impulse that was initially performed by the support objects through mirroring, idealization, or twinship. Self-support replaces those support objects that were essential in early life and which, following Kohut, we could call archaic. If there is no transmuting internalization, the individual will be a prisoner of his archaic support objects, without developing a capacity for self-support and to enrich his life experience with the acquisition of new support objects.

Interestingly, the notion of optimal frustration had already been articulated by Kohut & Seitz (1963, p. 142) in a discussion of a structural model à la Hartmann. They have shown that an area of progressive neutralization can result from the internalization of many experiences of benign frustration. According to them, the difference between traumatic and optimal frustration is like the difference between a harsh "NO!" from a poorly empathic mother and a loving "no" from a supportive mother. Or the difference between the behavior of the father who reacts to a temperamental tantrum of a child with an outburst of anger and hostility, and that of the father who in the same situation takes the child in his arms and, showing love and affection, manages to calm him down with a firm but non-aggressive attitude.

Winnicott (1949) mentions the capacity usually found in mothers to produce a gradual failure of adaptation according to the child's increasing ability to support them. Winnicott (1953) emphasizes the role of the good-enough mother, capable of actively adapting to the child's needs. This adaptation has the fundamental feature of losing importance as the child's ability to tolerate frustrations grow. There is no possibility of mental health for a human being who has not started life with a good enough mother. In the beginning, the ego support provided by the mother naturally compensates the immaturity of the ego. Over time, the individual becomes able to renounce the mother's real presence or that of a mother substitute. Winnicott (1959, p. 126) notes the child absorbs "supporting ego elements" from the mother that make him capable of being alone without frequent reference to her or other adults. If all goes well, the child's mind will gradually internalize a supportive environment, allowing him to engage alone in ludic activities.

What exactly changes in the individual's mental organization when transmuting internalization occurs? It happens that the ego incorporates some new pfunctions capable of producing the same effects that until then resulted only from the actions of support objects and identifications. They do this by neutralizing older pfunctions that have been incorporated into the ego to suppress non-supervised ludic activities. These new pfunctions can be defined as superego pfunctions, as they result from symbolic constructions produced by identification processes and become eventually automatic.

In identification by idealization, for example, the boy seeks to imitate his father to capture his attention and be supported by a powerful and competent individual. Still, he has not yet developed the fantasy of being himself like his father. There is still a realistic perception of the difference between his condition as a fragile and inexperienced boy and his father's idealized *imago*. Transmuting internalization happens when the child develops the fantasy that he is as powerful and competent as his father. This supporting element of self-confidence becomes automated and possibly unconscious. When this happens, identification by idealization is no longer necessary, as it is an archaic and relatively inefficient support mechanism. The illusion of power that produces the feeling of self-confidence becomes an authentic feature of the boy's personality, a "second nature" that allows him to neutralize the inhibitions produced by the repressive pfunctions of the ego and to develop his ludic activities autonomously.

It is important to emphasize this difference between ludic identification and transmuting internalization. In identification, there is an interest in copying as many of the father's ways and behaviors as possible. The idea is that the broader and more detailed the imitation, the higher its power to attract adult attention. Of course, this is what produces the desired ludic support effect. In the case of internalization, the child no longer seeks to be like the father in everything. The focus is only on absorbing paternal-behavior dimensions that serve the purpose of ludic-drive support. This point was emphasized by Kohut (1971, p. 50) when he wrote that in an effective internalization process, leading to the formation of a psychological structure, depersonalization of the introjected image must occur. The internal structure that now performs the same functions that the support object used to perform has been divested of most of its personal features.

Similarly, transmuting internalization may also have identification by mirroring as a starting point. In this case, the child constructs the fantasy that he is himself a partner who supports his ludic activities, without the need for the presence of an empathic mother, or an alter-ego, or even a participatory father. It can also occur in cases of false or fanciful identifications, which probably tends to complicate the pathological effects resulting from these perverse support mechanisms.

The set of pfunctions produced by transmuting internalization defines the "support superego." It is a mental structure rather different from the traditional Freudian superego. The Freudian superego represses sexual and aggressive impulses; the support superego prevents the ego from restraining the ludic impulse.

It is interesting to note that the notion of good behavior on the part of the Freudian superego has sometimes appeared in psychoanalytic literature. For Schafer (1960, p. 186), there is a part of the superego that can be described as loving and loved. It represents beloved and admired parents who provide love, protection, comfort, and guidance in the phase before the Oedipus complex. Afterward, even in their punitive activities, they still have valuable expressions of parental care, contact, and love. The maturing child identifies with these parenting aspects and eventually reaches the position of being able to love, protect, comfort, and guide himself and his children after him. Sandler (1960, p. 39) notes a strong tendency in psychoanalytic literature to neglect the positive side of the child's relationship with his superego. It is a relationship based on the fact that it can also be a splendid source of love and well-being. The superego works both by disapproving and by approving. However, this conception of a benign Freudian superego was limited by the classic understanding of drives, which assumed only sexual and aggressive impulses, without giving any space to the notion of ludic-impulse support.

The only exception was Sandler in a discussion of sublimation. He admits that "drives whose discharge produces a pleasure of non-erotic sort form the basis for later ego development" (1987, p.195). In his analysis of what he called the security principle, as an intermediary between the pleasure principle and the reality principle, he proposes the notion that a feeling of security produces an affective background for all our experiences. Nevertheless, he was never genuinely willing to desecrate the Freudian totem with the explicit incorporation of a ludic drive, although he did mention the possibility of a non-erotic work pleasure, as suggested by Hendrick.

Let me try now to explore more thoroughly the relationship between the Freudian superego and the support superego. As will be shown in detail in Chapter 26, we will only have a Freudian superego when identification with relevant adults has occurred in such a way that their "civilized" behaviors effectively become second nature for the child. But this is not necessarily produced just by the threat of breaking the primary affective relationship with these adults in the Oedipus complex. The child can only incorporate a set of precursor superego pfunctions that operate as a kind of false superego. In that case he/she uses civilized behaviors only in the proximity of some adult, and these pfunctions may never evolve into authentic superego pfunctions. This behavior can even lead to a case of psychopathy if it persists in the adult.

What we must recognize is that the Freudian superego is not only heir to the Oedipus complex, but also to the phenomenon of ludic-impulse support. Ludic identification and the support superego will appear first and then give rise to the Freudian superego. We can understand this schematically as a three-step transformation process. In the first stage, ludic identification with parental *imago* occurs. My father is strong and powerful, and by identifying with him, I guarantee better support for my ludic activities. Of course, it can also work with the mother, with some alter ego or other relevant adults.

In the second stage, the internal absorption of these support pfunctions occurs through the optimum frustration that produces the transmuting internalization. Those pfunctions, capable of producing the same effects resulting from the support objects' performance, are incorporated. Thus, the support superego (or part of it) appears. It is a symbolic construction of the type "My *father is strong and powerful, and I am like him, not necessarily a faithful copy of his personality, but certainly with the incorporation of those aspects that produce the desired support of my ludic drive.*"

In the third stage, the Freudian superego appears. Note that when the support superego appears, the mind has possibly already incorporated superego precursors, resulting from a previous oedipal situation. It may also happen that the support superego appears before the Oedipus phase, in which superego precursors arise. Anyway, the internalization of all kinds of ludic identifications will eventually incorporate rules and civilizing prohibitions of the parents that will become second nature, forming the Freudian superego. These behaviors, when adopted, encouraged, recommended, or explicitly approved by the relevant adults, are deeply rooted as authentic personality-defining characteristics. The individual starts to behave within civilized rules simply because it is the right thing to do and because he expects ludic support from the civilized world.

The conclusion is that wherever there is a Freudian superego, there will also be a support superego. However, it may happen that a robust support superego, which effectively supports ludic activities, appears alongside a weak Freudian superego, with little power to control and inhibit behaviors. This may be the case with psychopaths. But the opposite situation of a weak support superego with a strong Freudian superego can produce a pathological state of low self-esteem and chronic depression.

The role played by the Freudian superego in classical neuroses is well known. On the other hand, the support superego is crucially important in Kohut's narcissistic personality disorders. To have an idea of the great diversity of pathologies that can result from the formation and coexistence of these two superegos, consider the possibility of having different types of internalized support pfunctions with greater or lesser intensity, and that may include support by mirroring, idealization or twinship, in addition to perverse identifications of the false-self and fanciful type.

7. Self Psychology and Winnicott

This chapter examines connections between Kohut's self psychology and my reformulated Freudian model, and it ends with a brief note on Winnicott. First, we must acknowledge that self psychology has gone through two consecutive stages of theorization. Let me call them the "transformation model," first used in Kohut's 1966 paper on forms and transformations of narcissism and later also in *The Analysis of the Self* of 1971, and the "self-model," developed in *The Restoration of the Self* of 1977 and later works.

The transformation model uses a modified version of the intricate Freudian notion of narcissistic libido. Freud (1940a, p. 20) wrote that the ego first stores up the whole available quota of libido, the sexual-drive energy, in an initial state of absolute primary narcissism. This changes only when the ego begins to invest (cathect) ideas of objects with libido. In this way, some of the narcissistic libido eventually transforms itself into object libido. Throughout life, the ego remains the reservoir from which libidinal cathexes are sent out in search of objects and to which they may return in the same way as an amoeba behaves with its pseudopods.

After Hartmann's correction (1950), psychoanalysis redefined narcissism as the libidinal investment in the self. Ego psychology made the distinction between the Freudian narcissism phenomenon and an independent neutralization phenomenon. In the latter libidinal and aggressive energies are transformed into non-sexual energy to sustain certain adaptive functions of the ego. This neutralization does not affect narcissistic libido, which preserves the same original sexual aim.

Kohut's transformation model postulates that some of the libido invested in the self also undergoes a qualitative change different from the neutralization of ego psychology. For him, narcissism should be "defined not by the target of the instinctual investment (*i.e.*, whether it is the subject himself or other people) but by the nature or quality of the instinctual charge" (1971, p. 26). This transformed libido, which he also called narcissistic libido, not only loses its sexual aim but also *"supplies the instinctual fuel for our ego-syntonic ambitions and purposes, for our ability to enjoy our activities and for important aspects of our self-esteem"* (Kohut, 1971, p. 27). He makes a distinction between idealizing narcissistic libido and narcissistic-exhibitionistic libido. The first is *"the main source of libidinal fuel for some of the socioculturally important activities which are subsumed under the term creativity"* (1971, p. 40). The second is responsible for manifestations of early grandiose fantasies which tend to develop into the grandiose self, but after the child learns to accept realistic limitations, *"are* pari passu *replaced by ego-syntonic goals and purposes, by pleasure in his functions and activities and by realistic self-esteem"* (1971, p. 107).

Since Kohut offered no reasonable explanation, this idea of libido transformation was hard to understand and accept. Stolorow, for example, complained it was a highly speculative proposition that just produced a conceptual "mulberry bush."[7]

In a narcissistic object relationship the object is invested with narcissistic cathexes. But what is a narcissistic cathexis? In struggling to reconcile his excellent clinical observations with an outmoded economic concept of narcissism, Kohut presents us with either a tautology or a notion that there is a *qualitative* difference between

---

7   In other words, a conceptual tangle. This seems to be an allusion to the old English children song that never comes to an end, in which the chorus line is "Here we go round the mulberry bush; on a cold and frosty morning". See Halliwell-Phillipps (1849) or Bryson (2011).

narcissistic energies and object-related energies—a highly speculative proposition (Storolow,1975, pp. 200–201, also in Morrison, 1986, 201, original's italics).

With this kind of criticism coming from a non-hostile commentator, Kohut could not help noticing that his attempt to integrate a new set of relevant clinical observations into the traditional body of psychoanalysis was not working well. Hence, in *The Restoration of the Self*, he developed the self-model, a "decisive shift in the focus of psychoanalysis" (1994, p. 358), fully dismissing the drive concept.

We may note that after the *Restoration*, the term "narcissistic libido" disappears from Kohut's work. The last quick mention I find occurs in the 1976 text on Freud's self-analysis. In the self-model, the notion of narcissistic libido as an "engine" of human motivation for nonsexual activities seems to be replaced by the notion of a "maturational push" that was made explicit only in his posthumous book, *How Does Analysis Cure?* (Kohut 1984, p 78). But it was clearly implicit in all his theorizing since the *Restoration*. In a normal childhood, a nuclear self is created from archaic undifferentiated mental contents, in a process analogous to Mahler's transition from the symbiotic to the separation-individuation phase (Mahler, 1975). This structure is "the basis for our sense of being an independent center of initiative and perception" (Kohut 1977, p. 177). There is somehow embedded in it a development program that leads to the acquisition of core ambitions and ideals. In normal development, ambitions are acquired in early childhood (second, third, or fourth year) and ideals in later childhood (fourth, fifth, or sixth year). The nuclear self may also incorporate core skills and talents acquired during the latency period (Kohut 1977, p. 179).

Kohut speaks of the presence of a tension gradient[8], an action-promoting condition that arises "between" a person's ambitions and his ideals. There is a flow of actual psychological activity that induces the person towards essential (nonsexual) pursuits, so that "he is driven by his ambitions and led by his ideals" (Kohut, 1966, p. 250 and 1977, p. 180). But the fuel for these activities (and their emotional and motor consequences) can only be the mysterious maturational push supposedly embedded at birth or early childhood in our minds. Kohut points out that "the maturational push that was thwarted in childhood will begin to reassert itself spontaneously as it is reactivated in the analysis in the form of a selfobject transference" (Kohut 1984, p. 78). In other words, a self-psychology informed analysis puts again in movement the normal development program that was somehow pre-defined in our nuclear self and has been interrupted by lack of selfobject support. Note the apparent similarity in the maturational push's roles in the self-model and the earlier transformation model's narcissistic libido.

It is worth noting how Kohut gradually moved away from the classical drive conception of Freudian psychoanalysis (Siegel, 1996), and how this became a full rupture as he neared death. In the address on empathy he delivered three days before his death, he pointed to one of "the worst distortions of the perception of man that psychoanalysis is guilty of: the introduction of the drive" (Kohut, 1981b, p. 529). In his posthumous paper on the semicircle of mental health, he wrote that the drive concept "has had

---

8   An awkward term that sounds like physics or electrical engineering, reminding me of Breuer's notion of a tonic excitation flowing in a cerebral structure, much like an electric system. (Breuer & Freud, 1974, III. 2). Kohut also mentions "a tension arc from basic ambitions, via talents and skills, toward basic ideals" (1984, p. 4) and "the energic field that established itself between the patient's nuclear ambitions and ideals (1984, p. 99). He concludes that the basic feature of an essentially cohesive self is "the existence of an energic continuum between ambitions and ideals" which is the *sine qua non* of the capacity to lead a fulfilling life (1984, p. 211, n. 1). It is hard not to find the use of these energy ideas strange in this context.

significant deleterious consequences for psychoanalysis," and it does not "belong in a system of psychology" (Kohut, 1981b, pp. 553–554).

This book proposes the opposite movement: a return to drive theory. It shows that with the hypothesis of a ludic drive, there is no need for such intricate notions as narcissistic libido or maturational push to explain the fuel driving nonsexual ludic activities. The whole theoretical argument becomes surprisingly simple. In the narcissistic phase (equivalent to Mahler's symbiotic phase), the ludic-drive object is self-representation, with limits not precisely defined at the beginning of life. It typically includes relevant adults, such as the mother and possibly others, as parts of the self. As the individual matures and leaves this primary narcissistic position, the ludic drive's object moves towards the outside world and its infinite and exciting possibilities for generating ludic pleasure and the feeling of joy associated with it. I have already discussed the ludic drive's vicissitudes and the roles played by support objects, ludic identifications, and the support superego. Support objects are equivalent to Kohut's selfobjects. On the other hand, the support superego results from the same transmuting internalization process, which for Kohut constructs, with the help of identifications, the adult self as a center of initiative. The support superego may be strong or weak, just as Kohut's adult self may be cohesive or fragmented. Note how even these rapid observations are sufficient to show that we have a relatively simple way to reconstruct self psychology using the ludic drive notion.

Yet we must acknowledge that Kohut's self-model has an implicit fundamental innovation that is not usually emphasized, perhaps because it is not well understood. It is the hypothesis that it is possible to derive joy and pleasure not only from ludic activity, but also from the very experience of being supported. We do not find this hypothesis clearly stated in the transformation model, even though in *The Analysis of the Self*, Kohut had already pointed to an *"undisguised pleasure in being admired"* (1971, p. 25). It is a subtle notion that came to play a fundamental role only in the self-model.

We value ludic support, in the first place, for the joy resulting from the ludic activities it makes possible. But we also value it for the pleasure derived from the feeling of being supported in these activities. In other words, the experience of being supported is itself a source of joy, and therefore it may also be a primary ludic object.

In the transformation model, the ludic drive is the fuel for the pure ludic motivation, the direct search for ludic activities. In the self-model, the ludic drive is also the fuel for a narcissistic ludic motivation, which is the search for the experience of being supported, involving multiple dimensions of exhibitionism and grandiosity. To simplify, we can speak, in an abbreviated form, of ludic motivation and narcissistic motivation, always remembering that the fuel is the ludic drive in both cases.

Let me try to clarify this hypothesis of crucial importance in Kohut. Consider first the case of a young child with ludic motivation to engage in a sensory-motor activity. The ludic drive results from an innate instinctive tendency to seek action and stimulus. In other words, from aversion to inactivity. When the child dedicates himself to the ludic activity, this produces a pleasurable sensation of joy associated with realizing the aim of the ludic drive. A support object facilitates this, as it increases the confidence that the activity poses no risk of accidents. In principle, therefore, support does not generate pleasure by itself. It only produces a state of trust that allows the pursuit of pleasure through ludic activity. With the child's growth and the appearance of a symbolic ludic capacity, this starts to change. He begins to derive joy directly from the experience of being supported. We do not know precisely why this happens. It may have to do with the fact that firm and explicit support in the present generates the expectation of adequate support in the future. There may also be an element of fantasy at the root of narcissistic motivation.

Narcissistic motivation means that even someone lying on a bed can derive a joy-type pleasure from imagining how his presence at an event will produce supportive responses later in the day. The individual seeks narcissistic relationships to obtain reassuring support for his ludic motivation, but also because he wants to have that same experience of being supported once more. It is as if ludic narcissism had turned into an addictive drug.

Of course, we can have combinations of the two motivations with different intensities. In young children, pure ludic motivation is dominant, but eventually, narcissistic motivation gains importance. When an older child likes to play wearing superheroes or princesses' costumes, she seems to be responding to a narcissistic motivation. She does not merely want to engage in a ludic activity, like running or having fun in an amusement park; she also wants to do this while personifying the fantasy of representing individuals influential and widely admired by adults. In this case, it is as if the ludic drive produces an internal yearning for exhibitionism and grandeur.

In one of his earlier papers, Kohut (1970, p. 556) had already identified the addictive nature of narcissistic motivation, both on the side of "addiction-like praise-seeking" and on the side of the "compulsive search for idealized selfobjects." It becomes rather evident when a traumatic frustration occurs that causes the child to become insatiably hungry for mirroring, affirmation, and praise (1970, p. 558). Kohut also notes that these demands may become sexualized, producing different forms of sexual perversion (1970, p. 556).

It is easy to confirm through empathy and introspection that ludic activities' support can become a primary ludic object. Groos (1896, p. 290) already called attention to the pleasure resulting from the element of conquest and victory in play. For example, with adolescents and adults, a play activity is rarely wholly disinterested, and participants in organized games are often very much interested in the results of their efforts. In sports and team games, there is a definite increase in interest and pleasure when there are awards for performance and records to be broken. By introspection, we observe that we feel joy by thinking we are being applauded or valued in our activities, even when these efforts do not produce very satisfactory results. I may know I have poor golfing skills; still, I feel pleasure in achieving a better result than a friend that happens to be an even worse player. And I am delighted to report this at a meeting of mostly lousy golf friends. I can even feel pleased with the fantasy of becoming a great player admired by lots of people.

This discussion of the self-model makes clear what is different in Winnicott and Kohut. As I will show in detail in Chapter 18, Winnicott developed a theoretical construction almost identical to our analysis of pure ludic motivation and its vicissitudes. The notion of a good-enough mother who functions as a support object for her child's ludic activities is analogous to the notion of the mother as the first selfobject. The notion that the child's mind will eventually internalize a series of gradual adaptation failures in a favorable supportive environment is analogous to the notion of the transmuting internalization process generating a support superego. It roughly corresponds to Kohut's transformation model, albeit with a more concentrated emphasis on mothers and children (though fathers may also be implicit). However, it turns out that Winnicott did not realize the parallel dimension of narcissistic ludic motivation. He did not go through anything like Kohut's transition from the transformation model to the self-model.

8. Summing up and the Self Problem

This chapter presents a summary of ludic-drive psychology with occasional references to insights from self psychology. It also discusses the problem of defining exactly what Kohut meant by the word "self." The starting point is the aversion to inactivity and boredom that gives rise to the ludic drive, an impulse (*Trieb*) that may realize its aim with any activity. Of course, it means that we may often have a confluence of drives, for example, when a sexually motivated activity also achieves the ludic drive's aim, which is to avoid inactivity, in conjunction with the sexual aim. But the ludic drive may also motivate activities not aiming at sex, aggression, or self-preservative needs. At the beginning of life, sensory-motor activities predominate, as a typical manifestation of Hendrick's drive to master. Later, symbolic ludic activities arise and become dominant in adulthood.

The ludic drive is the fuel for ludic motivation that leads the child to explore a universe of pleasurable possibilities. But this is inhibited by the reality principle, which quickly teaches: ludic activities without the participation of trusted adults can lead to accidents and produce pain of different intensities. It may even sometimes be life-threatening. A conflict situation, in which the ego represses the ludic impulse emerging from the id, can only be overcome through support objects. These, like Kohut's selfobjects, can be of three types: mirroring, idealization, and twinship.

However, support objects are a mixed blessing, because dependence on them creates the possibility of frustrations. It is never possible to guarantee that these early support objects, which Kohut called archaic selfobjects, will always offer an adequate support dose. When they fail, the ludic impulse will be harmed or even aborted. Hence, the human mind builds ludic identifications to avoid this. These are processes through which the ego tries to become like its support objects. This way, it hopes to attract attention, sympathy, and preference in their care. Ludic identification can occur in any of the three "healthy" dimensions of support: idealization, mirroring, and twinship. It may also happen in the two "perverse" dimensions of the false self and fanciful idealization.

Ludic identification helps but does not fully solve the problem of fully supporting ludic activities. Frustrations keep happening. A definitive solution is only reached with the transmuting internalization process that produces a series of frequent and low-intensity disappointments accompanied by empathic compensatory reactions from relevant adults. Kohut (1977, p. 32) describes this as "innumerable processes of microinternalizaton." Hence, from this optimal frustration the individual develops an internal capacity for self-support and incorporates a set of pfunctions, capable of automatically performing the same support actions that used to be provided by those essential archaic support objects at life's beginning, Kohut's archaic selfobjects. This set of pfunctions constitutes what I call the support superego. Kohut would say that in this case, the individual has achieved a healthy self-structure, a cohesive self that makes possible a meaningful, joyful, and fulfilling life.

This normal development process, which goes from the ludic drive to the support superego, applies equally to pure ludic motivation and narcissistic ludic motivation. In the latter case, as the support experience itself becomes a primary ludic object, it is possible to have narcissistic support objects to mirror exhibitionism and confirm grandiosity, somewhat independently of any ludic activity. These support objects, in turn, create the possibility of narcissistic identifications with a symbolic construction such as: *"I am just like you, so you'll want to mirror my exhibitionism and confirm my grandiosity."*

These identifications can also be internalized in a transmuted form in the support superego.

Note the duality between the classic Freudian superego and the support superego. The first represses sexual and aggressive impulses, while the second supports ludic impulses, so that the ego's insecurity does not end up restraining them. Strictly speaking, we are dealing with a conflict between agencies of the mental apparatus in both cases. In the first case, there is a conflict between the Freudian superego and the id on whether to repress socially inappropriate impulses. In the second case, there is a conflict between the support superego and the ego on whether to avoid ludic drive's repression. Hence, in both cases, we have situations of internal conflict.

In normal development, the support superego first arises before the oedipal conflicts that produce the Freudian superego. It is expanded and strengthened by new experiences of support and transmuting internalization throughout life, including narcissistic transfers in psychoanalytic clinic situations. Archaic support objects and children's identifications tend to disappear as they become unnecessary. The result of this process can be the consolidation of a strong support superego with the complete elimination of all archaic support mechanisms. It is what Kohut used to call a cohesive and well-structured self. It may occur, however, that the process does not conclude adequately. The result may be a relatively weak support superego that coexists with residues of archaic support mechanisms.

Kohut (1984, pp. 76-77) suggests that the consolidation of a support superego, or a cohesive self, also allows the replacement of archaic support objects (*i.e.*, archaic selfobjects) by the empathic resonance emanating from support objects acquired through adult life. For example, at the age of forty, Mr. X decides to learn to play golf and use as support objects a professional teacher from the club and another beginner partner to accompany him in the first games. At the age of sixty, he decides to write a book on psychoanalytic fundamentals, using his former analyst as a support object.

Or, at age seventy, he finds a new friend who offers empathic resonance for his expressions of exhibitionism and grandiosity. But these adult ludic support objects are different from the archaic ones. He no longer depends exclusively on them for an adequate disposition for ludic activities if he has a well-developed support superego. Consequently, the frustration of a support relationship with objects acquired in adult life has a much less significant impact on self-esteem.

This discussion has shown that there are obvious connections between Kohut's self psychology and ludic-drive psychology. But a significant difference is that the latter, like classical Freudian metapsychology, does not depend on the obscure Kohutian notion of the self. As we will see in detail in Chapter 25 of Part V, the concept of self-representation has a precise definition that William James (1890, ch. X) summed up, more than a hundred years ago, as the sum of everything that an individual can call his own. More precisely, it is the set of memory records that define a person's identity. The same, however, cannot be said of Kohut's imprecise notion of the self. Hartmann (1950) saw the self as the whole psychic apparatus, that is, id plus ego plus superego plus memory. Kohut appears to have something different in mind when he states in *The analysis of the self* (1971, p. XV) that the self is a "content of the mental apparatus, but not one of its constituents."

Self psychology has the disturbing feature of not having an exact definition of its main object of study. Kohut's first definition in *The Analysis of the Self* (Preface, pp. xiv to xv) is quite confusing. He argues that the concepts of ego, id, and superego belong to "a specific high level, i.e., experience distant, abstraction in psychoanalysis: the psychic apparatus." In contrast, his idea of self is a notion close to experience (experience-near), not an agency of the mind but a structure within the mind, invested (cathected) with instinctive energy and with continuity over time. Later on, his *Restoration of the Self* (p. 97) has no better explanation. It just states that "it is possible to discern a self which, while it includes drives (and/or defenses) in its organization, has become a supraordinate configuration, whose significance transcends that of the sum of its parts."

This notion of a supraordinate configuration is, at first sight, hard to understand. Cooper (2005d, p. 27) seems to agree when he notes that "the concepts of the supraordinate self, with its bipolar character, appear ... to be concepts of high abstraction, no longer simply phenomenological." He adds that "the connection of the concept of self with a set of adjectives such as 'enfeebled,' 'firm' or 'vigorous' is problematic."

Lynch (1991) tries to summarize the concept of Kohutian self as a psychic structure that is the core of our personality, but this is tautological. Another attempt by Treurniet (1980, p. 325) proposes that "the self is the universe of conscious and unconscious feelings which the individual has about himself as the center of experience and initiative." However, this latter definition seems incompatible with Kohut's tendency to think of the self as a mental structure rather than a set of feelings. It is difficult to disagree with the conclusion of some authors that the "self" is the most problematic concept of self psychology.

Yet, we may associate the Kohutian concept of the self with the idea of a support superego. A cohesive and well-structured self seems to be the same as a cohesive and well-structured support superego, where cohesive means not fragmented. A fragmented self is a support superego with some deficiencies, in which some archaic support objects and some ludic and narcissistic identifications have not been adequately internalized. In his 1966 article, Kohut wrote that the interplay between the narcissistic self, the ego, and the (Freudian) superego determines the characteristic flavor of the personality. We can naturally translate the "narcissistic self" as the support superego. The episode reported in the article, of the grandiose flying fantasy in Churchill's biography, can be understood as resulting from a strong support superego's interaction with an equally strong Freudian superego. The first produces an excess of self-confidence because of intense mirroring and idealizing internalizations. The second does not accept the possibility of defeat and insists that it is better to take the risk of getting hurt than to lose the game. In other words, in this case, the Freudian superego has directly affected ludic behavior. On the other hand, one can think of situations in which the support superego affects sexual behavior.

Our impression is that when Kohut uses the term "self," he may be referring to two distinct concepts that we can only identify individually by the context of the argument. One is the support superego, a set of pfunctions, or, as it is common to say in psychoanalysis, a mind's structure. It provides support for ludic activities, including, of course, activities driven by narcissistic motivations. The other concept is the self-representation, which, as we will discuss in Chapter 25 of Part V, consists of a set of memory records somehow related to the individual himself and his life experience. This second concept is associated with the notion of the self as a center of initiative with continuity over time.

Kohut (1981, p. 234) wrote that we experience ourselves, that is, our self, as a center of initiative, having a feeling of comparative independence, assertiveness, and initiative. Another feature of the self is a feeling of cohesion in space and continuity in time. He adds that in the healthy self, there is "a sense of cohesion versus fragmentation, a sense of the harmony of oneself versus a sense of chaos of oneself, a sense of strength about the self versus weakness, lack of vitality." In summary, there is a feeling of being truly alive. Of course, this has to do with self-representation, our memory records relating to our life experience regarding ourselves, and the things and people that concern and interest us. It has nothing to do with the notion of the self as a mental structure, or as a support superego.

Note that ludic-drive psychology has the advantage over self psychology of allowing a non-conflictive integration with a reformulated Freudian metapsychology. The radical position we sometimes observe in Kohut, notably in *How Does Analysis Cure?*, of dismissing the pathological consequences of sexual phenomena, often downgrading them to the category of derivatives of narcissistic disorders, makes no sense The pacific coexistence of ludic-drive psychology (and hence self psychology) with the Freudian model's fundamentals can only be good for psychoanalysis.

On the other hand, the Kohutian narrative, which we could summarize as the typical story of the self and its difficulties, has some literary charm and strong communication potential. It can undoubtedly help the analyst in the working-through process. Talking about the reconstruction of a self whose development was inhibited in childhood by insufficiently empathic responses from relevant adults, or talking about fragmentation, cohesion, and strengthening of the self, may be more effective than talking about archaic support objects of the ludic drive and about reconstruction of a deficient support superego.

A compromise between the communication potential of self psychology and the scientific rigor of ludic-drive psychology is perhaps possible if we understand the self (now indeed!) as a suprarordinate configuration composed of two parts, a structural component and a memory component. The structural component is the support superego; the memory component is the traditional notion of self-representation. With this understanding, Kohut's work can be easily understood without any ambiguity. You have just to check whether each reference to the self is dealing with the "structure of the self" or the "memory of the self."

9. Drives, Relationships, and Reflexes

A psychoanalyst friend often complained that this book was going in the wrong direction by proposing a "return" to a modified version of the classic drive model when the bulk of the profession seems to be moving towards relational psychoanalysis. Greenberg (2012, p. 24) summarizes the difference between the classic drive model and the new relational model. The first has a conception of the mind as energized by the need to satisfy impulses that originate in the human organism's pre-social somatic nucleus. The second has a conception of the mind, including its fundamental motivations, as structured by the lasting influence of relationships with other people in childhood.

Cooper (2005b), in his classic article on new wine in old bottles, pointed that many analysts have perceived that children are motivated by strong desires for stimulation, the satisfaction of curiosity, communication, and learning. They require empathic contact and a safe and stimulating relationship with those adults that are their caretakers. For Cooper, the Freudian drive theory cannot explain these demands. He thinks that some psychoanalysts that were still recently speaking of drives, such as Otto Kernberg (1984) or Margaret Mahler (1975), understood this concept quite differently from Freud's original idea. When Sandler (1987) speaks of the need for security as a central motivator, or Winnicott (1971) speaks of the central role of ludic development, and, I may add, when Kohut (1977), speaks of the self as a fundamental personality structure, they are talking about something quite distinct from what Freud intended with his metapsychology.

But this opposition between drive and relational conceptions is a false dichotomy, as shown by my ludic-drive psychology. The apparent dichotomy is just a result of the enormous resistance of psychoanalysis to accept anything that means a desecration of the old Freudian totem. In that same text, Cooper (2005b, p. 54) makes this explicit when he comments that psychoanalysts cling to Freudian language to preserve their identifications with Freud. For him, only a fearless and foolish psychoanalyst could want to break away from this magnificent identification. But as ludic-drive psychology demonstrates, when we defile the totem with a modified version of the Freudian model, incorporating the ludic drive and using information instead of energy, the dichotomy disappears. With the same model, we can put together both drive and relational aspects of human behavior. It is possible to preserve all of Freud's brilliant insights on the vicissitudes of the sexual drive and the genesis and treatment of neuroses, and at the same time, within the same theoretical framework, add a deep understanding of the impact of childhood relationships upon mental development and upon the genesis and treatment of narcissistic pathologies (and also, as we will see in Part III, a deep understanding of aggression, its genesis and vicissitudes).

The option of replacing the drive model with a new relational paradigm uses the hypothesis that human beings are born pre-programmed to seek relationships with other human beings. They can only achieve and maintain their mental health through these interactions. The primary motivational need is not the pleasure resulting from the realization of instinctual impulses, but rather the building of relationships. There is an innate tendency of the human mind to seek interaction with other minds. Without these interactions, it would not be possible to build something that we could identify as a human mind.

It is easy to think of a phylogenetic explanation for the hypothesis of an innate relational tendency, since the great success of the human species suggests that it may have significant survival value. The problem is how to find a minimally reasonable ontogenetic explanation. Daniel N. Stern (2005) is a useful reference, on account of his systematic search of theoretical foundations for an intersubjective approach. I focus here on his work only because it is a technically well-developed example of this line of thought.

According to Stern, a possible ontogenetic explanation could be the notion of mirror neurons. A series of experiments by Giacomo Rizzolatti and associates (Rizzolatti et al. 2001, Gallese 2001, Rizzolatti et al. 2004) implanted electrodes in the brains of monkeys. When a monkey noticed a hand movement of the investigator, some neurons in the monkey's brain related to hand movements were activated. It was as if it were the monkey itself doing the action. For these authors, this property defines the mirror neuron.

Stern proposes that the experimentally proven existence of this type of neuron is a sufficient neurological basis for the psychological hypothesis that human beings have an innate capacity to participate in other humans' experiences. From this indirect participation, a sense of sharing emerges, as well as an understanding of other humans' intentions and emotions. It should happen even with children in the early stage when there is no clear differentiation between self and others. Stern speaks of core intersubjectivity and argues that the evidence from many studies of child development suggests that children live in an intersubjective matrix since birth. He notes that some studies suggest newborn babies tend to imitate actions of the experimenter's face, such as showing the tongue. It cannot be considered a reflex and suggests a primitive form of intersubjectivity resulting from mirror neurons.

The problem with this line of theorization is that Freudian metapsychology also sees the human child as born within a matrix of relationships, despite being driven by instinctual impulses. These relationships will affect the whole of his later development. Freud (1910, 1912) notes the infantile fixation of tenderness upon the mother, which he sees as the primary infantile object-choice. The mother is the first love object for both men and women, and this has nothing to do with mirror neurons or intersubjectivity. We may say something similar about the relationships that result from the ludic drive, as we have seen here. From the fact that human babies and primates develop in a matrix of relationships, it is not possible to infer that there is an innate tendency to relate that does not depend on drives as a motivating mechanism.

The evidence about mirror neurons only suggests that humans and at least some primates are born with a neurological mechanism that facilitates imitation! As noted by Piaget (1951), this process is fundamental to the development of sensorimotor intelligence and associated ludic activities, which are shared by men and some animals. Furthermore, in humans, imitation facilitates the evolution in the direction of symbolic ludic activities, with all its fantastic consequences for the development of our civilization. There is no doubt that mirror neurons may have had an essential role in our species' evolutionary success, but this in no way implies that we should discard the drive model.

We can make a similar assessment of a second option, suggested by Stern, of an ontogenetic foundation for the relational model. This option, based on Husserl's phenomenological philosophy, proposes that the mind is by its very nature "open to intersubjectivity" since it can only be built through interaction with other minds. It emerges and exists owing to the permanent communication of mental processes with the environment created by other minds. Without this constant interaction, there would be no such thing as mind.

In the same vein, Robert Stolorow (2011) proposes a psychoanalytic phenomenology. He uses the concept of the "experiential world" of the individual as his central theoretical foundation. This "world" evolves organically from the person's encounter with the critical forming experiences that make up his unique life story. It is somewhat surprising to see, in the twenty-first century, the use of a philosophical argument in a scientific discipline, even in the case of non-experimental human science. It was quite common in the past when psychology was still seen as just a chapter of philosophy (Hunt, 2007; Makari 2015).

For Stern, the "phenomenological view" results from the fact that every human mind is necessarily intertwined with other human minds, being itself the result of a joint creation through this interaction. This sentence immediately suggests a simple question: can the same be said for other animals? It is interesting to examine the case of animal species, such as most reptiles, in which interactions throughout life with other individuals of the same species are minimal. In this case, should we conclude that lizards and frogs have no mind?

Homeostasis alone is enough to create a mind in most animal species, that is, to build a set of standard responses to somatic needs, such as hunger or sexual appetite. These responses are processed by a mental device, that is, a mind, which is just the brain's "software" (if you do not believe in the soul or something similar). In his 1940 *Outline*, when Freud pondered if there were a superego in animals, he was implicitly acknowledging that there is an ego in animals. As we will see in Chapter 26 of Part VI, the correct answer to Freud's doubt is that animals cannot have superegos, but this does not mean that there is no mind in a lizard or frog. They certainly have a rudimentary mental apparatus, although their interactions with other lizards and frogs are minimal. Naturally, in humans, the normal socialization process and the sophisticated capacity for symbolic thinking causes part of the mind to result from interaction with other minds. There is no doubt that this affects both the ego and Freudian and support superegos. In this sense, there is no doubt that the human mind is the result of a process of joint creation with other human minds, but to understand this, we do not need Husserl's old phenomenology.

A third option mentioned by Stern for an ontogenetic foundation of the relational model is John Bowlby's attachment theory. It is a theory that, at first glance, seems to represent the most significant challenge ever presented to Freud's theory of the mind. However, we find it is not strictly incompatible with the existence of drives and, on the contrary, may even represent a valuable contribution to that theory.

Bowlby (1969) develops attachment theory from three criticisms of the foundations of classical psychoanalysis. First, he puts away the Freudian notion of psychic energy, which he considers rather obscure, and uses a cybernetic notion of biological control systems. In other words, information replaces energy precisely as we are doing here. He also argues that evidence produced by direct observation of children and animals' behavior should be considered valid substrates for theoretical elaboration. There is no problem in accepting this second criticism if we add the *caveat* that direct observation cannot completely replace the "natural experiment" *par excellence* of the discipline that occurs in clinical activity. The Appendix B at the end of this book has a detailed discussion of the concept of natural experiment and other methodological issues.

The third criticism is the most important. It concerns the traditional Freudian notion that there is a special connection between the baby and his mother as a consequence of being fed by her. Bowlby (1988, ch. 2) exaggerates here since this connection results from a confluence of self-preservative drives with the sexual and ludic drives. For him, however, this phenomenon has nothing to do with drives. The propensity to make intimate emotional bonds with preferred individuals is a fundamental characteristic of human nature that is already present in germinal form in the newborn and continues to be present throughout adult life. Like the offspring of some other species, the human child is pre-programmed to develop in a socially cooperative manner. Consequently, a reasonably devoted common mother can turn herself into a "secure personal base." From that secure base, the child can go out to explore the world with the certainty of being allowed to return from time to time, or in extraordinary circumstances when disturbed or frightened.

The third and final volume of his *Attachment and Loss* (1980, pp. 38-43) presents an excellent summary that I will try to reproduce schematically. What he proposes is a new paradigm. Despite incorporating many notions of psychoanalysis, it differs by adopting principles derived from ethology and control theory. That allows him to dispense with concepts such as psychic energy and drive. In fact, at this point, Bowlby commits the same fallacy that Gedo (2005, p.6) attributed to the "students of Rappaport" (G. Klein, Schafer, Holt, and Gill), and we can still find in contemporary authors such as Wilma Bucci (1997). The fallacy is that if we abandon the concept of psychic energy, we must necessarily abandon the drive idea as well. This book shows this is not true.

Bowlby (1980, pp. 39-40) summarizes the main propositions of his theory:

a) People have an attachment behavior that allows them to reach and retain the desired closeness to some other preferred individual (such as the responsible mother). Under normal conditions, this behavior consists of little more than brief eye contact. Still, in certain circumstances, it can manifest itself as a search for proximity (following), as grabbing behavior (clinging), as a cry for help (calling), or merely as outright crying.

b) Attachment behavior has its proper dynamics, distinct from self-preservative and sexual behaviors.

c) Under normal conditions, attachment behavior leads to the development of affective bonds, initially between children and parents, but later between adults throughout the life cycle.

d) The purpose of attachment behavior is to preserve a certain degree of proximity and communication with specific preferred figures. It works as a kind of homeostatic system with the capacity for self-correction.

e) When an attachment link arises, the various forms of behavior that contribute to it are only activated when required. For example, in situations of strangeness and fatigue, or in the presence of anything frightening. They may also be activated in the case of absence or lack of adequate response from the object of attachment.

f) The uncontested maintenance of a satisfactory attachment bond is experienced as a security source, and the renewal of that bond as a source of pleasure/joy. As noted in Bowlby (1988, p. 69), this bond creates a secure base from which the individual can explore the world and return when he feels the need. It consolidates sets of cybernetically organized behavioral systems that can mediate both an attachment behavior pattern and an exploratory behavior pattern.

g) Many species have incorporated attachment behaviors in their natural development because they contribute to the individual's survival by keeping him in contact with adult caregivers, thereby reducing environmental and predator risks.

Examining this summary of attachment theory, we see in item (b) that Bowlby is not proposing a new paradigm that entirely replaces the drive model as he does not intend to say anything about behaviors related to self-preservative needs (such as food) or sexual urges. We may also notice that he says nothing about ludic-driven behaviors; that is, why an individual decides to leave his safe base to explore the world. Wouldn't it be more comfortable and pleasurable to remain indefinitely in the warmth of the secure base? Bowlby (1980) emphasizes that attachment behavior should never be considered pathological, but this contradicts Kohut's self psychology understanding of the pathological nature of an unusually long dependence on archaic selfobjects. Or, in terms of our ludic-drive psychology, it contradicts the conclusion about the pathological nature of the inability to replace primitive support objects by a support superego.

The most relevant part of Bowlby's formulation, which I see as a significant contribution to the drive model, is his detailed explanation of the mental processes that give rise to attachment behavior. It is something that we can better understand in his first article on this topic published in 1958. Bowlby, in 1986 added a footnote warning that this old contribution no longer adequately represented his thinking. But the fact is that the fundamentals of this theory remained the same, only with greater emphasis on what he called "cybernetic systems of behavior."

The 1958 article explains that attachment is a consequence of what Bowlby called component instinctual responses. It is an analogy with the *Three Essays'* Freudian conception that the sexual drive is the result of a set of individual instinctual components that initially operate with relative independence, but later merge into adult sexuality. The idea is that these partial instinctual responses are at work in activities such as sucking (typical of human newborns) or grabbing (typical of monkeys), and in behaviors such as following an imprinting figure (as in ducks) and smile or cry (as in human babies). The attachment would result from the fusion, in varying dosages depending on the animal species, of these five partial instinctual responses. Bowlby, who recognizes a strong influence of research in ethology, emphasizes that these automatic responses are very different from a drive (*Trieb*) of psychoanalysis. They produce precise and observable patterns of behavior, common to all members of the species, and primarily determined by heredity.

Bowlby is right! These instinctual responses are not drives; obviously, they are reflexes. Freud (1915), in his text on the vicissitudes of instinctual impulses, had already noticed the difference between a drive (*Trieb*) and a stimulus (*Reiz*). The latter results from a reflex arc scheme (*Reflexschema*) and is the same as the modern concept of reflex. For Freud, the stimulus (*Reiz*) has a single trigger originating outside the organism and automatically produces an action directed to the outside world. We can add that the reflex can also have a trigger internal to the organism, such as in the cough reflex. The drive (*Trieb*), on the other hand, always originates from within the organism and operates as a force that persists over time, creating a need that remains in operation until it is satisfied. Or, more consistently with our concept of drive as information, we can add that this need remains in operation until it is met or rejected. Unlike the drive, therefore, the reflex is automatic, instantaneous, and cannot be modulated or rejected by the mental process. The reflex always produces a peremptory motor command whose execution overrides any other command generated by the drive's' action in the mental process.

Human beings, like other animals, are born with a set of pre-programmed reflexes. Some are difficult to understand in evolutionary terms, as in the patellar reflex, activated in response to an impact on our knee, or the yawning or tickling reflexes (Phillips 1993). Others represent a straightforward contribution to survival, such as the sucking reflex that allows human infants to feed, or the reflex of moving your hand away when touching a hot object.

A reflex is activated independently of the mental processing of drives. The experience of a reflex generates memory registers that can be accessed later and define its "trigger." The trigger is the set of memory registers of people or things that activate the reflex. For example, a young child can quickly learn that a plugged electric iron is a possible trigger for the reflex of moving the hand to avoid being burned. Note that conditioning can modify any species' innate reflexes by a learning process that changes its triggers. Thus, reflexes are initially pre-programmed, but actual life experiences can change them.

In Attachment Theory, partial instinctual responses are reflexes that have the mother as their trigger and induce empathic and supportive reactions from her. The mother's breast is the trigger for the sucking reflex, and from it, develops the primary form of feeding for the newborn. The smile reflex induces a supportive response from the mother, who is proud of her initial contact with her son. The reflexes of seeking closeness, having physical contact, asking for help or crying produce similarly positive welcoming responses in the case of a mother who is good enough (to use Winnicott's term) and from this set of interactions, a secure basis arises, which is the fundamental concept of the theory.

We cannot deny the relevance of Bowlby's contribution, as an extensive body of evidence supports it. What, however, we perceive immediately is that there is no justification for excluding the role of drives in attachment formation. See the suction case in which we start from an innate reflex to understand the mechanism of suckling as a realization of the self-preservative drive of feeding. It is evident that, after the baby has discovered the functionality of the breast to satisfy his hunger, the activity is no longer a mere reflex and has a drive motivation. On the other hand, the erotogenic pleasure derived from suckling also activates the sexual drive, transforming the breast into the first libidinal object. One can even think, as suggested by authorities like Melanie Klein or Winnicott, that the breastfeeding activity soon acquires the characteristics of ludic activity. It is clear, then, that we have here the confluence of the innate reflex of sucking with the food, sexual and ludic drives.

Consider the reflex of smiling, which only appears after the second or third month of life. The smile has an immediate impact on the mother. For the first time, she has the impression that her efforts to pamper the child are successful. It is only a reflex, but it is as if the child shows that there is indeed a personal relationship. It motivates the mother and other relevant adults to dedicate themselves even more to gestures, touches, and speaking ways. Consequently, the baby learns that his smile generates a joyful and dedicated reaction from the mother. The reflex is conditioned and from that moment a crucial partnership of ludic activity starts to be built, in which the mother becomes what Stern (2010) defined as a show of light and sound, with sequences of mutual smiles, delicious interactions, and exciting games and rituals that fill the whole day.

We have already seen that Bowlby's formulation has three underlying problems. First, it does not consider the participation of drives in the emergence of the initial attachment situation. Second, it does not offer an alternative explanation for eating and sex behaviors (item b of the summary above). Also, it has nothing to say about ludic-motivated behaviors, that is, about why an individual decides to leave his safe base to explore the world. It is assumed to be just an innate exploratory behavior different from the attachment behavior.

Even the concept of a safe base remains poorly explained since Bowlby (1988, p.4) has only the phylogenetic argument that puppies close to their mothers are more likely to survive. The biological function of this behavior would be protection against predators. But Bowlby lacks an ontogenetic argument to explain from whence comes the feeling of security that the child experiences when he is with his mother. We know that the only reasonable answer is that she becomes a ludic support object after the separation-individuation stage of child development.

To finish this chapter, we need to face the following issue. The ludic drive has a reasonable biological plausibility. Its inclusion in a Freudian model modified by the substitution of energy for information produces many impressive theoretical results. Freud (1915c) himself could have done this when he wrote that no objection could be made to anyone employing the concept of a ludic drive (*Spieltrieb*), or a destruction drive (*Destruktionstrieb*) or a sociability drive (*Geselligkeitstrieb*). Still, he preferred to focus on what he called primal drives (Ürtriebe). We will address the possibility of a destruction drive in Part III. Let me explain here why I discard the alternative of a sociability drive.

In principle, I have no objection to an attempt to add this type of drive to an expanded Freudian model. It could be a kind of libido, as imagined by Fairbairn (1952, ch. VII), essentially object-seeking. That is, the drive's aim would be the establishment of relationships. In practice, however, we can see

82

two strong arguments against this expansion of the model. First, we cannot see a minimum biological plausibility. What natural homeostatic mechanism can be a reasonable ontogenetic explanation for this type of motivation? Second, this proposal to expand the model does not resist the Occam's razor principle. This methodological principle, attributed to the English Franciscan friar William of Ockham (or Occam), recommends that a simpler model with fewer assumptions and variables should always be preferred to a more complex model if the two produce equally satisfactory explanations for a given set of phenomena.

The inclusion of the ludic drive is sufficient to eliminate a significant gap in classical drive psychoanalysis, which was the absence of satisfactory explanations for many types of human relationships. Ludic psychology allows integrating relational phenomena into the drive model without any significant loss for the classic foundations of the discipline. Therefore, there is nothing to be gained by adding a socialization drive.

PART III. AGGRESSION AND MELANIE KLEIN

10. Freud and Lorenz

Despite almost five decades of continued effort in the construction of psychoanalysis, Freud was unable to discover a satisfactory solution for the great enigma of aggression. How can civilized people living in advanced cultures commit countless acts of aggression, destruction, and cruelty against their fellowmen? How to understand the human tendency to get involved in conflicts and wars? How to solve the riddle of large-scale genocides that frequently haunt the news?

Freud eventually put forward the death instinct as an explanation, but even in his *Beyond the Pleasure Principle* he had some words of critical reflection:

> It may be asked whether and how far I am myself convinced of the truth of the hypotheses that have been set out in these pages. My answer would be that I am not convinced myself and that I do not seek to persuade other people to believe in them. Or, more precisely, that I do not know how far I believe in them (1920, p. 332)

The vast majority of psychoanalysts, with the exception perhaps of the Kleinian, were equally dissatisfied with the death-instinct solution and ended up adopting in practice the notion of an aggressive drive as an experience-near intuitive hypothesis, as advocated by Hartmann, Kris & Loewenstein (1949).

Still, it is interesting to examine how Freud's thinking evolved until he reached his "mythology" of Eros and Thanatos. He informs us in his 1930 book on the problem of Civilization that he initially decided to work with two classes of drives. He had been inspired by the poet-philosopher Schiller, who wrote that hunger and love are the movers of the world. This hunger-love duality results from the interaction of self-preservative drives, which aim to preserve the individual, with the sexual drive, which seeks to preserve the species. In this scheme, there was no room for an additional aggression drive, since each of the drives considered could by itself become aggressive in certain situations. He indeed used this argument in Section II of the third chapter of the Little Hans case history (1909) to reject Adler's proposal of a third independent aggression drive. In sadism, we can perhaps see aggressive behaviors as a result of the sexual drive, but in most cases, these behaviors are just manifestations of a self-preservative motivation:

> The ego hates, abhors and pursues with intent to destroy all objects which are a source of unpleasurable feeling for it... Indeed, it may be asserted that the true prototypes of the relation of hate are derived not from sexual life, but from the ego's struggle to preserve and maintain itself. (Freud 1915, p. 136).

In other words, aggressiveness was not understood as a drive in the early days of the Freudian model, but only as a reaction to certain external stimuli, using as "fuel" the energy of the self-preservative drives.

Freud informs us that this first solution to the puzzle was later made unfeasible by the concept of narcissism, which allowed him to advance in the understanding of traumatic neuroses and of many pathological manifestations associated with psychoses. A consequence of this theoretical innovation was that it was no longer possible to distinguish between the energy of the self-preservative drives and the energy of the sexual drive now invested (cathected) in the ego:

Since the ego-instincts, too, were libidinal, it seemed for a time inevitable that we should make libido coincide with instinctual energy in general, as C. G. Jung had already advocated earlier. Nevertheless, there still remained in me a kind of conviction, for which I was not able to find reasons, that all of the instincts could not be of the same kind (Freud 1930, p 77).

A mischievous reading of this text could infer that this conviction for which he could not find reasons resulted only from his difficulty in recognizing his defeat in the long and fierce intellectual dispute with Jung. Freud was always concerned with defending what he considered his most significant discovery, the thesis that neuroses are pathologies of sexual origin. He thought that conservatively motivated interests were trying all the time to review or neutralize this conclusion. His conflict with Jung mainly resulted from this issue. Could libido be understood as instinctive energy of a general nature acting on all types of human motivation, or did it have to be recognized as the exclusive energy of sexual motivation? One gets the impression that in all of Freud's "notable" disagreements, involving Adler, Rank, and Jung, the relationship problems resulted mainly from his suspicion that those authors' proposals for theoretical innovations could have the shady objective of eliminating the sexual focus of psychoanalysis. His engaged and robust position on this issue became evident when in the *Introductory Lessons* (1916), he demonstrated his contentment with the discovery of the notion of narcissism. He wrote that perhaps libido theory could now celebrate its triumph along the whole line, from the simplest neurosis to the most severe alienation of personality (Freud 1916, p. 534).

We don't have to assume that Freud's accounts of the evolution of his thought have high historical precision and were free from unconscious distortions of memory (such as those he discussed in his 1899 text on "screen memories"). However, there is a reasonable technical justification for his difficulty of accepting that libido always energizes aggression. After all, in the original conception, libido had sensual pleasure as its aim. We may understand that there is an element of aggressiveness mixed with sexuality in perversions, but how can we admit that aggressive behaviors of a non-sexual nature may be motivated by a sexual impulse that should, by definition, seek sensual pleasure? How to acknowledge that the individual who kills his fellow man is enjoying sensual pleasure? How to admit that both cruelty and sexual activity produce the same feeling of pleasure?

Freud's solution was to introduce the death instinct, an impulse of destruction he postulated based on weak psychological evidence and with an equally weak argument of biological plausibility, inspired by an obscure morphological theory of August Weismann. The theory was that there is germplasm, an immortal part of the body built to ensure the survival of the species, while on the other hand, the rest of the body was built to die. This theory is certainly not consistent with further advances in genetics.

In Freud's new conception, aggressive behavior would result from a mixture or fusion between a self-preservative motivation, mobilized by the energy of ego instincts, that is, by the same libido that motivates sexual activity, and a destruction motivation, mobilized by the energy of the instinct of death. The interaction between these two forces would determine all human behavior. The two basic instincts operate against each other or in combination. For example, eating is the destruction of an object with the ultimate goal of incorporating it into the ego. Sexual activity is an act of aggression to obtain the most intimate union with another person. This simultaneous and mutually opposite action of the two basic instincts gives rise to the great variety that we observe in life's phenomena, and changes in the proportions of this fusion produce consequences. An excess of sexual aggression can turn a passionate lover into a sexual killer, while a marked decrease in this factor can make him shy or sexually impotent.

As always, Freud used his new understanding of the sources of human motivation with great skill. However, in this case, neither his brilliance nor his masterly communication skills were sufficient to achieve high adherence in the psychoanalytic community. The new theory was very complicated, without a respectable biological basis, and still called into question the pleasure principle, one of the foundations of psychoanalysis. See, for example, Fenichel's (1935) strong adverse reaction:

> ... it seems to me characteristic of psychoanalysis as a scientific psychology that it integrates itself with biology and regards mental life only as a special case of life in general. It explains psychological phenomena as the result of an interplay of biological needs and influences of the external world. "Instinct" is the concept which reflects for us those "biological needs"; therefore it is an indispensable bridge between our science and biology... instinctual need is the "demand made by the body upon the psychic apparatus" ... A "death instinct" does not fit in with such a definition of instinct (p. 366).

The near-experience alternative suggested by Hartmann, Kris, and Loewenstein avoided the complications of Freud's mythological model, but it was also unsatisfactory. It is not easy to accept the notion that there is some psychic energy that aims at the destruction of its object, in an activity that produces a particular type of pleasure different from that resulting from meeting self-preservative needs, the sensual satisfaction of libido, or even the joy of the ludic drive. It ignores the question of biological plausibility. The difficulties become even more severe when we abandon the old energetic model and start to work with the conception of the mind as an information processor and with the understanding that drives are homeostatic impulses. In this case, what would be the homeostatic imbalance that makes the body produce an input of information to the mental apparatus, demanding an angry reaction or an act of cruelty or the destruction of an object? We can imagine the biological mechanism at work when people say they are hungry or sexually excited or wanting to develop some activity to break the monotony. What, however, is happening when someone attacks another person or decides to do some cruel act?

The study of animal behavior may help us unravel this enigma, and for this, the best starting point is still the classic *On Aggression* by Konrad Lorenz (1963). Lorenz shows with countless examples that aggression is of great importance for the preservation of species in the process of natural selection. He concludes that, far from being the "destructive and diabolical" principle of psychoanalysis, it is an essential part of the psychological organization that has as objective the preservation of life. Naturally, he referred to Freudian mythology and the death instinct, this notion that living beings, despite their natural expansiveness, have a dark side and a "diabolic" tendency to self-destruct, which occasionally turns into aggressive impulses.

Lorenz notes that even aggression between animals of the same species can have survival value, since it is always beneficial for a species when the strongest of two rivals become the master of a "territory" or ensures exclusive access to all females. This behavior may be sexually motivated, but the territorial definition may also bring an ecological benefit:

> The danger of too dense a population of an animal species settling in one part of the available biotope and exhausting all its sources of nutrition and so starving can be obviated by a mutual repulsion acting on the animals of the same species, effecting their regular spacing out... This, in plain terms, is the most important survival value of intra-specific aggression (Lorenz, 1963, p. 31).

The dispute for hegemony between rivals can also result in a higher level of security for the group:

The most important function of rival fighting is the selection of an aggressive family defender, and this presupposes a further function of intra-specific aggression: brood defense ... its truth can be demonstrated by the fact that in many animals, where only one sex cares for the brood, only that sex is really aggressive toward fellow members of the species (Lorenz, 1963, p. 43).

Ethology seems to indicate that aggression, far from being an innate tendency to produce damage, pain, and destruction, as proposed in the psychoanalytic tradition, is innate to ensure the preservation of the species. However, a phylogenetic argument does not explain why any individual in a given situation adopts aggressive behavior that may cause destruction and cruelty. The question of biological plausibility is how to find an ontogenetic explanation for this kind of behavior.

11. Animal Aggression

Lorenz produces valuable insights when he focuses his analysis on the typical situation of the struggle between a predator and a resistant prey. It is a scene that, in the past, could only be observed by researchers in fieldwork, but today it is widely available in videos on the Internet for the most varied types of species and circumstances. We may note that there is a big difference between the predator's behavior that engages in hunting and the violence and despair with which the non-docile prey reacts to defend itself:

> ... the fight between predator and prey is not a fight in the real sense of the word: ... the inner motives of the hunter are basically different from those of the fighter ... The differences in these inner drives can clearly be seen in the expression movements of the animal: a dog about to catch a hunted rabbit has the same kind of excitedly happy expression as he has when he greets his master or awaits some longed-for treat. From many excellent photographs it can be seen that the lion, in the dramatic moment before he springs, is in no way angry. (Lorenz, 1963, p. 25)

Lorenz notes that the aggressiveness that seems absent in the hunter's behavior is evident in the desperate struggle for survival of the trapped prey, which he calls the "critical reaction":

...we call this... behavior pattern the critical reaction. The expression "fighting like a cornered rat" has become symbolic of the desperate struggle in which the fighter stakes his all, because he cannot escape and can expect no mercy. This most violent form of fighting behavior is motivated by fear, by the most intense flight impulses whose natural outlet is prevented by the fact that the danger is too near, so the animal, not daring to turn its back on it, fights with the proverbial courage of desperation. Such a contingency may also occur when... flight is prevented by lack of space, or by strong social ties, like those which forbid an animal do desert its brood or family. (Lorenz, 1963, p. 28)

This analysis highlights a difficulty common to many discussions on aggression, of not precisely defining the specific type of behavior considered. Indeed, we must make a distinction between the predator's assertiveness and the aggressive prey defense reaction. The hunter's assertiveness has a playful element, a pleasure in performing a task well, and the primary motivation to get food. This assertiveness is motivated by some combination of the ludic drive and the self-preservative drive of hunger. Lorenz does not consider it correct to call this aggression. For him, aggression is what we see in the critical reaction, in the prey's desperate struggle to defend himself.

Contrary to the hunter's assertiveness, where we can perceive both the hunger motivation and the ludic impulse, the critical reaction seems to be driven by some combination of fear, despair, and anger. Pfaff (2007) coined the name "impulsive aggression" for this reaction that appears explosively, usually accompanied by anger and rage.

The notion that assertiveness and aggression are fundamentally different phenomena has received broad support in the literature. Leider (1998) has a good survey, with references to Kohut (1972), Parens (1973; 1979), Stechler & Halton (1987), Lichtenberg (1983; 1989), Mitchell (1998), Fosshage (1998) and Ornstein (1998). The psychology textbook by Gleitman,

Reisberg & Gross (2007) correctly identifies the non-aggressive nature of the predator's assertiveness. It notes that predators hunt and kill for food, but do so in a completely dispassionate manner. There is no sign of discomfort or anger. A hunting dog does not show typical signs of aggression, such as growling or having its ears laid back. Panksepp & Biven (2012) note that when predatory animals chase and kill their prey, they seem to experience only an anticipatory pleasure from the next meal rather than discomfort or anger. Naturally, if the victim resists vigorously and manages to escape, the predator will be irritated and angry, as it now lost the homeostatic gratification expected from the food.

However, there is a problem with using the term "assertiveness" in the case of the predator's behavior in Lorenz's combat scene. After all, it is the victim and not the aggressor who should define whether a particular action of the latter is aggressive. For the predator, hunting can be just a moment of ludic assertiveness or self-assertion. Still, it is a real threat for the prey, fraught with risks to its integrity and survival. For the victim, a hunting activity with it as the target is an act of cruelty. It aims to inflict suffering and pain. There is no doubt that it is aggressive behavior, something very different from a peaceful activity. From the predator's point of view, however, what stands out is that the action does not involve any emotion of anger. In this case, instead of talking only about assertiveness, it seems more informative to talk about assertive aggressiveness, understanding that we are dealing with zero-anger behavior.

On the other hand, the defensive action of the trapped prey does involve an aggressive reaction with a strong component of anger, in which case we can follow Pfaff in using the term "impulsive aggression." For the victim, there is no difference between assertive and impulsive aggression. Still, for the aggressor, the difference is the presence of a component of rage and anger in the second case.

What interests us is to understand in greater depth the mechanics of the critical reaction. We can assume that in this situation, the prey has two defense strategies to try to survive its predator: fight or flight. We know that the type of defensive behavior can vary between different species. For example, in some cases, the escape is replaced by thanatosis, which occurs when the prey pretends to be dead, causing a predator stimulated by movements to abandon the predatory action. However, this behavior is more common in insects and reptiles than in mammals, so we can focus on the case of the prey that defends itself through fight or flight.

In this case, we may understand the escape behavior as a reflex triggered by the threatening proximity of the predator. The experience of fear, which is an anticipation of that trigger and its consequences, typically precedes the escape. The prey starts to monitor the predator's behavior from the moment it enters its field of vision and collects information through sounds and smells. Then it goes into a state of alert, experiencing physiological changes such as sweating, rapid breathing, muscle contraction, and an increase in heart rate. The predator's perception in the vicinity operates as a generator of fear and discomfort/stress until, when its proximity becomes very unsettling, or its movements assume very threatening characteristics, the escape trigger is activated. The escape experience is always unpleasant, with intensified physiological changes to allow escape. The fleeing animal feels significant discomfort and has high energy expenditure.

The prey situation becomes critical when it realizes that its defense through the escape reflex has become either unviable or undesirable. There may be some physical constraints for the escape route. But even when escape is possible, it may be highly undesirable owing to the need to protect the young or its territory. In this case, the level of discomfort/stress quickly rises above a critical limit value, and what we may call "aggressive mobilization" occurs, putting into operation a set of reflexes typical to the species. In some animals, this defensive behavior against a predator may include the ejection of ink (in squid) or luminescent material (in some crustaceans). In most mammals, including primates, the mobilization resulting from an excessive level of discomfort/stress produces a reflex of impulsive aggression. The prey assumes an attack posture, even though there is a definite physical capacity disadvantage. The intensity of the prey's reaction, which Lorenz associates with the expression "fighting like a cornered rat," together with movements, postures, and threatening noises, often achieves the goal of scaring the predator and driving it away.

What matters here is to make it clear that in impulsive aggression, it is an excessively high level of discomfort/stress produced by the approach of some potentially threatening animal that triggers the reflex. It can occur in the fight between predator and prey, as seen above, or in several other typical situations of conflict between members of the same species or different species. This level of critical discomfort, which generates an aggressive mobilization, can be hereditary, but fighting games involving adults or siblings can also modify it. These games develop combat and attack techniques that increase the chances of successful aggressive mobilization, causing the now-conditioned reflex to emerge in relatively lesser levels of discomfort. That is, the animal will have become "more aggressive." The fundamental point, which we want to emphasize, is that we need neither the mythology of the death impulse nor an aggressive drive à la Hartmann, Kris, and Loewenstein to explain the reflex of impulsive aggression.

We can make an interesting parallel with the analysis of affective neuroscience by Jaak Panksepp (1998). Pankseep identifies four emotional operating systems capable of generating organized sequences of behavior. The most important is the SEEKING system, which commands actions aimed at goals and which we can associate with the realization of the self-preservative, sexual, and ludic drives. Then we have the three systems called Fear, Panic, and Anger. With some imprecision, we can think of the the aggressive reaction of the trapped prey as using these last three systems in sequence. The presence of the predator generates fear and flight. The perception that it will not be possible to escape causes panic and discomfort/stress. The aggressive critical reaction as a result of the discomfort appears as a manifestation of the anger system. Panksepp believes that these emotional systems are genetically implanted neural circuits that can be evoked by localized electrical stimulations.

We can see that some animals do not seem able to develop aggressive mobilization when encountering one of their predators. They are easy prey, such as African gazelles, that even when cornered keep trying to escape. It can also happen that they are frozen in shock, failing to offer any resistance to the predator, which is very convenient for it. For example, for a lion, it is much less work to eat a gazelle that usually does not offer much resistance than to eat a wild boar, which both screams and kicks frantically while remaining alive. Often these docile animals are not endowed with sufficient physical resources for an effective defensive reaction against a strong predator. Typically, they have an innate pattern of non-aggressive behavior. In general, we can see that they are not carnivores and do not have the experience of killing to eat, which may be part of the explanation for their relative passivity. For some reason, in these animals, we cannot observe the type of angry, aggressive mobilization that, in certain situations, transforms the flight behavior into impulsive aggression.

Lorenz points out that the critical reaction of the trapped prey does not necessarily aim to destroy the hunter and may only aim at making possible an escape. Here we have another essential dimension, the difference between destructive and non-destructive aggressiveness, behavior with or without intention to destroy. Assertive aggression is always destructive, since the aggressor wants to eat the victim, but impulsive aggression may not be. Of course, it has to do with the aggressor's intention; from the victim's point of view, aggression is always destructive. Here we are thinking about destructive ex-ante behaviors that, for different reasons, fail to be realized and so turn out to be non-destructive ex-post.

Lorenz also notes that impulsive aggression in animals is generally non-destructive. For example, when large male predators, such as lions, fight for dominance over territory or for a group of females, the result is rarely the destruction of the loser, who usually moves away alive when defeated. The coral fish in the Lorenz aquarium only end up killing their opponents of the same species because they have no way to chase them away on account of limited space. In nature, the result of conflict is usually only the weaker flight, with the consequent demarcation of territory.

Aggressiveness between animals of the same species can play a role in preserving the species, reducing the danger of a very dense population's using the same part of the available biotope and depleting sources of nutrition. Mutual repulsion, not necessarily destructive between males of the same species, usually has a strong sexual motivation and also produces an ecological benefit, insofar as it guarantees separation between families. On the other hand, the non-destructive dispute for hegemony between rivals may result in a higher security level for the group, as it selects an aggressive defender for the family and, especially, for the brood.

Lorenz acknowledges that some cases seem, at first glance, to contradict the conclusion that impulsive aggression is non-destructive, but notes that these cases do not stand up to further analysis. See the "counteroffensive" of a group of animals against one of their predators. Some social animals take every chance to attack an "enemy eater" that poses a potential threat to their security. He calls this phenomenon "mobbing." Several types of crows or birds, for example, produce group attacks against their nocturnal predators (such as cats) when they see them during the day. These manifestations of group aggression have vital survival value. They teach younger and inexperienced members to quickly identify their dangerous enemy eater, which is something they do not know how to do instinctively. From an ontogenetic point of view, what probably happens is that the encounter of a group of prey with a predator triggers critical reactions in all individuals in the group, and this collective movement ends up destroying the aggressor. It does not mean that each individual attacked initially intends to kill and not just chase away the predator.

Another complicated case is infanticide, which seems to be quite common among animals (Hrdy 1979, Packer & Pusey 1984, Packer 2001). We know that male lions kill offspring that have been bred by females in their group with other males, and sexual motivation often explains this as females do not become receptive until their offspring are at least eighteen months old. That is, killing cubs facilitate their sexual activity. However, this behavior presupposes an extraordinary learning ability and level of intelligence in this wild animal. Another possible explanation may be that there is some sensitive marker, such as some special odor, that the dominant male somehow associates with his adult females and his own young and leaves them safe from his instinctual attack. It seems to be a kind of sensory safe-conduct. Any other animal without this marker that appears in his territory, whether adult or young, will be immediately perceived as an invader, and this demands impulsive aggression that usually ends with death in the 'cubs' case. Lorenz notes, from the observation of a group of Eskimo dogs, how the puppy seems to invite dangerous adults to do an odor test to confirm the legitimacy of its presence. As soon as the adult's approach occurs, the puppy sits on its back on the floor, exposing its belly and ejecting a few drops of urine. These are immediately sniffed by the adult, thus confirming its recognition as a member of the group.

The analysis of the destructive dimension of animal behavior has the obvious limitation that we cannot ask them about their ex-ante intentions in each specific case. We must rely on empirical observations or experiments. We know that there may be an intention to destroy that does not materialize, so that the ex-post verification may not be very informative about the ex-ante purpose. The problem is much less severe in humans, because in this case, we can also count on the two powerful instruments of psychoanalysis: empathy and introspection.

12. Human Aggression

The previous chapter identified two types of aggressive behavior in animals: assertive aggression and impulsive aggression. A distinguishing feature of assertive aggression is the total absence of anger and rage. From the aggressor's point of view, aggressive behaviors may or may not have the intention to destroy, but aggression is always potentially destructive from the victims' point of view.

Our analysis of aggressive behavior in animals did not allow us to identify anything like a death instinct or an aggressive drive. Assertive aggression typically results from a combination of the ludic drive with the self-preservative drive of hunger. Impulsive aggression results from aggressive mobilization produced by an excessively high level of discomfort/stress. It is a reflex whose trigger is activated when the discomfort reaches intensity beyond a critical limit value. It may result from the perception of a real risk or fear condition. It may also result from the irritation and resentment produced by the unwelcome presence of a stranger, or even from the behavior of anyone impairing the satisfaction of some instinctual drives. These may be self-preservative, or sexual, or even ludic. Internal conditions can also act to intensify discomfort. For example, any circus tamer knows that even a trained lion can become dangerous when suffering from visceral pain. The critical limit value that triggers the aggressive reflex must be innate and does not seem to be present in docile animals. Nevertheless, even in aggressive animals, it can be changed by learning from experience or fighting games with adults and siblings. The aggressive reflex is innate, but experience may condition it.

How can we apply these conclusions to the case of our species? It seems reasonable to suppose that the first aggressive mobilization experience for any human being occurs with an explosive newborn cry. In a footnote to his *Two Principles* (1911), Freud observed that the baby in early life demonstrates dissatisfaction with unsatisfied needs through the motor discharge of screaming and hitting the air with arms and legs. It is an angry demonstration in which he seems to be trying to attack anyone nearby. The volume and stridency of the scream appear designed to have an irritating impact on responsible adults. Darwin (1872, ch. VI) observed that infants, when suffering even slight pain, moderate hunger, or discomfort, utter violent, and prolonged screams. For Tomkins (1963) and Wolff (1969), crying is an automatic response that signals a state of discomfort. Walter (2007) notes that in the first months of life, we have a simple way of expressing fear, loneliness, pain, or any other discomfort: we bawl, long and loudly. Konner (2010) notes that human crying in the first months of life does not have the same social dimension that it assumes later; it reflects only a state of physical discomfort.

The phylogenetic explanation for the phenomenon is evident. Humans are probably the animal species in which newborns are least prepared to face life outside the mother's womb. Konner notes that human infants are the less competent in motor, social, and even perceptual abilities among primates. Therefore, the explosive crying of the human baby must have some benefit for the species. The evolutionary advantage is to enlist the help of adults in addressing the child's deficiencies, avoiding survival risks. Lutz (1999) notes that puppies that can communicate when they are hungry tend to be better fed than those that cannot. Given the enormous human dependence on maternal care, there would be a high risk of starvation if there were no crying.

Nelson (2005) explains why the cry of the human baby has a fundamental adaptive role. Beginning in childhood, she says, the function of our crying is to attract the attention of our caregivers to keep them close, nurturing, and willing to guarantee the meeting of our needs. Crying upsets other people, so they know they must come and help us. It not only alerts responsible adults that we need them, but it also bothers them to the point where they feel viscerally compelled to respond, even when it is unpleasant or inconvenient. Indeed, crying, as suggested by Bowlby, is one of the innate reflexes that produce the attachment behavior that is fundamental for survival and human development. Konner (2010) points out that crying can only be stopped by nutritious substances and by physical proximity, factors that support life, reduce the risk of predators, and maintain adequate body temperature.

This phylogenetic explanation does not, however, fully solve the problem of biological plausibility. We also need to understand the mechanism that produces aggressive mobilization and angry crying in babies. We have already seen that aggressive mobilization is a reflex that is triggered when the level of discomfort/stress experienced by the individual reaches an intensity higher than a critical limit value. We can extract from tips manuals for good parenting a list of five primary sources of discomfort that can produce crying in babies: hunger, pain, temperature (too cold or too hot), wet diaper, tiredness/sleep. Nelson (2005) proposes an expanded list including colic, the transition state of awakening, illnesses, scares in general, the discomfort of gases from swallowing air, thirst, diapers with feces and harmful stimuli such as bitter taste or loud noises. For the human newborn, the critical limit value for any discomfort is practically zero. As every mother knows very well, the child is entirely intolerant to any item on these lists, however insignificant. In other words, the human baby goes into aggressive mobilization and produces an outburst of violent, angry crying in response to any slight feeling of discomfort. He is born with total intolerance to discomfort.

A noteworthy important phenomenon is that this intolerance decreases with the child's development, notably after the fourth month of life (Blatz & Millichamp [1935]; Charlesworh & Kreutzer [2006]; Konner [2010]). It probably occurs because opportunities to obtain pleasure from ludic, sexual (with the use of a baby pacifier), or even self-preservative drives begin to appear, which are incompatible with explosive crying. These new opportunities for pleasure start to function as compensations for a transient situation of discomfort. Life experience transforms the aggressive mobilization into a conditioned reflex, opening space for a higher level of peaceful tolerance to the normal setbacks of life.

Here we have an interesting technical question to clarify. Aggressive mobilization is triggered when the total level of discomfort experienced by the individual has an intensity higher than the critical-limit value. The question is how the mind performs the task of measuring this level. Discomfort is a sensation that can be produced by three different types of information. First, it may be the signaling of a homeostatic demand that can be self-preservative (hunger, thirst, heat, cold) or sexual (sensual interest or desire) or ludic (boredom or the urge to do something). Second, it can be the signaling of an external disturbance capable of producing fear, irritation, or anger. And third, it can be the signaling of a stimulus associated with an arc reflex pattern (the Freudian *Reiz*), with an origin both internal (like colic) and external (like unexpected noise). The problem is how to measure the intensity of these different signals and aggregate them into a single indicator of total discomfort.

It is a neurology problem that goes beyond the scope of this book, and we can only speculate on it. Imagine an individual with two homeostatic imbalances: hunger and the urge to urinate. While the imbalances remain, the mind receives a sequence of signals related to them. The frequency of these signals informs the relative intensity of the imbalances. Observing how many times per second the "eat" and "urinate" signals appear allows this information to be "read." If the urinate signal appears more often than the eat signal, this means that the urge to urinate is more intense than hunger.

Consequently, if the mind focuses on the frequency of the two signals, it can build an indicator of the total discomfort resulting from them. It is precisely the total amount of signals sent per unit of time. It may be how the ego decides its course of action when it must determine which homeostatic demand must be met as a priority when there are several simultaneous imbalances. A simple rule of thumb is to meet the demand that is being signaled most often per unit of time.

The reduction of intolerance to discomfort begins at about the same time as the phase that Mahler called separation-individuation. In this phase, the child has an increased motor capacity and can dedicate himself fully to ludic activities of the sensory-motor type. She then learns to "attack" material things, biting every kind of object she can catch and throwing it hard on the floor. This behavior must, in the beginning, be only motivated by curiosity. For a young child in an intense learning process, biting an object or throwing it away can be very informative about its physical nature and dynamic properties. Is it hard or soft? Which noises occur when we bite it or throw it away? What happens when it hits the ground? At least initially, there is no intention to damage, destroy, or make the thing disappear.

This peaceful mood begins to change when material things do not behave in the way the child wants, becoming agents of frustration in his ludic activities and sources of discomfort. If the child were still a small baby, his reaction would be an aggressive mobilization, producing an intense burst of crying. But now he/she is less intolerant of discomfort and has learned he/she can eliminate it with a direct attack. The discomfort disappears if the frustrating thing is destroyed or removed from its playful environment.

The next development is to target this attack behavior learned in dealing with material things to people who may be acting as agents of frustration. The child says, "I want to go into the pool now," but the mother says, "No, now you can't because it's too cold and you must still have lunch." In response, the little one tries to hit or bite the mother. Charles Darwin (1877) already noticed this behavior in his children aged 11 months to two years. Usually, the mother and other responsible adults will know how to suppress this infantile aggression and, if they do not, significant deformations may result in the adult personality. Freud (1930) taught that this is an educational task of the utmost importance for the construction of human civilization. We know, as will be seen in detail in Chapter 26, that this repression will be internalized in a superego precursor and, eventually, in a Freudian superego.

This evolution eventually leads to the full development of impulsive aggression in human adults. The repression by the superego, along with natural conditioning throughout the child's development, tends to reduce intolerance to discomfort by raising the critical threshold value that triggers aggressive mobilization. On the other hand, life experience with R&T (rough-and-tumble) games among children and sports and combat games among adults significantly increase the effectiveness of the human attack. It can be particularly dangerous when the individual develops the ability to deal with modern instruments of destruction through, for example, sport shooting training or military service.

When comparing men and animals, it is evident that civilization has had enormous success in mitigating impulsive aggression among humans. Paul Seabright notes in his *The Company of Strangers* (2004) the carnage that would result if you tried to put a group of chimpanzees inside a commercial plane like those that routinely transport thousands of people peacefully across the world. The modern man no longer needs to carry out impulsive aggression to exclude intruders from his territory or defend his wife and family. He may need a critical reaction against a predator only if he is on an Africa safari or in proximity to a still- isolated indigenous Amazon tribe.

Of course, in the daily life of urban men, moments of discomfort and very intense stress may arise, which end up producing impulsive aggression reactions, sometimes with tragic consequences. Fortunately, the penal systems in modern societies are relatively successful in limiting and discouraging this behavior. The angry response from the man who discovers that his wife has betrayed him often results in passionate murder, as we see all the time on the news. Interestingly, the reaction of women tends to be less aggressive. In similar situations, they often resort to crying rather than to physical aggression, a behavior that suggests a regression to the typical pattern of aggressive mobilization used in childhood. It may also have a cultural explanation, as in many modern societies, women don't develop combat and destruction skills.

As for assertive aggression, human civilization has also produced significant changes. Modern man no longer needs to kill to eat; a supermarket trip is enough to guarantee his usual supply of proteins. The slaughter of animals has become a big industry, and assertive aggressiveness is needed only for those responsible for this industrial activity, which is increasingly done by machines and robots. In this case, the motivation, as in any other human labor activity, is the result of a mixture of self-preservative drives with the ludic drive. For example, the engineer who developed an automated chicken-slaughtering system that practically requires no human intervention may have the world's most docile personality, almost like an African gazelle. He feels only the narcissistic satisfaction of having produced a highly admired and profitable technological advance.

At first glance, the claim that civilization may have somehow reduced human aggressiveness seems inconsistent with the common observation of modern world's great cruelties, such as the great wars of the 20th century, the Nazi holocaust, or the nuclear attacks to Japan. However, this fact is mainly a consequence of technological progress that has dramatically increased the effectiveness of assertive aggression. The pilots of the bomber plane that carried atomic bombs to Hiroshima and Nagasaki were just doing their job and fulfilling their duty without any emotion of anger. Even fighter pilots who engage in aerial combat intending to destroy enemy planes are only performing their mission, primarily with ludic and narcissistic motivation. The proof of this is evident in the way they happily display and comment on the statistics of their victories.

The great cruelties of the modern world probably have more to do with sociology and politics than with psychology. Modern societies where there is no democracy (but sometimes also in democracies) often place powerful instruments of mass destruction created by technology in the hands of sadistic psychopaths. Their assertive aggressiveness, which has no regard for the rest of humanity, may produce great genocides.

Military training is an interesting case of institutional development of assertive aggressiveness. The recruit is initially subjected to significant deprivation to put him in an almost permanent state of discomfort, always on the threshold of aggressive mobilization. This discomfort is then directed towards improving his willingness and ability to destroy the enemy. The training also aims to strengthen the esprit de corps between companions (the so-called "band of brothers") who help each other in adversity. It generates an essential incentive for impulsive aggression (and heroism) in combat situations when a companion is lost.

This discussion on human aggression implies that the usual hypotheses of a death instinct or an aggressive drive lack any empirical basis and are entirely unnecessary. Aggression can be assertive or impulsive. Assertive aggression is a behavior that results from a combination of self-preservative, sexual, and ludic drives. Impulsive aggression is not a drive (*Trieb*), but just a reflex action that arises from aggressive mobilization triggered by an excessively high level of discomfort.

13. Melanie Klein

At first glance, when we replace psychic energy with information and conclude that there is neither a death instinct nor an innate aggressive drive, we will have to abandon all the contributions of Melanie Klein and associates. But this is not true. In the theoretical framework introduced in this book, we preserve an essential part of her contribution, with only a few changes in the original formulation. True, it will also be necessary to desecrate a sort of Kleinian totem, venerated and protected by a significant part of the psychoanalysis community that would not be happy with the blasphemy. However, the result of a few small changes may be the preservation of a valuable contribution to the discipline, allowing it to be better understood and evaluated by "non-converts."

We can take as a starting point a very illuminating passage from Melanie Klein's essay on "Love, Guilt and Reparation":

> The baby's first object of love and hate—his mother—is both desired and hated with all the intensity and strength that is characteristic of the early urges of the baby. In the very beginning he loves his mother at the time she is satisfying his needs for nourishment, alleviating his feelings of hunger, and giving him the sensual pleasure which he experiences when his mouth is stimulated by sucking at her breast... But when the baby is hungry and his desires are not gratified, or when he is feeling bodily pain or discomfort, then the whole situation suddenly alters. Hatred and aggressive feelings are aroused, and he

becomes dominated by the impulse to destroy the very person who is the object of all his desires and who in his mind is linked up with everything he experiences—good and bad alike. In the baby hatred and aggressive feelings give rise, moreover, to most painful states, such as choking, breathlessness and other sensations of the kind, which are felt to be destructive to his own body (Klein, 1937, p. 58).

From this text, we can summarize some fundamentals of Klein's theoretical construction in a simple schematic way. The baby early in life develops a love-hate relationship with his mother. Love results from the fact that the mother's breast functions as a "good breast," a vehicle for obtaining food as breast milk and a source of sexual pleasure through the activity of sucking. Hate stems from the fact that the breast is sometimes unavailable when the baby needs it. In this last case, frustration awakens an aggressive impulse to destroy this "bad breast" perceived as the cause of suffocation, shortness of breath, and other equally unpleasant sensations.

The impulse to destroy gives rise to the phenomenon of projective identification. Its target is perceived as a persecuting agent who threatens to reciprocate with a similar intention of destruction. At this point, the child is in the so-called "paranoid-schizoid position" and sees the world as polarized in good and bad objects, even when, in reality, the relationship is limited to the single person of the mother. This primordial polarity generates anxiety and will be a pattern that will repeat throughout life in an expanding universe of relationships. Eventually, the child manages to evolve to the so-called "depressive position," with the understanding that the mother, like other people encountered throughout life, actually has a mixture of good and bad qualities, being worthy of both love and hate. In this case, the consequence of the destructive impulse is not paranoid anxiety, but a feeling of remorse, sadness, and guilt.

The problem is how to save this construction when we rule out the possibility of destructive impulses in the baby? The obvious fact is that the human being has no innate capacity to destroy anything. The very notion of destroying does not make sense when applied to a newborn. Our previous chapter explained that this is something the child has to learn over time, mainly through ludic activities and the inevitable frustrations that occur in them. As the newborn has zero-tolerance for any discomfort, in the primordial situation described by Klein, aggressive mobilization will result in a violent crying spree. Still, it will not produce any destructive impulse.

Klein needs the notion of a destructive impulse in the child to define the concept of a "bad object," of fundamental importance in her theoretical construction. But to achieve this we only need to introduce the new notion of a *frustration object*. It is a kind of inverted version of the idea of support object, which, as we have already seen, has the function of facilitating and supporting the realization of a drive. The frustration object has the purpose of restraining and jeopardizing the realization of a drive.

Early in life, the good breast that satisfies the baby's self-preservative demands is a support object. In contrast, the bad breast perceived as preventing the satisfaction of these demands is a frustration object. In general, for any drive, we can think of both a good supporting object and a bad frustration object. With these concepts, we can reformulate the elaborate construction of the Kleinian canon without the absurd notion of an innate destructive impulse in the baby.

The notion of projective identification also loses importance, but there is no need to dismiss it wholly. As we showed in the previous chapter, children around three to five years of age discover they can destroy material things. They now believe it is possible to launch a direct attack to destroy anything that becomes a source of frustration and discomfort. Similarly, children also learn that they can hit, kick, and bite people when they become frustration objects for some drive. Usually, this occurs with the ludic drive, but sometimes also with sexual or self-preservative drives.

Note that this is precisely what would happen if there were an innate impulse of destruction. In this case, projective identification will work, as in the Kleinian canon. The desire to attack a bad object because it restrains a drive may turn it into a persecutory agent that may counter-attack. Hence, it is useful to distinguish between merely bad objects that operate as frustration objects for some drive, and persecutory (bad) objects, which have already gone through projective identification.

The concepts of bad objects and paranoid-schizoid and depressive positions are ingenious and exciting and should undoubtedly be considered relevant contributions to psychoanalysis. Melanie Klein also attaches great importance to her notion of the inner (or internal) world, and we can directly quote from her "Mourning and its Relation to Manic-depressive States":

... the process of introjection and projection from the beginning of life lead to the institution inside ourselves of loved and hated objects, who are felt to be 'good' and 'bad', and who are interrelated with each other, and with the self: that is to say, they constitute an inner world. This assembly of internalized objects...is, according to my findings, a complex object-world, which is felt by the individual in deep layers of the unconscious, to be concretely inside himself, and for which I and some of my colleagues therefore use the term 'internalized', or an internal (inner) world. The inner world consists of innumerable objects...corresponding partly to the multitude of varying aspects, good and bad, in which the parents (and other people) appeared in the child's unconscious mind through-out various stages of his development. Further, they also represent real people who are continually becoming internalized in a variety of situations provided by the multitude of ever-changing external experiences as well as phantasied ones. In addition, all the objects are in the inner world in an infinitely complex relation both with each other and with the self (Klein, 1940, in J. Mitchell, 1986, p. 166).

Klein seems overjoyed with the relevance of her innovation:

An understanding of this complex inner world enables the analyst to find and resolve a variety of early anxiety situations which were formerly unknown and is therefore theoretically and therapeutically of an importance so great that it cannot yet be fully estimated (Klein, 1940, in J. Mitchell, 1986, p.167).

The text speaks of an assembly of objects internalized in deep layers of the unconscious. Freudian tradition understands an object as a memory register (or a set of registers) with a drive-associative key. The unique associative key of this drive tags all memory registers associated with impressions related to the fulfillment of its aim. This is how the Freudian concept of cathexis or drive investment is understood when the mind is an information processor. With the expansion of the object concept in this book, as a result of the introduction of support and frustration objects, we also have to consider associative keys for these secondary objects. These associative keys define the inner world, an assembly of unconscious objects corresponding to good and bad aspects of parents and other people experienced over the child's development and continually internalized over life in various situations.

The following set of brief notes summarizes Melanie Klein's main contributions to psychoanalysis:

1) In Freud, an object is always "good" and associated with the pleasurable realization of a drive. It can be either a primary or a support object, a differentiation we introduced in Chapter 4. The

aim of a drive is always the realization of a homeostatic impulse. A primary object is something or someone in which the aim is achieved. A support object is something or someone through which the aim is achieved. This differentiation comes from Freud's (1915c) definition of an object as "the thing in regard to which or through which the instinct is able to achieve its aim." The support object has the role of facilitating, reinforcing, or supporting the drive.

2) Klein introduces the notion of the bad object. It acts to frustrate the realization of the aim of some drive and may have gone through a projective identification process. By definition, there is no unpleasant realization of a drive, but its frustration will always be unpleasant and uncomfortable. Caper (1988, p. 104) notes that Klein distinguishes between a bad object that is merely frustrating and a bad object that is also destructive and hateful. The distinction has to do with whether or not it had a projective identification.

3) Klein highlights the weakness in the Freudian tradition of never having been concerned with the possibility of unconscious objects, that is, objects not accessible to conscious mental processing. Arlow (1980), for example, defines an object as a set of memory traces of pleasant sensory impressions connected with an external person. This notion of sensory perceptions inevitably leads to the conclusion that we are talking here about conscious objects, that is, memory registers that were created by a conscious mental process and can be recovered and used again by the flow of consciousness.

As will be further discussed in Chapter 24 of Part V, it is possible to admit the existence of an associative key that tags the recording of conscious information in memory. We know that a conscious mental process uses only memory registers that contain this key (a kind of consciousness registration key). Freud (1915b) wrote that these are memory registers that have the property of "being capable of becoming conscious" (to use Breuer's expression: p. 175). However, suppose mental processing took place subconsciously without ever becoming conscious, but still generating traces of memory associated with the realization of a drive. In that case, it will have created an unconscious object that may affect the thought process.

4) Klein introduces the notion of an internal or inner world. She notes that traces of memory from unconscious sensory impressions can arise in the process of fantasy. These are unconscious objects, and the set of these objects can be called the inner world. Of course, there is another set of conscious objects of the Freudian tradition, which are the only ones that can be accessed by conscious mental processes. Unconscious mental processes can act freely on the whole memory, accessing both unconscious and conscious objects.

5) Freud (1940) explains how memory registers can affect human behavior and, consequently, several pathologies. The mind interposes between the demand made by a drive and the action that satisfies it a thinking activity that involves two stages. In the first stage of experimentation, it uses memory registers from previous experiences and, through imaginary experimental actions, seeks to determine the consequences of several possible courses of action and thereby find an optimal solution. As the optimization criterion is probably that of limited rationality (as we explain in Chapter 27 of Part VI), routines and procedures that have worked well in the past will strongly influence this process. This stage, which Freud refers to as imagination, is followed by a reality testing stage, aiming to determine whether the information recorded in memory is still relevant to the current reality.

6) If bad objects, which act as frustration objects for a drive, are present in memory, the realization of its aim may be impaired or even aborted in the imagination stage. This is even more so if they have been

subjected to projective identification, thus becoming frustrating and persecutory. Consider, for example, the case of the individual who is compelled to speak in public but is anxious at the prospect that his speech may be a failure. However, if the discourse becomes a success, the individual will enjoy the joy of the satisfaction of this ludic drive despite the transitory displeasure of anticipating failure. In this case, the fantasy of failure, which resulted from previous experiences and therefore functions now as a bad ludic frustration object, can be neutralized by a new good object that is the record of this experience of a successful speech. The next time the individual must make a speech, he will be able to remember (even if unconsciously) both objects, bad and good. He will more easily overcome the anxiety of anticipating failure and dedicate himself more calmly to his goal of making the speech. That is how it can work in a healthy adult, who may feel anxiety in certain stressful situations, but learns to manage them through favorable experiences.

7) The presence of bad objects becomes even more damaging when they are unconscious frustration objects, particularly if they have been subjected to projective identification, thus becoming frustrating and persecutory. Typically, these bad objects are products of fantasy, often internalized in the early years when the child's imaginary life can be dramatic, violent, and frightening. From this fantasy world, inhabited by witches and monsters, an assembly of evil persecutory objects may arise that will affect the individual throughout his life and result in pathological conditions of greater or lesser severity.

8) Klein also developed other concepts relevant for the clinic, such as reparation, envy, and gratitude, but I think her most important contributions were the notions of bad object, inner world, and projective identification.

Let me now speculate on a possible connection between ludic-drive psychology (and, for that matter, also Kohut and Winnicott) and the Kleinian construction. In the former, the initial acquisition of support objects (or Kohut's archaic selfobjects) is a simple eventless matter once the child enters the separation-individuation phase. But for Klein, it may be a rather complicated process. It occurs when the child is moving from a paranoid-schizoid position into a depressive position. Any support object brings together the possibility of an attached frustration object if it does not perform well. In ludic drive psychology or self-psychology, failures of a support object will trigger defensive processes of identification and transmuting internalization. However, in Klein, it may trigger a regression to a paranoid-schizoid position that only reinforces earlier persecutory fears and schizoid phenomena. For her, this may turn out to be the source of various forms of schizophrenia and psychotic phenomena in later life (Klein, 1946, p. 190).

Heinz Kohut was always critical of Melanie Klein's work. In a letter to Anna Freud in October 1966, talking about Klein's many followers in South America, he wrote that he "often predicted that they would finally die out because of the sheer boredom which their formulations must cause them" (Kohut, 1994, p.147). Even for private correspondence, this is a rather unfortunate commentary, and the only excuse is that Kleinian texts use a rather difficult dialect for the uninitiated. Yet when we convert Melanie Klein's arguments to a more accessible language and articulate them logically and consistently, we must recognize the importance of her contribution to psychoanalysis.

PART IV. THE LUDIC DRIVE IN PSYCHOANALYSIS

14. Freud and Schiller

Some mental processes are entirely logical. For example, I decide to use an umbrella because I think it will rain. Other mental processes have an instinctive nature: I choose to eat because I am hungry. I do not make up my mind to eat because I know I need some nutrient intakes to keep me alive. I eat moved by the impulse to satisfy an urge to eat. Of course, the biological need to consume nutrients is at the root of the urge to eat when my body needs nutrients, but this does not eliminate the urge's instinctive nature. The decision to eat does not result from a logical mental process. It is an instinctive impulse generated by an unconscious mental process that drives me to act to satisfy the need to eat. It was this way that Freud introduced the concept of sexual drive (*Trieb*) in the *Three Essays on the Theory of Sexuality* of 1905, still in the early stages of the development of psychoanalysis. Just as hunger is an instinctive impulse that leads me to act to satisfy a need to eat, the sexual drive is an instinctive impulse that leads me to act to meet a sexual demand.

This notion of impulse or drive has some semantic subtleties. By choosing to translate the "*Trieb*" of the German original as "instinct," the editors of the *Standard Edition* added unnecessary confusion to our understanding of this fundamental concept. Freud only used the term "*Instinkt*" when referring to animal behavior. He always preferred the term "*Trieb*" for that idea of human motivation that occupies a central position in his theoretical construction. In the General Preface of the *Standard Edition*, the translator James Strachey complained of excessively harsh criticisms for his choice of the term "instinct." His defense, along with Ernest Jones, was that in general the meaning of the word "*Trieb*" in Freud's work seems closer to the usual sense of the word "instinct" in English, basically suggesting the notion of an innate and hereditary trait (Jones 1958).

Why did Freud choose not to use the term "*Instinkt*"? One possible explanation is that the use of the word "*Trieb*" for human motivation was already deeply rooted in German thought. For example, it appears quite frequently in Kant's work (Paccioni, 2002), particularly in the *Critique of the Power of Judgment*. This book had a substantial influence on the poet-philosopher friends Johann Goethe and Friedrich Schiller. We know Freud was well acquainted with Schiller's work, as he quoted him often. In the catalog of Freud's private library to be found at the Freud Museum in London, there are four volumes of Schiller's *Werke* and several volumes of his correspondence.

Goethe was following Kant and the physician Johann Blumenbach (the original author of the idea) when he used the notion of the *Bildungstrieb*, a formative impulse or epigenetic motor force that determines the reproduction of form in plants, animals, and humans (Richards 2000, MacCord 2014). In all living beings, there would be this hereditary impulse that remains active throughout life and regulates the appearance, preservation, and sometimes even the restoration of its specific form. It was the basis for Goethe's studies on botanical and zoological morphology.

On the other hand, Schiller was influenced by Kant in writing his short book of 1795, *On the Aesthetic Education of Man*, based on a series of letters addressed to a Danish prince who had offered him a generous monetary contribution[9]. Freud never quoted this specific essay by Schiller, but it

---

9   The prince was Friedrich Christian von Schleswig-Holstein-Augustenburg, and the aid amounted to one thousand thalers per year for three years. This figure was at least four times higher than the average income of a university professor. The offer was prompted by gossip that Schiller was badly ill, perhaps on the verge of death. In fact, his health was

seems unlikely that he had never seen it. Disappointed by the course of the French Revolution, of which he had initially been a vigorous advocate, Schiller now argued that humanity would only be ready for political freedom after developing an adequate sensitivity to beauty. Through art, aesthetic education would be the real awakening of human culture, freeing man from his animalistic desires.

Schiller argues that there is a conflict between animal impulses and rationality, between sensations and reason, which dominates human existence:

> ...we are urged by two contrary forces which, because they impel us to realize their object, are very properly called impulses [*Triebe*]. The first of these impulses, which I shall name the *sensuous*, proceeds from the physical existence of Man or from his sensuous nature... The second of these impulses, which we may call the *formal* [or rational] impulse, proceeds from... his rational nature and strives... to maintain his person throughout every change or circumstance. (Schiller, 1795, pp. 64–65)

This reasoning seems quite like Freud's thinking in the early days of his intellectual development: the sexual impulse competing with a self-preservation impulse, the pleasure principle in conflict with the reality principle.

At a certain point in the book, the sensuous impulse looks quite like the notion of Eros adopted in Freud's later formulations: "The object of the sensuous impulse... may be called *life* in the widest sense of the word; a

---

already quite shaken, but he would still live for fourteen years. Anyway, the news mobilized Jens Baggesen, a Danish literary critic employed with the prince. Being a great admirer of Schiller, he convinced the prince of Augustenburg to offer the aid. The original letters sent to the prince were later destroyed in a fire in his palace, but Schiller had preserved copies and eventually published an expanded version. See Barbosa (2004, in Portuguese).

concept which express all material being and all that is immediately present in the senses." (Schiller, 1795, p. 76)

Like Freud, Schiller notes the role of human culture in managing this conflict:

> To watch over these two impulses, and to secure for each its boundaries, is the task of *culture*, which therefore owes justice equally to both, and has to uphold not only the rational impulse against the sensuous, but also the latter against the former. (Schiller, 1795, pp. 68–69)

However, culture does not offer a wholly satisfactory solution to the conflict, since the separate activity of only one of these impulses leaves human nature without full realization. For this, we need the action of a third impulse that combines the two others. Schiller used the term *Spieltrieb* for this third impulse, which we can translate as play impulse (literally) or as ludic impulse (my preference):

> ... the impulse in which both are combined, allow me to call it ... the *ludic impulse* ... In proportion as it lessens the dynamic influence of the sensations and emotions, it will bring them in harmony with rational ideas; and in proportion as it deprives the laws of reason of their moral compulsion, it will reconcile them with the interest of the senses. (Schiller, 1795, p. 74)

For Schiller, by allowing the union of reality with formality, contingency with need, freedom with discipline, the ludic impulse enables the full realization of human potential. Only it can make man complete by reconciling his dual nature. Ludic activities produce a sensation of freedom that necessarily leads to aesthetic contemplation and art. Through aesthetics, one can transform the sensual man, dominated by senses and emotions, into a rational man.

Note that when Schiller writes on *Spieltrieb*, he does not seem to be referring specifically to children's play. There is no mention of childhood, kids, or children's games in this little book, most likely reflecting the fact, mentioned by Ariès (1978), Fass (2013) and others, that the very concept of childhood is a relatively recent construction in human history. Schiller's ludic impulse seems to be associated with creativity and artistic productions—that is, with adult activities free from both formalism and sexual desire.

Snell (2004) tells us that Von Humbolt once said that no one could know if Schiller was a poet who did philosophy or a philosopher who did poetry. There is not any doubt, however, that Schiller was never a real scientist, and, in this respect, there is a great distance between him and Freud. His use of the notion of impulse (*Trieb*) was almost impressionistic. Despite the surprising parallels with Freud, his ideas are far from making a consistent contribution to the theory of mind. On the other hand, even though Freud never quoted Schiller's book on aesthetic education, the possibility of influence cannot be ruled out.

Another possible influence on Freud's decision to use the term *Trieb* was the book *The Play of Man (Die Spiele der Menschen)* published by Karl Groos in 1899. Groos was a German philosopher who knew Schiller's work well and, like him, had a particular interest in aesthetics. He was also one of the pioneers in the study of animal play, a subject to which we will later devote much attention. In that book, which was often quoted by Freud, Groos argues that the notion of instinct ("*Instinkt*"), with its usual connotation of an automatic association between stimuli and specific bodily reactions, may be useful for understanding animal behavior, but not human behavior. For a man, it would be more appropriate to speak of a natural or hereditary impulse (*natürliche oder ererbte Trieb*). Here we may also have a possible channel of influence of Shiller on Freud, through Groos.

These thoughts on Freud's use of the term *Trieb* are just speculative exercises in the history of ideas. Better let Freud himself clarify the precise meaning of his *Trieb* concept. He does it in *Instincts and their Vicissitudes* of 1915, by showing the differences from the physiological notion of a stimulus (*Reiz*). A drive (*Trieb*) arises from inside the organism, never from the outside world. Further, while a stimulus always has a single impact resulting in a specific reaction, the drive operates with a constant pressure force. The essential nature of the Freudian *Trieb* is its origin inside the organism and an impact that extends over time.

Anna Freud put forward a compromise solution to this problem of the correct translation of *Trieb* when she used the term "instinctual impulse" in her 1937 book on defense mechanisms. This way, she was implicitly rejecting the term "instinct" introduced by Strachey and Jones. An analogous solution by Hartmann (1948) was the term "instinctual drive," and after that, English-language psychoanalysis converged in the preferential use of "drive." In this book, we use both "drive" and "instinctual impulse," and sometimes just "impulse," as adequate translations for the Freudian *Trieb*.

15. The Drive to Master

Ives Hendrick (1898-1972) was probably the first psychoanalyst to work with the notion of a ludic drive. He is almost unknown now, despite having been one of the founding members of the Boston Psychoanalytic Institute and president in 1954 of the American Psychoanalytic Association. After graduating in medicine from Yale and working at hospitals in Boston and Baltimore, he was analyzed by Franz Alexander in Berlin and became a professor at Harvard Medical School. His 1934 book, *Facts and Theories of Psychoanalysis*, is still a readable survey of classical psychoanalysis.[10]

Hendrick put forward the concept of an "instinct to master," a drive to master that he defined as an inborn urge to do and to learn how to do. In his 1942 essay entitled "Instinct and the Ego during Infancy," he argued that psychoanalysis was neglecting the overwhelming evidence on the existence of a need to learn "how to." This need becomes apparent when the child uses his sensory, motor, and intellectual resources to control (or become "master of") his environment. In the first two years of life, this seems as crucial for the determination of a child's behavior as the quest for sensual pleasure. It is an instinctive impulse with a non-sexual nature and independent of libido. The aim of the sex drive is always a sensual pleasure, while the aim of the drive to master is the pleasure of learning how to perform some function, regardless of its sensual value.

---

10   For biographical information, see the website of the Boston Psychoanalytic Society and Institute, http://www.bostonpsychoanalytic.org

Hendrick notes that this impulse can be identified even in first-life activities, as the child needs some practice time before achieving a fully efficient performance. For him, this is the pattern of development of the drive to master: a merely reflexive first stage evolves through intensive training into a phase of acquired ability and gratification with mastery. He points out the importance of the initial development of sensory skills as essential tools for survival. Available evidence indicates that, in the face of the challenges of adapting to variable external conditions, the organs of hearing, sight, touch, and other motor and intellectual capacities require periods of concentrated practice. Each neuromuscular resource appears at a well-defined moment of the child's development, but practical use is not achieved immediately. It needs practice for days, weeks, or months.

The drive to master is what turns this essential learning of children into a distinctly compulsive activity that becomes less intense only when the intended function is effectively mastered and the drive diverted towards new mastery challenges. This pattern is particularly evident in the development of the ability to walk. At first, the boy tries to take a step hesitantly, supported by an adult on both hands. He then repeats the process with a single hand and then stops using his hands as he tries to walk quickly between two safe supports. Later he gains the confidence to walk without any support. Much of his attention is focused, during all these weeks, on the repetitive practice of each stage in this process of learning to become master of the physical space using just his legs. It produces an enormous satisfaction in the child, who feels amazed by a new sense of power. But once he has effectively learned to walk, this compulsion to repeat indefinitely specific movements and maneuvers of locomotion without a clear goal disappears, and the function is incorporated into the repertoire of active functions of the ego. From this point, however, the function ceases to produce anything comparable to the joy felt in learning, and we have the complete satisfaction of this drive to master.

The development of ego functions in the first years of a child's life consists of a sequence of learning experiences. This sequence comprises three phases. In the first, reflex phase, the function is made available by the neurophysiological apparatus. Then there is a learning phase that brings to perfection the function through an almost compulsive practice and training effort. In the last maturity phase, the function is fully mastered and incorporated into the ego's available capacities. Throughout the first two years of life, in the early stage of ego development, the compulsion to repeat every sensory or motor function appears as soon as it becomes physiologically feasible. For example, this happens with the capabilities of ocular fixation, grasping, phonation, or locomotion. But as soon as there is efficient mastering of the function, the evidence of repetition disappears, and the new ability becomes available for any use intended by the individual.

The research of Margaret Mahler and her associates confirmed the occurrence of a period in early childhood in which the primary focus of the child's activity is the development of ego functions through training. Mahler, who is one of the few modern authors in psychoanalysis that made direct reference to Hendrick[11], regards this period as the second sub-phase of the separation-individuation process and calls it the practicing phase. See how Mahler and Hendrick have similar views:

The child's first upright independent steps mark the onset of the practicing period *par excellence*, with substantial widening of his world and of reality testing. Now begins a steadily increasing libidinal investment in practicing motor skills and in exploring the expanding environment, both human and inanimate…The child concentrates on practicing and mastering his own skill and autonomous

---

11   Other exceptions were Erikson (1950, p. 259), Brenner (1990, p. 195) and Pine (2005, p. 10).

(independent of other or mother) capacities. He is exhilarated by his own abilities, continually delighted with the discoveries he makes in his expanding world and quasi-enamored with the world and his own grandeur and omnipotence. (Mahler 1975, p. 71)

Unlike Mahler, however, Hendrick (1942) argues that we cannot explain this behavior in terms of libidinal investment, as driven by sexual motivation. For him, the "compulsive quality" of child learning is clear evidence that another instinctive impulse is in operation, independent of the sex drive. The child must learn to control his neuromuscular equipment to ensure independent survival before he can devote himself to any other goal. He achieves this by intensive and compulsive training, which produces the necessary adaptations in his original reflex apparatus. There is nothing sensual about this need to practice a partial function indefinitely until you reach proficiency in your performance. It seems clear that the motivation here is non-sexual. Indeed, it is objective evidence of the drive to master in operation.

Hendrick has a close-to-experience concept in his drive to master, while Mahler has a notion of vital energy similar to Freud's Eros when referring to a libidinal investment. For Hendrick, the drive to master is an independent instinctive impulse complementary to libido. In early childhood, approximately for the first two to three years of life, it is the primary determinant of human behavior.

By proposing a new instinctive impulse independent of libido and articulated with Freud's theoretical framework, Hendrick was indeed making a frontal attack on the Freudian totem. Therefore, it is not surprising that this somewhat naïve proposal produced an avalanche of criticisms that led him to publish a note to defend himself:

In two recent contributions... I have introduced the theory of an 'instinct to master'. This hypothesis was suggested to provide a dynamic explanation of the force impelling the development and exercise of ego functions.

Adverse criticism of these papers has centered almost entirely on this hypothesis…a hypothesis is not imposed irrefutably upon us like data but is designed to facilitate comprehension and discussion of a certain category of facts. The problem is not so much whether it is right or wrong, but whether it is a useful intellectual tool, and whether it serves not only its proponent but his colleagues in formulating their mutual problems.

The primary aim of our hypothesis is… to establish a concept explaining what forces make the ego function. Our starting point is Freud's general concept of the instincts as forces whose source is biological, producing tensions whose release is experienced as pleasure. Furthermore, instincts are classified by Freud according to their goals; the ego goals do not appear adequately defined by the libido theory, yet they are more specific than those of the 'life instincts' as described by Freud. (Hendrick, 1943b, pp. 562–563)

It is a brave and naïve defense that reminds us of Galileo Galilei in the famous Brecht play, when he tries to induce Aristotelian philosophers to look at Jupiter's satellites with his telescope. In the face of criticism, Hendrick still seeks to defend himself by mentioning the precedent of authors like Thorstein Veblen (1914), with his "instinct of workmanship," and Karl Bühler (1930), with his *Funktionslust*. For him, these authors were precursors to the idea of a drive to master in human beings. He also quotes Siegfried Bernfeld (1929), one of Freud's first disciples and a close friend of Anna Freud, who also came close to accepting the idea. But the discomfort of his heterodox position already seems quite evident in how he ends his second article on this subject:

In conclusion, let me say that I feel that possibly my discourse is after all only a fancy version of plain 'common sense.' Yet it is a common sense which the best analysts have always applied in their appraisal and treatment of human problems. But perhaps it is the inclusion of this common sense ... within our formal theoretical framework that our science needs. (Hendrick, 1943a, p.328)

The *coup-de-grâce*, which practically banned the idea from the universe of psychoanalysis, was issued a few years later by Hartmann (1948):

This may be the place to say a few words about what psychologists call pleasure in functioning (*Funktionslust*), the pleasure in activities themselves, or in overcoming difficulties. The child's enjoyment in the exercise of a recently learned function ... as contrasted with the pleasure we get from the effect of an activity. Its developmentally important role can be traced partly to the fact that through maturation and learning a series of apparatus in the nonconflictual sphere of the ego ... become available to the child ... *Somewhat similar ideas are expressed in a paper by Hendrick (1942), but I am not convinced that the introduction of what he calls a basic "instinct to master" is really unavoidable.* (Hartmann, 1948, p. 84, my italics)

It is not surprising that Hartmann should have dismissed Hendrick's theoretical innovation in this way, as diplomatic as definitive. In *Psychology of the Ego and the Problem of Adaptation* (1939), his main contribution to psychoanalysis was the notion of a conflict-free sphere in the ego. This hypothesis became the cornerstone of Ego Psychology that dominated American psychoanalysis for a long time. In Freud's theoretical scheme, all psychic energy came from the id. For there to be a conflict-free sphere in the ego, this energy had to be neutralized or "desinstinctualized," which for Hartmann (1955) was a generalization of the classic mechanism of sublimation. Ego psychology was advanced as a development of Freud's thinking, focusing on the functioning and vicissitudes of this neutralized instinctive energy.

Now, what Hendrick was proposing when suggesting the inclusion of his new drive to master side by side with the traditional drives was ultimately to render irrelevant all theoretical innovations of ego psychology, and therefore to initiate a new research agenda on an entirely different basis. Indeed, Hendrick's papers were only a rather timid initiative in this direction, which may show that he was not fully aware of the extent of the possible implications of his suggestion. Hartmann, however, reacted predictably to defend his intellectual property.

The problem with the drive to master was that it could cast doubt on the need for the hypothesis of a conflict-free ego sphere to address a series of ego mechanisms and functions that classical analysis, based on the repression of sexual and aggressive drives, could not explain. The new drive and its vicissitudes could now explain these mechanisms. Hartmann seems to have reacted instinctively to Hendrick's heterodoxy, realizing that it could be dangerous, if not irrelevant. Hence this proposal of a new drive to master just disappeared from the main body of psychoanalysis.

Interestingly, in the same paper that disqualifies Hendrick's suggestion, there is a reference to the "biological theory" of play advanced by Groos. This theory explains ludic activity as a training exercise that makes the child fit for situations he may encounter in future life. But this reference to the theoretical analysis of play activity in animals and children, obviously related to the drive to master, has all the signs of a faulty act (Freud's *parapraxis*). It was as if Hartmann unconsciously was trying to assert his intellectual superiority over Hendrick by indicating that, if that unorthodox suggestion had been his own, he would undoubtedly have referred to this relevant literature on animal play.

I believe Hendrick should have a place in psychoanalysis history, not just for his suggestion of the instinct to master. He had a concept of "ego defect neurosis," similar to Kohut's concept of narcissistic personality disorder. He argued that the proper development of ego functions depends on the child's formative environment, the frustrations imposed on him, and the tolerance shown by parents and other relevant adults. This development depends heavily on adequate identifications with these people's behavior and attitudes (Hendrick, 1942, p. 52). Consequently, some severe personality problems cannot be adequately explained within the framework traditionally applied to psychoneuroses, which uses concepts such as conflict, repression, defense against castration anxiety, and loss of love (Hendrick 1943a, 312). These problems result only from defects in ego functions:

> In several papers I introduced the extensive and difficult topic of the relationship between adult ego-functions and early development of the ego, especially during the first two years of life. The need for such studies had been indicated by several clinical analyses ... which showed that the pathology of psychoses, and also that of many character problems, was primarily the result of defect in functions usually considered components of the ego. Theses personalities differ in their essential dynamics from what is characteristic of the psychoneuroses. The symptoms are not primarily the result of a healthy ego's defense against an unresolved infantile conflict; they result from a fundamental inadequacy of some essential function of the ego itself. These studies suggested, therefore, that such defective functions are end results of failures in ego development. (Hendrick, 1951, p. 44)

This innovative notion of ego-defect neurosis makes me think that Hendrick has never received due recognition. In his view, these ego pathologies resulted from vicissitudes of a new instinctive impulse, the drive to master. Still, unfortunately, Hendrick chose not to fight for his innovative ideas, letting them fall into oblivion. The most significant evidence of this is the third edition of his introductory book on psychoanalysis, Hendrick (1966, with a preface dated 1963). There, the idea of a drive to master hardly appears, receiving only a mention in a footnote (page 121).

16. Animal Play

Karl Groos, the author mentioned by Hartmann, was the leading pioneer of a biological research area focused on animal play. Fagen (1981), Bekoff and Byers (1998), Power (2000), and Burghardt (2005) are recent reviews of the relevant literature. As we shall see, what Hendrick identified as the development of ego functions in childhood through intense training is quite like many forms of animal play studied in this literature. Hendrick's drive to master is nothing more than the ludic impulse identified by these researchers in both animals and humans.

The presence of ludic activities in many animal species is an undeniable phenomenon for any attentive naturalist, but it is somewhat paradoxical. Ludic activities practiced by animals, young or adults, require time and energy while creating the risk of accidents. They do not produce any apparent immediate benefit in preserving the individual or the species. This seems inconsistent with the Darwinian mechanism of natural selection. Why does a living organism allocate precious parts of its energy to activities that seemingly contribute nothing to its survival chances?

There is much controversy regarding the precise definition of what is a ludic activity in an animal. Still, the literature is abundant in describing these activities in the most varied species, not only in mammals (*e.g.*, Fagen 1981 or Burghardt 2004). Karl Groos has the great merit of producing the first systematic study of the phenomenon, and a theoretical explanation still quite influential in the field.

We have little biographical information on him. We know he lived between 1861 and 1946, studied at Heidelberg, and was a philosophy professor at the universities in Giessen, Basel, and Tübingen. Freud was never quoted in any of Groos' books but made several references to him in many of his books. *The Three Essays on the Theory of Sexuality* of 1905 mentions two books by Groos, *The Play of Man* of 1899, and *Das Seelenleben des Kindes* (The Mental Life of Children) of 1904.[12] The second footnote to Chapter II of the *Three Essays* notes that *The Play of Man* presents evidence on a sex drive's possible presence in children. But there is no indication that Freud ever encountered Groos' previous, 1896 book, *The Play of Animals*.

The *Play of Man* is also widely quoted in Freud's book on jokes (1905b). For example, in Section 2 of the fourth chapter on the mechanism of pleasure and the psychogenesis of jokes, he wrote: "Play... appears in children while they are learning to make use of words and to put thoughts together. This play probably obeys one of the instincts [*Trieb*] which compel children to practice their capacities (Groos, 1899; Freud, 1905b, p.157).

There is an unexpected coincidence in the works of these two authors. In *Civilization and its Discontents* (1930, p. 74), Freud states that his point of departure for the theory of drives was a statement by the poet-philosopher Schiller that "hunger and love are what moves the world." In his *Play of Animals*, Groos' first concern was to correct the attribution to Herbert Spencer of a theory on animal play that was, in fact, rightly due to the same poet-philosopher Schiller (1795). That is, in a somewhat surprising way, Schiller seems to be at the origin of these two lines of thought.

In a chapter on "Aesthetic Sentiments" included in the second edition of his *Principles of Psychology* (1872), Herbert Spencer presented a thesis on animal

---

12 This book, which is available only in German and had a fifth edition in 1922, does not refer to Freud but mentions Alfred Adler in a footnote. It says the term "*Trieb*" is a notion used only by psychologists (ein psychologischer Begriff). Yet, Groos himself uses the term "*ererbte Trieb*" (hereditary impulse) in the introduction of his *Play of Man*.

play's origin. Spencer stated that his inspiration came from a German author he had read somewhere, but whose name he could not remember. Groos corrected Spencer's lapse by identifying the German author as Schiller and the correct reference as the little book of 1795 on man's aesthetic education. In letter 27, Schiller notes that animals driven in most of their activities by vital survival and reproduction needs also seem to engage in unnecessary ludic activities. His thesis is that this happens when they have an excess of unnecessary energy.

> Nature has indeed granted, even to the creature devoid of reason, more than the mere necessities of existence....When hunger no longer torments the lion, and no beast of prey appears for him to fight, then his unemployed powers find another outlet. He fills the wilderness with his wild roars, and his exuberant strength spends itself in aimless activity...The animal works when some want is the motive for his activity, and plays when a superabundance of energy forms this motive—when overflowing life itself urges him to action. (Schiller 1795, p. 133, quoted by Groos, 1896, p. 2)

Of course, physical fitness and energy availability are prerequisites for the vigorous activity that occurs in any animal's ludic activities. Even among humans, we can see that children abandon their most vigorous play when they become ill. The return to more intense play activity is always an unmistakable sign of the end of the disease. This thesis of energy over-abundance explains why an individual well supplied with energy is ready to engage immediately in some activity. However, it does not explain why all individuals of a given species present the same pattern of ludic behavior, with a design that is typical of the species and different from those of other species (Groos, 1896, pp. 11–12).

Based on this criticism, Groos presented an alternative theory, which became known as the Practice Theory. This term was coined by J. M. Baldwin, one of the pioneers of American psychology (Baldwin 1902). Baldwin's daughter, Elizabeth Baldwin, was Groos' translator. In the foreword to the English edition of *The Play of Animals*, Baldwin suggested that the theory that regards play as a native tendency of animals to practice certain special functions that can be useful for them in the future, be called the "practice theory" of play (Groos, 1896, Editors Preface, p. vii).

For Groos, the origin of ludic activities is instinctive and hereditary. The presence of sufficient physical force may be favorable, but the real foundation and motivating force are always instinctive impulses. His Practice Theory's central thesis is that these instinctive impulses appear early in life, giving certain animal species (including humans) a critical evolutionary advantage:

The play of youth depends on the fact that certain instincts, especially useful in preserving the species, appear before the animal seriously needs them...This anticipatory appearance is of the utmost importance and refers us at once to the operation of natural selection; for, when the inherited instinct may be supplemented by individual experience, it need not be so carefully elaborated by selection, *which accordingly favors the evolution of individual intelligence as a substitute for blind instinct.* At the moment when intelligence reaches a point of development where it is more useful than the most perfect instinct, natural selection will favor individuals in whom instinct appears only in imperfect form, manifesting itself in early youth in activity purely for exercise and practice—that is to say, in animals which play... *the very existence of youth is due in part to the necessity for play*; the animal does not play because he is young, he has a period of youth because he must play. (Groos, 1896, Author's Preface, p. xx, italics in the original)

Baldwin gives a good explanation of why this instinctive impulse that benefits the species tends to be logically favored by natural selection:

> Its utility is ... twofold. First, it enables the young animal to exercise himself beforehand in the strenuous and necessary functions of its life and so to be ready for their onset; and, second, it enables the animal by a general instinct to do many things in a playful way, and so to learn for itself much that would otherwise have to be inherited in the form of special instincts; this puts a premium on intelligence, which thus comes to replace instinct. (Groos, 1896, Editors Preface, p. v)

A modern version of Groos' Theory of Practice, after half a century of scientific developments, can be found in Fagen (1981, p. 19):

> Animals risk time, energy, and injury to play ... Through play, the cerebral cortex is stimulated to grow, to develop, and therefore to take a larger role in control of behavior, making that behavior more flexible. Simultaneously, play experience produces adaptive modifications of effector structures, such as muscle, bone, and connective tissue ... Through play, animals acquire physical ability and develop social relationships.

The instinctive origin of ludic behavior is evident when we observe its hereditary transmission, in a differentiated and specific way for each species. This impulsive nature is also apparent when we see its compulsive quality, which Hendrick also mentioned concerning the drive to master. Groos (1896, p. 20) notes that both children and young animals only abandon their playful activities when they need to eat, and they tend to stick to them all day long until at night they collapse exhausted to bed. The ludic impulse seems to persist indefinitely until these compulsive activities give rise to a state of complete exhaustion and the need for restorative rest and sleep.

Do we also have ludic activities in adult animals? In other words, are we talking about an instinctive impulse that appears in childhood and disappears at maturity, or are we talking about a permanent drive that only changes throughout the life cycle, as it happens with the sexual instinct in a man? Ludic activities in adult animals are less evident than in young animals, but are well documented; for example, Fagen (1981, pp. 438–448), Hall (1998), Pellis & Iwaniuk (1999; 2000), Burghardt (2005, p. 201) or Lewis (2005).

Modern literature on animal play identifies three major categories: locomotor play, play with objects, and social play. Locomotor play is typically the first to appear in the life cycle. It is a solitary activity in which the animal does intense and repetitive movements with its limbs, often producing locomotion or rotation. These activities develop motor coordination and some species-specific skills, such as running or jumping in non-predatory mammals. They are predominant at an early age but practically disappear in adulthood.

Playing with objects usually appears later than locomotor play, encompassing manipulating objects with paws, mouth, and other parts of the body. It is less frequent among adult animals than young animals, but it cannot be entirely discarded (Hall 1998). Fagen (1981) uses the term "post-mastery manipulation" for this type of activity, which reminds us of Hendrick's notion of a drive to master. Mahler also puts forward the idea of a sub-phase of practicing in the process of separation-individuation. Like Hendrick, she has also considered these two modalities of play in the development of the human child, locomotor play, and playing with objects.

The most common ludic activity among adult animals seems to be social play, with more than one animal and often taking the form of a play-fight, which is sometimes called "rough-and-tumble" (R&T). Fagen (1981) distinguishes four types:

- Play activities between adults of the same sex.
- Play activities between adults of opposite sexes, often as a preliminary of mating.
- Play activities of groups of more than two adults.
- Play activities of adults with younger animals of the same species.

The incidence of these activities varies significantly among different species. The most common is the play of adults with youngsters of the same species, most of the time a mother and a member of her litter. Fagen wonders why an adult animal, whose daily activity of self-preservation and, sometimes, reproduction already produces a good dose of stimulus, still loses time in ludic activities with his puppy. For species preservation, these activities' benefits are evident since they facilitate the learning of basic survival techniques by new generations. However, from the side of motivation, the interest (and patience!) of adults in these activities can only be explained by the permanence of the ludic drive throughout the entire life cycle.

The intensity of the ludic impulse may be lower in adulthood than in childhood, but there is no clear evidence. The adult animal certainly has a higher demand for its reproductive and self-preservative activities and, consequently, has less time and energy for ludic activities. From the Theory of Practice, it may seem that the ludic drive is unnecessary for adult animals that already have well-developed repertoires of useful behaviors. On the other hand, adult play activities can be a way for the animal to maintain proficiency in some actions of vital importance, such as hunting, without the costs, troubles, and unforeseen risks of the real activity.

Many activities of the adult animal, such as sex or hunting, have a ludic element (Hall 1998, pp. 52–56), so the adult may also be "playing" while "loving" or "working." For example, it is evident in the behavior of a domestic cat killing a captured rat, or a leopard seal killing a penguin (Hiruki et al., 1999), or an orca whale killing a seal (Heimlich & Boran, 2001). There is also evidence that orcas develop ludic activities with shallow-watering offspring as training for future seal hunting, and that training is an essential determinant of adult hunter efficiency (Rendell & Whitehead 2001). Playful activities associated with sexual interest between potential partners (courtship play) or simulating the sexual act (pseudo-sexual play) are also mentioned, for example, by Fagen, (1981, p. 439) or Hall (1998, p. 41).

The literature on animal play is vibrant and exciting. We have seen here a small sample, but sufficient to document the occurrence of a ludic impulse in animals. There is an obvious similarity of this impulse with the drive to master, identified by Hendrick in humans' case, showing that the two phenomena must be related.

17. Human Play

It is quite surprising that Groos, a German professor of philosophy, mainly interested in aesthetics, should have devoted so much effort to researching animal play. In the tradition of the poet-philosopher Schiller, his real goal was to explain the higher manifestations of the human spirit, both in art and creativity in general. He elaborated this theme mainly in *The Play of Man*, which tries to show how his Practice Theory developed to explain animal play can be expanded to deal with more complex human behaviors. The basic argument, already hinted in the final chapter of *The Play of Animals*, identifies the pleasure derived from the ludic impulse with Hendrick's joy of mastery:

> The feeling of pleasure that results from the satisfaction of instinct is the primary psychic accompaniment of play... it is also delight in the control we have over our bodies and over external objects. All [animals at play] experience the pleasure in energetic activity, which is, at the same time, joy in being able to accomplish something. (Groos, 1896, pp. 288-290)

This pleasure derived from an instinctive impulse is what moves the animal (and man) to seek increasingly elaborate modalities of ludic activities throughout the life cycle. Naturally, the priority of any living creature is the mastery of its own body, which results from activities involving movement and experimentation. Next, the ludic activity focuses on the manipulation of inanimate objects. As if moved by a higher aspiration, the animal goes after social activities and seeks others from the same species for playful chase and mock combats. Some animals pretend to escape from his pursuer playfully. Often, the satisfaction seems to be increased by the difficulty of overcoming opposition, perhaps because there would be no clear perception of the value of what was being conquered without this. That is as true for a simple motor challenge as for a game of chess (Groos, 1896, pp. 290–291).

Of course, Groos exaggerates on animal capabilities, but his real focus was on human play. For him, there is a progressive development, starting initially with activities that aim at the satisfaction of an instinctive impulse and that obey a hereditary propensity, and then progressing into activities of make-believe with fictitious representations of reality. When the memory of these activities' pleasurable quality becomes the dominant motivation, there occurs the transition from the playful activity to the artistic activity itself. In this case, the memory of pleasurable ludic experiences reinforces the strength of the instinct. Here there is the development of superior forms of intelligence. When, despite recognizing that this type of activity is just a farce, the individual continually repeats it, he is genuinely elevating it to the sphere of conscious illusion and reaching the threshold of artistic production.

An essential point in this analysis by Groos is the idea of a typical trajectory of development of the ludic drive throughout the life cycle, going through different stages of increasing complexity. This notion was developed in great depth by Jean Piaget (1962). He identified three phases in the development of human play: a sensorimotor phase, a symbolic phase, and a phase of games with rules.

The first phase corresponds to animal play, being distinguished by the absence of any element of symbolic imagination or social norms. Piaget quotes and endorses Groos' practice theory to explain animal play and sensory-motor play in humans. He even refers to these activities as "mere practice games" that do not use symbols, fantasies, or rules. They are only training exercises that put into action a varied group of behaviors with no other purpose than the pleasure of functioning. They typically involve the almost integral reproduction of adaptive behavior that may be useful in the future, but that the child repeats out of context only for the pleasure of exercising and of being assured of his power.

The next stage in Piaget's scheme, which usually appears at some point in the second year of life, is characterized by the symbolic component, which results from the appearance of the ability to fantasize or "pretend":

> ...there is a relatively clear dividing line between sensory-motor and symbolic games since the latter involve make-believe and imagination and the former do not. In contrast to practice games, which involve neither thought nor any specifically ludic representational structure, symbolic games imply a representation of an absent object, since there is comparison between a given and an imagined element (Piaget, 1962, pp. 109–111).

A symbol appears when a given object (or action) becomes a representative of another object that is not currently present. The symbolic intent overlaps the actual object, and the child experiences it in a non-literal way. For example, an object represents not what it is, but what is determined by fantasy (Smith, 2005).

Symbolic thinking appears only in human development. Careful research by Gómez and Martín-Andrade (2005) on the possibility of finding it also among great primates reached a contrary conclusion. The authors note that it is possible to identify just a few of its prerequisites or precursors in primates. It doesn't matter if they are in nature or have been raised as children by human experimenters. Some manifestations of fantasy or imagination seem to emerge for so-called acculturated or "linguistic" monkeys, who undergo specialized training. Still, there are essential differences in both quantitative and qualitative terms compared to the human child (Gómez, 2004). The primary benefit of these experiments with primates is to help us understand the evolution of symbolic thinking in man. The mind of a chimpanzee placed in a typically human environment seems to reveal some of the components from which the ability to fantasize may have emerged in human evolution. However, it is only a rough outline of the direction in which the mind of a monkey could perhaps begin to evolve towards the invention of symbols (Gómez & Martín-Andrade, 2005, p. 168).

For Piaget, human play, after incorporating the symbol, still evolves to the third stage of games with rules. Unlike symbols, rules necessarily imply social relations. The group imposes them to organize the relationships among the participants of the ludic activity. Some penalty often occurs after the violation of a rule. Therefore, we can say that for mental structure, training, symbol, and rule are the defining properties of the three successive stages in the development of the human play.

The evolutionary sequence is well defined, but the emergence of a new stage does not necessarily eliminate occasional manifestations of previous stages. It happens even in sensory-motor play, which is the first form of play in children. The training exercises that define this type of activity do not occur exclusively in the first two years of the pre-verbal period but can also be found throughout childhood whenever a new skill is acquired. Together with the pleasure derived from the activity itself and a sense of power, these experiences indicate that a new adaptive behavior is under construction. Something similar often happens with adults as this kind of play may reappear with each acquisition of a new skill far beyond childhood. However, it does not mean that training games are widespread at all ages. As new physical skill acquisitions become increasingly rare and playing with symbols and rules more frequent, sensory-motor play declines continuously over time, particularly after the onset of language.

The three types of ludic may coexist throughout the life cycle, but the predominance of one of them in each successive phase is unequivocal.

For example, training games tend to evolve with the child's intellectual development: they either become symbolic through the addition of representative imagination, or become socialized as games with rules, or become a real-world adaptation moving from the ludic area towards practical intelligence. The same happens with symbolic games, which become less frequent after the fourth year of life. As the child gradually adapts to the natural and social world, she relies less on symbolic distortions. Instead of "assimilating" the outside world into the ego, she gradually subordinates the ego to reality.

In human evolution, the dominant play form of each stage of intellectual development is often embodied at a later stage in a more sophisticated form. Games with rules, for example, may result from sensory-motor activities that have become collective. They may also result from symbolic games that have lost part of their creative content and symbolism in addition to becoming collective.

The typical play activity in the adult is the game with rules. Both the purely sensory-motor play and the purely symbolic play (which is symbolic, but not collective) tend to lose importance with maturation. Still, games with rules remain and even develop throughout life like sports, games with cards, chess, etc. For Piaget, the explanation for this late appearance and the prolonged continuation of these games is straightforward: they are the play activity par excellence of the socialized being.

But of course, we don't have to assume a somewhat limited definition of adult play activities. As suggested by Schiller, Groos, Csikszentmihalyi, and others, the concept of an adult ludic activity can be extended to a wide range of artistic or creative activities, applying even to productive activities usually understood as "work." The distinction between a ludic activity, which has itself as its goal, and a non-ludic or work activity, which has a practical purpose that transcends the activity itself, is very restrictive. In many cases, work can incorporate an important ludic component, especially in the typical modern man, who lives in cities and performs activities in the provision of services with some intellectual elements. It is particularly evident in the case of workers who live of their artwork's fruit, such as musicians, plastic artists, or theater actors.

Piaget himself shows how to justify expanding the concept of ludic activity in the adult. What defines it is neither a particular class of behaviors nor some specific kind of activity. The ludic nature of an action is primarily a result of the orientation and tone of the behavior. In other words, the definition of an adult ludic activity lies less in the characteristics of the behavior performed than in its performer's mood. All ludic activities produce the same kind of pleasure, which Groos so aptly defined as the delight and enchantment of accomplishing something. All ludic activities originate from the same instinctive impulse, and this pleasurable feeling of joy is only a natural consequence of its realization. Its manifestations may be of different types, but they always follow a typical developmental trajectory throughout the human life cycle.[13]

The possibility of identifying a playful "tone" in almost all modern civilized man activities led historian-sociologist Johan Huizinga to propose, in his book *Homo Ludens*, that ludic motivation is at the root for the development of all human culture:

It has not been difficult to show that a certain play-factor was extremely active all through the cultural process and that it produces many of the fundamental forms of social life. The spirit of playful competition is, as a social impulse, older than culture itself and pervades all life like a veritable ferment. Ritual grew up in sacred play;

---

13   Piaget makes a distinction between recreational activities (which seek to "assimilate" the reality into the ego) and imitation activities (which attempt to "accommodate" the ego to reality). I think this is, strictly speaking, unnecessary. There is no difficulty in understanding imitation as a particular manifestation of play (with characteristics of both pre-exercise and symbolic games). The two activities result from the same instinctive ludic impulse.

poetry was born in play and nourished on play; music and dancing were pure play. Wisdom and philosophy found expression in words and forms derived from religious contests. The rules of warfare, the conventions of noble living were built up on play-patterns. We have to conclude, therefore, that civilization is, in its earliest phases, played. It does not come from play like a babe detaching itself from the womb: it arises in play, and never leaves it. (Huizinga, 1944, p. 173)

This beautiful book by Huizinga is rich in historical material and has given rise to the research field of play sociology.[14]

The historian scientist Jacob Bronowski also sees the ludic impulse in all great cultural achievements of man:

The most powerful drive in the ascent of man is his pleasure in his own skill. He loves to do what he does well and, having done it well, he loves to do it better. You see it in his science. You see it in the magnificence with which he carves and builds, the loving care, the gaiety, the effrontery. The monuments are supposed to commemorate kings and religions, heroes, dogmas, but in the end the man they commemorate is the builder. (Bronowski, 1973, p. 116)

---

14   See, for example, Brunner (1976), Pellegrini (1995), Pellegrini & Smith (2005), Henricks (2006 and 2015) or Mielicka-Pawowska (2016).

18. Winnicott

There can be no doubt that Hendrick, Groos, Piaget, and Huizinga were examining the same phenomenon, albeit with different angles and in both animals and humans. Ludic activities or playing also appear in the work of a famous psychoanalyst, who came close to following Hendrick's heresy of explicitly assuming the existence of a third drive independent of sex and aggression. We are thinking of Donald Winnicott and, more specifically, of his *Playing and Reality* (1971), a book full of valuable insights.

To understand Winnicott's thinking, take as a starting point his observations on how psychoanalysis fails to cover the play phenomena adequately. He states that "there is something about playing that has not yet found a place in psychoanalytic literature" (Winnicott, 1971, p. 41). For him, even the literature specializing in child analysis, including Melanie Klein's, focus only on the content of the symbolic play, understood as a close substitute for patient-therapist communication in the psychoanalytic setting, and ignoring the play phenomenon as an object of study. The psychoanalyst seems so busy using the content of play to understand children that he has forgotten to focus on the nature of the play activity itself.

Winnicott notes there is an association between playing and mental health, as playing facilitates growth and leads to group relationships. He even states that psychoanalysis has been developed as a highly specialized form of playing. The therapeutic process itself is a ludic activity—a game with rules between two people, as Piaget would say—and psychotherapy heals insofar as it eliminates the inhibition of play in the patient. When playing is not

155

happening, the work of the therapist is to bring the patient from a state of not being able to play to a state of being able to play.

Mental health is, therefore, the condition of being able to play, that is, a state of non-inhibition of play. This incapacity for ludic activities can be understood as a mental disorder. A psychically satisfying life requires an experience of creativity that can only be obtained through the ludic drive, and the psychiatric literature confirms this. For example, Brown (1998) reports that several field trials with homicides concluded that normal playful behavior could hardly be found in the lives of very violent people with socialization problems, regardless of demographic factors. He concludes, from research in educational institutions for gifted individuals and some high-performing scientists, that a pleasant disposition for ludic activities is a common feature of children who are creative in their learning and that this disposition remains active in scientists whose productivity remains high despite aging.

For Winnicott, playing is always a creative experience (1971, p. 50). In the ludic activity, both the child and the adult feel free to be creative. However, it is necessary to understand the exact meaning in which he uses the term "creativity." It is not restricted to the production of some remarkable work of art or to a highly successful achievement. It just has to do with a specific coloring of the individual's attitude towards external reality. In other words, creativity in Winnicott's sense is not the privilege of the great artist, the successful entrepreneur or the acclaimed intellectual, but something that manifests itself in the daily life of any individual mentally healthy with a productive life.

Playing and creative living are necessary conditions for mental health. In non-creative living there is a feeling that nothing means anything, a sense of futility in which the individual seems to be always saying, "I couldn't care less." But if mental health is associated with creative living, what mechanism produces this condition? Why in specific individuals, it seems so deficient that therapy is needed? Winnicott emphasizes that the usual notion of sublimated libido cannot explain the motivation for playing and creative living. He thinks it has to be studied as a subject on its own, independent of sex sublimation. He points that when a child is playing, the masturbatory element is essentially lacking. Indeed, it can be seen that "when the physical excitement of instinctual involvement becomes evident, then the playing stops, or is at any rate spoiled" (Winnicott,1971, p. 39).

Note that Winnicott had put himself in a somewhat contradictory position when he recognized the motivating force of the ludic impulse and the pleasure associated with creative living, but at the same time, denied that the phenomenon results from a sublimated sexual impulse. The introduction of a third drive, independent of sex and aggression, would solve the contradiction, and in fact, Winnicott came very close to doing this when he emphasized that "the creative impulse is something that can be looked at as a thing in itself" (1971, p. 69).

His concept of "creative impulse" is very similar to the idea of the ludic impulse we find, explicitly or implicitly, in Hendrick, Groos, Piaget, or Huizinga's works. Winnicott, however, was not willing to propose the introduction of a third non-preservative drive. After all, the pediatrician and therapist par excellence, the pleasant man who managed to remain neutral in the poisonous debate between the Kleinian and Freudian factions of the English IPA, would not venture into a frontal attack on the Freudian totem, as done by Hendrick in the 1940s. Nor was he willing to incur the personal cost of becoming the leader of a new heterodoxy, as happened with Kohut and his self psychology.

His more straightforward solution was a strategic retreat towards an object-relations concept, which he called cross-identification. The thesis was that there are significant relationship mechanisms, even in ludic activities, which are not drive-determined, having more to do with affection than instinct. We spend much of our lives constructing and maintaining these relationships based on cross-identifications (Winnicott, 1971, p. 137).

Yet, even though not having taken the logical step of proposing a new drive, Winnicott was one of the psychoanalysts who best explored the ludic phenomenon and its consequences. If mental health is only possible with the creative living that results from the ludic impulse's free course, a deficiency in this area can be a significant pathology. We may identify its origin in certain limitations of early childhood's emotional environment that may have somehow affected and severely inhibited the individual's ability to play. Creativity in human beings is related to the "quality and quantity of environmental provision" at the beginning of life (Winnicott, 1971, p. 71).

He notes that the development of playing, starting from the primary sensorimotor type and evolving into more sophisticated symbolic or social play, occurs throughout a process of gradual independence and separation from the mother. Margaret Mahler (1975) used the name "separation-individuation" for this process. For this to happen in a healthy non-traumatic way, it is fundamental that the child experiences an appropriate emotional environment that only a good enough mother can provide.

The good-enough-mother initially produces an illusion of omnipotence in the child, which later gradually transforms into adaptation to reality through a process of optimal frustration. This process must be very careful and delicate, as good mothers know instinctively. The migration from the nirvana of childhood omnipotence to the day-by-day experiences of the reality principle is a challenging and potentially traumatic transition. Only with a sufficiently supportive environmental provision will the child be able to cope with "the immense shock of the loss of omnipotence" (Winnicott, 1971, p. 71).

At the beginning of life, the mother must produce the necessary illusion of omnipotence, with her breast being part of the infant and under the baby's magical control. The same must occur with infant care in the quiet times between excitements, as she must give sufficient opportunity for illusion. Subsequently, the mother's adaptation to the baby's needs must be gradually relaxed in order to produce a gradual disillusionment.

The good-enough mother will adapt progressively less and less to the child's needs, while at the same time, the child learns to cope with these new imperfections. When there is appropriate management of this process, the result will be the establishment of a trusting relationship between child and mother, which will become a sense of self-confidence and allow the emergence and development of ludic activities and creative living. Winnicott uses the metaphor of a "potential space" (sometimes also called an "intermediate area") to describe this relationship of trust that will gradually turn into self-confidence. The transformation of a feeling of trust in the mother into self-confidence, which is the very essence of mental health, depends on the introjection of experiences with a reliable mother and other environmentally friendly elements. Essentially, the potential space can be understood as a feeling of security that allows the unrestricted manifestation of the ludic impulse in play and creativity.

This feeling of security is fundamental for the development of ludic activities, not just because the outside world may seem initially quite threatening, but also because playing does sometimes create real threats, and children can indeed get hurt while playing. Winnicott notes that, for the small child, playing is always liable to become frightening; and we may think of games and their organization as attempts to forestall this frightening aspect. This is also the reason responsible adults must be available when children play, though it does not mean they should enter into the children's playing.

Winnicott's concept of potential space bears some resemblance to Piaget's notion of compensatory play (1951, p. 134), a frame of mind in which the child takes refuge through voluntary illusion and in which he feels free from the pressures for accommodation from the outside world. Winnicott adds that playing will flourish only if the child feels safe within the potential space. This is possible only if the presence of a protective mother can be somehow assumed, a mother always ready and able to help in case of need. Groos (1896, pp. 324-325) also reported this phenomenon, stating that playing is a world by itself, into which we enter voluntarily and from which we exit whenever we want to. Inside, a conscious process of self-delusion makes us feel free from any need.

For Winnicott, the potential space allows the emergence in the child of a paradoxical mental state that is necessary for the development of the ludic activities, the state of "being alone in the presence of someone" (1971, p; 47). The child plays with the unconscious assumption that a loving reliable person is immediately available if needed. This person is felt to be monitoring what happens in the playing. Feeling safe while playing alone, which is the essence of the potential space, is a prerequisite for social play (as in Piaget's rule games) and human relationships.

In his 1958 article "The Capacity to Be Alone," Winnicott had already highlighted the fundamental role of this "ability to play alone" in mental health. This ability to be truly alone results from the early experience of being alone in someone's presence, which usually happens at an early stage of life when ego immaturity is naturally offset by ego support from the mother. Throughout life, the individual introjects this support, becoming able to be alone without the need for frequent reference to the mother, to some maternal symbol, or to some other responsible adult. We need not emphasize that this thought by Winnicott seems to make an obvious reference to the process of building a support superego we have already discussed.

With this understanding of the concept of potential space and its importance for creative living, it is easy to see how the incapacity for ludic activities that resulted from an inadequate emotional environment in early childhood can lead to pathology. In that case, a healthy potential space, that depends on good living experiences for its existence, does not develop. There is no built-up sense of trust matched with reliability. Lack of trust in a not-good-enough mother turns with maturity into a lack of confidence in people and things in general, impairing the possibility of ludic activities. It reduces a person's ability to play and produces an impoverishment in his creative and cultural life.

19. Kohut

Heinz Kohut and Donald Winnicott were two giants of psychoanalysis in the second half of the 20th century. Their works have in common a concern with a type of pathology that does not fit into the classical model of neurosis studied by Freud. It was named *narcissistic personality disorder* by Kohut (1971) and *psychopathology in the area of transitional phenomena* by Winnicott (1953). Hendrick (1936) had also identified the same pathology using the name "ego defect neurosis."

The influence channels between these authors are challenging to determine accurately. There is a chronological order in the dates of the most relevant publications of each. They were mostly in the '40s for Hendrick; in the '50s and '60s for Winnicott and in the second half of '60s and '70s for Kohut. Winnicott never quoted Hendrick or Kohut, and we do not know if he ever read any of them. Kohut quoted Hendrick in *The Analysis of the Self* and quoted Winnicott in all of his books. Kohut certainly saw the concept of "the good-enough mother" in Winnicott's 1953 article, which he often mentions. Still, the influence may have been unconscious, since Kohut never explicitly refers to Winnicott in his discussion of the empathic mother's role in mental health. Kohut (1971, pp. 28–33) does speak of the "ego ideal as a transitional self-object" and explicitly discusses Winnicott's concept of the transitional object in footnote 17 of Chapter 1. But he never mentions his contribution when talking about the phenomenon of maternal mirroring in early childhood.

Strozier (2001, p. 226) has an interesting discussion of the intellectual link between Kohut and Winnicott. He notes that Paul Ornstein stated that Kohut certainly knew about Winnicott and regarded him as someone with interesting clinical ideas, but not as a prominent theorist. There is also a 1973 Kohut's letter commenting on Martin James's criticism of plagiarism, which states that "even the importance of good mothering, to which Dr. James refers, pales as a vague generality from the vantage point of my work" (Kohut, 1994, p. 282).

Hendrick, however, was the first to recognize the critical role of the empathic mother in this type of pathology.

> ... those identifications which contribute to the basic structure of the ego occur very much earlier in life. They ... are established at a stage of development when the foundations of the personality are not yet stabilized ....In contrast to super-ego formation, early ego-identifications are derived largely from the mother's way of doing certain things, rather than from the prohibitions against what the child wants to do (1951, p. 50).

Hendrick already had a clear perception of the mechanism of "empathic frustration," later emphasized by Winnicott and Kohut:

> Mother (in whatever degree she is mentally represented) becomes at once not only a source of pleasure, but a source of pain as well. Emotional need for her immediately subjects the infant to emotional frustration by her, and henceforth the balance of gratification and frustration will be a constant determinant of its life experience ....Bit by bit, many devices for dealing with failure to obtain gratification are developed (1951, p. 55).

Of the three authors, Kohut certainly has the work of higher density and theoretical ambition, as he presents self psychology as an alternative or complement to Freudian metapsychology. It is true that, unlike Hendrick and Winnicott, there is never an explicit focus on ludic activities or play in his work, but careful observation shows that these are implicit in much of it.

Kohut (1966) states that narcissism transformation allows a "healthy enjoyment of our activities and successes" (1985, p. 106). If the change is imperfect, we will see a lowering of the capacity for healthy self-esteem and ego-syntonic enjoyment of activities. People with this psychic dysfunction are either chronically incapable of work or can only work automatically, without pleasure and initiative, just responding passively to external cues and demands. A patient of this type who goes through a process of analysis "will one day report that his work has changed, that he is now enjoying it, that he now has the choice whether to work or not, that the work is now undertaken on his own initiative rather than as if by a passively obedient automaton and, last but not least, that his approach has now some originality rather than being humdrum and routine" (Kohut, 1971, p. 120). That is, he will report that his work has now a "ludic tone," as in Piaget, which is allowing a more productive activity, as in Hendrick, resulting in a feeling of high self-esteem, as in Groos, and with great satisfaction for his new creative way of life, as in Winnicott.

Kohut (1977) states that the psychoanalytic treatment of a case of narcissistic personality disorder comes to the point of termination whenever it manages to establish one sector within the self's realm through which an uninterrupted flow of narcissistic efforts can proceed toward creative expression. This happens, however limited the social impact of the personal achievements might be, and however insignificant this creative activity might seem. That is, Kohut is not thinking of the creativity associated with great works of art or outstanding intellectual achievements, but the creativity that happens in the day-by-day life of any healthy individual, and that is often relatively insignificant for other people. As Winnicott would say, creativity in this sense is a universal phenomenon that naturally belongs to "being alive," since everything that happens in an individual's life can be creative. It is a way of life, a specific coloring of one's attitude toward reality. Like Piaget, Kohut seems to be saying that this creativity corresponds to a particular "ludic tone" of ordinary life.

Adult mental health depends upon how parents behaved in early childhood, by accepting or rejecting a tentatively established, yet still vulnerable creative-productive-active self (Kohut, 1977, p. 76). In cases of rejection, the child abandons the attempt to obtain "the joys of self-assertion," resulting in a dysfunctional personality with symptoms such as apathy, lack of motivation and creativity, troubled working life and social relationships, hypochondria, and autoeroticism. Kohut builds a curious fictional passage about what a patient with narcissistic personality disorder would like to say to his analyst at the end of a properly conducted analysis:

We have been able to strengthen my compensatory psychological structures sufficiently so that I can now be active and creative; and I am now able to work toward meaningful goals. The devotion to meaningful goals and the very act of creating solidify myself, give me a feeling of being alive, real, worthwhile. And these attitudes and activities give me a sufficient amount of joy to make life worth living; they prevent the feeling of emptiness and depression (Kohut, 1977, p. 17).

Kohut (1985, p.74) indicates some features of the active and healthy individual throughout his creative and productive life: assertiveness, enthusiasm, joy, and a "sense of aliveness." Webster's dictionary indicates that "joy" is derived from the French "*joie*" and the Latin "*gaudium*," and means a feeling of gladness, happiness, or delight. In a letter by Kohut (1994, p. 343) to the person in charge of translating the *Restoration* into German, he insists on the distinction between "*Lust*" (pleasure) and "*Freude*" (joy).

He highlights the role of self-confidence by stating that a healthy individual can employ self-confident assertiveness in pursuit of goals. This self-confidence even allows the healthy child to move beyond the Oedipus complex phase without any trauma:

> ... the healthy child of healthy parents enters the Oedipal phase joyfully. The joy he experiences is due not only to the fact that he himself responds with pride to a developmental achievement, that is, to a new and expanding capacity for affection and assertiveness, but also to the fact that this achievement elicits a glow of emphatic joy and pride from the side of oedipal phase selfobjects. Owing to this joy and pride of achievement, the boy's affectionate attitude does not disintegrate into fragmented sexual impulses... (Kohut, 1984, p.14).

It is interesting to see how Kohut makes a sharp distinction between sensual pleasure and the deep sense of joy, a kind of delight and well-being that results from an experience of productive and creative self-affirmation:

> I do not use the terms joy and pleasure at random. Joy is experienced as referring to a more encompassing emotion such as, for example, the emotion evoked by success, whereas pleasure, however intense it may be, refers to a delimited experience such as, for example, sensual satisfaction... the experience of joy has a genetic root different from that of the experience of pleasure... each of these modes of affect has its own developmental line and ...*joy is not sublimated pleasure* (Kohut, 1977, p. 45, my italics).

Kohut is saying that the pleasure derived from a ludic and creative life does not result from sexual impulse or sublimated libido. What could be the source for this type of satisfaction he always calls joy and is so different from sensual pleasure? Kohut sent a letter to Fritz Morgenthaler in March 1969 in which he articulates explicitly the notion that creativity is the foundation of mental health and that it arises from a ludic motivation:

> ...I see the major issue of life... in terms of the outcome of the struggle to maintain assertive creativeness. Creativeness, however, depends in the last analysis on the ability to be in touch with *the playful child deep in the personality*, and thus on the ability to maintain the freshness of the child's encounter with the world (Kohut, 1994, p. 234, my italics).

The ludic drive is also implied in some of Kohut's reflections on his own creative activity: "...to my mind, all worthwhile theorizing is tentative, probing, provisional—contains an element of playfulness... The world of creative science...is inhabited by playful people" (1977, p. 207).

> ...the true scientist—the playful scientist...—is able to tolerate the shortcomings of his achievements...Indeed, he treasures them as the spur for further joyful exertions. [Scientific] ideals are guides, not gods. If they become gods, they stifle man's playful creativeness (1977, p. 312).

All of these quotes indicate that Kohut articulated a concept of mental health quite like Winnicott's. Both identified the existence of psychological structures in healthy adults that allow active and creative living. This way of life somehow connects with what Kohut calls "the playful child deep in the personality." It would be natural to associate these psychological structures with some specific impulse, such as a ludic drive, as explicitly or implicitly suggested in Hendrick, Groos, Piaget, Huizinga, and Winnicott. Winnicott speaks of a creative impulse in *Playing and Reality*. Otto Rank also mentions a play-impulse in Chapter Four of his *Art and Artist: Creative Urge and Personality Development*. He sounds much like Winnicott when he states that in therapy, "the neurotic must first learn to live playfully" (Rank, 1932, p. 108).

However, Kohut never showed any inclination to commit this aggression to the Freudian totem, which is quite understandable. Kohut was a respected insider in the American and world psychoanalytic community. Strozier thinks he could even be called "Mr. Psychoanalysis" at a particular stage of his life. Indeed, he was aware of Hendrick's daring adventure with his drive to master. He may also have seen how Winnicott avoided heresy with occasional references to an obscure object relation concept called "cross-identification," which he never bothered to explain in detail.

Kohut now had only two options: either a profound reformulation of the Freudian model or a new paradigm. In the first case, the logical path would be to follow Hendrick, giving an independent drive status to that kind of differentiated narcissistic energy. It is exactly what this book proposes when it states that Winnicott's creative drive, Hendrick's drive to master, and Groos's, Piaget's, and Huizinga's play drives are essentially the same thing—and something quite different from the sexual and aggressive drives of Freudian metapsychology. The alternative chosen by Kohut was to propose the new paradigm of self psychology.

20. Sublimation and Joy

It is impossible to see two leopard cubs engaged in fictitious combat or a domestic kitten manipulating a ball of wool without the impression that one is witnessing a manifestation of an instinctive impulse, as noted by animal-play theorists. Similarly, it is impossible to see a child learning to walk or absorbed in practicing a new activity for days or weeks without the impression that one is seeing an instinctive urge, as noted by Hendrick. The same drive element is also evident in Groos'human play, in Piaget's symbolic play, in Huizinga's play rituals, in Winnicott's creative impulse, or Kohut's narcissistic libido.

Nevertheless, psychoanalysis has always reacted with considerable skepticism to the evidence of a ludic drive. Take, for example, Robert Wälder's 1932 article on the psychoanalytic theory of play. He acknowledges the noteworthy fact that play activities take a considerable part of the growing child's day. He also considers that Bühler's thesis on the existence of functional pleasure must be "granted without reservation":

> According to Bühler, play...is connected with a form of pleasure other than the pleasure of gratification. Bühler speaks of the "functional pleasure," that is, of the pleasure experienced in pure performance without regard to the success of the activity. Gratification-pleasure represents pleasure in the success of an action, while functional pleasure represents the joy in the activity itself. The most vivid

example of a functional pleasure is the playing of children. (Wälder, 1932, p. 210-11)

He argues, however, that functional pleasure does not explain certain child games in which an unpleasant experience, such as the visit to a dentist, is repeatedly represented in symbolical form. In this case, Freud's explanation for play as an abreaction activity of traumatic experiences seems more pertinent. For him, this type of behavior results from the compulsion to repeat. It repeats a painful experience in a ludic form to enable its emotional assimilation, a kind of "rumination" process that allows the gradual digestion of disturbing impressions from real life. In this way, the child also replaces a passive position by an energetic attitude, creating the pleasant feeling that unpleasant aspects of reality can be dominated and controlled by his ego, at least through symbolic play.

This observation, however, does not conflict with the understanding of play activities based on functional pleasure. The ludic drive makes the child want to play instead of remaining inactive, or eating, or receiving attention and affection from adults, or even sleeping. In the sensorimotor phase, this impulse produces a vigorous form of play, full of physical activity. When the symbolic appears, the play activity gains content, since the operation of make-believe demands the choice of a theme, and sometimes it is controlled by rules, as in collective games. It is in the selection of the theme that Freud's phenomenon of abreaction of unpleasant experiences becomes relevant, in what Piaget called "compensatory play". Yet the driving power for the activity still comes mainly from the ludic drive.

Wälder recognizes the role of functional pleasure when he mentions the baby's activity of holding all the objects within his reach. This behavior appears already in the last months of the first year of life. Look at this passage from the article, in which he even speaks of an "instinct of mastery," curiously anticipating the concept that would be used by Hendrick ten years later:

This behavior is perhaps the first which may be regarded as a manifestation of the instinct of mastery. At this particular time the child has reached an age when it is slowly becoming aware of the world, and when objects in the outer world lose the originally menacing character to which the primal predominantly negative reactions of the child bear witness, so that the child finds pleasure in gaining mastery over more and more objects. The pleasure he feels in this is perhaps remarkably similar to the one designated by the term "functional pleasure," but we must not ignore the specific quality of mastery (Wälder, 1932, p. 222).

The final part of the text has an obscure reference to the "quality of mastery," explained in a footnote.

In the empirical sense one can confidently speak of an instinct of mastery, but by this term we do not mean the ultimate in the realm of instinct. From the standpoint of the theory of instincts, the mastery instinct, like all others, is a blending of love and destruction, a destructive instinct which has been turned outwards and rendered harmless through love (Wälder, 1932, footnote 1, p. 222).

In other words, for Wälder, at least in some cases, the drive nature of ludic activities must be recognized "in the empirical sense," but this evidence can be ignored for the benefit of the Freudian mythology of "primal impulses" (Ürtriebe in German). And notwithstanding Freud's statement that what characterizes a drive is its aim, not its source.

Wälder also mentions Groos and his theory of practice, which postulates that playing is a preparatory exercise for future functions. Despite not presenting any bibliographic references, this quotation shows that the Vienna's Wednesday meetings knew about Groos's ideas on play. Wälder even admits that functional pleasure represents experimental evidence that this preparation indeed happens. But this is soon dismissed in a footnote arguing that there are games where this preparatory character cannot be identified, such as when children pretend to be babies and "unlearn" functions already incorporated in the ego (as speech, for example). In the end, it seems that no argument or empirical evidence can disturb the religious faith in the prevalence of classical Freudian motivation, always resulting from a mixture of love and aggression.

An even more striking proof of psychoanalysis' skepticism on the ludic impulse was Otto Fenichel's (1995) frontal critique of Hendrick's drive for mastery. He argued that it is incorrect to infer the existence of this drive from certain child behaviors. For him, what happens is only that the mastery of a particular motor capacity eliminates the anxiety that results from insecurity about the ability to perform some activity. However, it produces a pleasurable feeling that is just the pleasure of enjoying one's abilities to achieve new and challenging skills:

> When the child discovers that he is now able to overcome without fear a situation that formerly would have overwhelmed him with anxiety, he experiences a certain kind of pleasure. Functional pleasure is pleasure in the fact that the exercise of a function is now possible without anxiety, rather than the gratification of one specific type of instinct. It is the same pleasure that makes children enjoy the endless repetitions of the same game or the same story, which has to be told in exactly the same words (Fenichel, 1995, p. 45).

For Fenichel, this understanding of functional pleasure resulting from anxiety inhibition is sufficient to destroy Hendrick's innovation: "This functional pleasure is not due to the satisfaction of a separate, specific 'instinct to master,' but may be experienced in the realm of any instinct when original hindrances and anxieties are overcome" (p. 480).

Fenichel here is just highlighting a feature of the drive to master that has been identified by various scholars of animal and human play. Groos in *The Play of Animals* (1896, p. 291) already pointed out that the feeling of joy associated with human play has a dimension of "joy in success, in victory." For him it is wrong to think of play as an aimless activity, performed only for its own sake. An energetic effort can generate pleasure, but it is not the only joy produced by play. There is always some goal that we seek in a ludic activity, an end to attain, though it may be an insignificant goal that only our imagination can enlarge. For example, players involved in games with rules are always interested in the results of their efforts.

Fenichel's critique of the ludic impulse has two serious problems. First, in the case of animal play, it is hard to think that anxiety may result from insecurity in these activities' performance. For example, this seems to make no sense when we see two leopard cubs engaged in a mock fight or a domestic kitten manipulating a wool ball. Moreover, the denial of the ludic drive means that some other instinctive impulse has to explain all those activities associated with it. Since they are not useful for self-preservation and have no aggressive motivation, the only possible explanation would be sexual impulses.

Sublimation has always been psychoanalysis's preferred explanation for ludic activities. They could be just different manifestations of a basic sexual impulse that, after being sublimated or "desexualized," has its original aim inhibited and diverted toward alternative goals. It is a somewhat speculative and far from experience thesis. Freud, in his posthumous *Outline of Psychoanalysis* (1940a), stated quite generically that drives could change their aims, and that any of them can take the place of another, transferring its energy to it. He recognizes, however, that this process is still not well understood (p. 18). When we replace the notion of psychic energy with the idea of information, it is indeed impossible to understand.

173

The notion that an instinctive impulse may go through a process of sublimation or neutralization that changes its aim is an undeniable deterioration of this concept's scientific status. If phenomenon A can be the cause of both phenomenon B and phenomenon C, it is impossible to construct a theory to explain why B happens instead of C. The concept of sublimation compromises psychoanalysis' logical rigor.

In his 1915 essay on instincts and their vicissitudes, Freud even explicitly acknowledged the possibility of a play impulse at a level of theorizing close-to- experience, but dismissed the idea with the argument that we should focus on what he called "primal instincts". He considered these to be more important and, in some sense, more fundamental for they "do not admit of further dissection in accordance with the sources" (p. 120). In this paper, he also mentions the possibility of a new gregariousness impulse, which might suggest something like Fairbairn's (1952) theorizing. Still, for him, these close-to-experience concepts were unnecessary and irrelevant. Psychoanalysis could proceed based solely on the two primal instincts identified by their sources, the need for self-preservation and the sexual libido. It was, of course, his position before replacing self-preservation by aggression, but, regardless of this change, ludic activities have always been understood by him as resulting from sexual drive sublimations. Yet on the same page of this paper, Freud states that the study of the sources of drives is outside the scope of psychology and that we can only distinguish between them by their aims. So how can we recognize different drives if each of them can unpredictably change its aim?

At a level of theorization close to experience, it seems hard to reduce the various manifestations we associate with the ludic drive to the status of mere manifestations of the sexual impulse. As noted by Winnicott:

... if we compare the happy play of a child or the experience of an adult at a concert with a sexual experience, the difference is so great that we should do no harm in allowing a different term for the description of the two experiences. Whatever the unconscious symbolism, the quantity of actual physical excitement is minimal in the one type of experience and maximal in the other (Winnicott, 1958, p. 35).

It is also implicit in Kohut's differentiation of sensual pleasure derived from the sexual drive from the experience of joy derived from narcissistic libido. Daniel Stern (1990) recognizes a similar difference between the pleasure derived from self-preservative or sexual drives, which he calls satisfaction, and the pleasure derived from the interaction of babies with their parents in the early months of life, which he calls joy. Stern seems mainly interested in these phenomena's intersubjective nature, but we cannot avoid the impression that he is genuinely thinking of ludic activities:

In an average ("good-enough") parenting situation, joy is probably the more frequent event, emerging from the many mutual chains of smiling between parent and infant, the many delightful exchanges, and the exciting games and rituals that punctuate a day (Stern, 1990, p .15).

Even Hartmann (1958, p. 47) makes a similar distinction between sensations of sexual pleasure that have strong somatic reverberation and the different feelings resulting from what he called "aim-inhibited sublimated activities," that is, from ludic activities. If, as Freud (1915b) argued, in mental life, we can only identify an instinctive impulse by its aim, then it seems evident that the presence of these differentiated sensations suggests the action of distinct drives. If an elephant is different from a hippopotamus, why use the same name for both, pretending it is just another quality of the same animal?

PART V. THE MENTAL APPARATUS REVISITED

21. Psychic Energy and Information

It is surprising how psychoanalysis has almost utterly forsaken Freud's structural model while still maintaining the proper liturgical posture of respect and reverence to the totemic symbol. After all, the model presented in the *Outline of Psychoanalysis* of 1940 is an intellectual construction of elegant simplicity and high explanatory power. If new phenomena and evidence emerged in the clinic that it could not fully explain, why wasn't it updated with reformulations or expansions? Why did psychoanalysis choose to move away from Freud's structural model while keeping it only as a sacred relic?

The usual explanation is that this stems from contemporary psychoanalysis' aversion to using the concept of drive, which it sees as an obsolete notion anchored on a "Cartesian assumption of isolated mind" with an inhibiting effect on the current effort to understand mental processes in the context of human relations. Cooper (2005b, p. 56) argues that several generations of analysts from different backgrounds have shown that the Freudian concept of drive no longer fits current clinical needs and contemporary theoretical models. Many prominent thinkers supported this position, and Gedo (2005) recalls the significant impact on American psychoanalysis of work by George Klein (1976a), Holt (1976), and Gill (1976). These Rapaport "students" (to use the term coined by Gedo) strongly contested Freudian metapsychology's biological underpinning.

Strozier, a staunch Kohutian, summarized what he thinks to be the widespread sentiment towards the Freudian model. His assessment is satirical and biased, but still quite representative:

... most respected analysts clung to the [drive] theory with some degree of respect, if ambivalence. Few felt really comfortable with words like "cathexis" or concepts like libido, or could figure out the intricacies of superego formation as opposed to that of the ego ideal. They stumbled on, however, muttering their incoherent phrases, because the theory seemed to capture a larger human truth. After Kohut, on the other hand, and a psychoanalytic theory of the self, only troglodytes would continue to speak of "cathexis" and "libido distribution." (Strozier, 2001, p. 225)

But in the same book, Strozier also quotes an unpublished excerpt from one of Kohut's interviews, where he says that basically, "man wants to fuck and kill" (Strozier, 2001, p. 25). Here we see no shade of doubt on the intuitive plausibility of the notion of a drive. There is nothing more evident than the close-to-experience definition of instinctual impulse or drive. People eat not because they rationally conclude that their nutrient reserves are deficient, but because hunger generates in their minds an urge to eat.

What seems to make Freudian theory unappealing to current psychoanalytic thinking is not the notion of "drive," but the notion of "psychic energy." The problem is not in the intuitive idea of instinctive impulse, but in the theory that an impulse consists of a certain quota of energy which presses in a particular direction (Freud, 1933, p. 120). It is hard to disagree with Mitchell (1988, p. 81) when he says that Freud built his theory on now obsolete ideas of nineteenth-century biology and neurophysiology. This is evident in concepts in his 1895 *Project for a Scientific Psychology*, such as the quantity Q of excitation or the principle of neuronic inertia. Although he never published a definitive version of the work (which he intended to destroy), there is no doubt that his thought was always implicitly supported by a version of this energetic neurological model. For example, in *The Ego and the Id*, he explains the thought process as a displacement of mental energy within the psychic apparatus:

...what about those internal processes which we may—roughly and inexactly—sum up under the name of thought-processes? They represent displacements of mental energy which are effected somewhere in the interior of the apparatus as this energy proceeds on its way towards action. (Freud, 1923b, p. 357)

Indeed, Freud himself never failed to recognize the fragility of the neurological basis of his theories, as he made clear in his 1940 *Outline*:

Here we have approached the still-shrouded secret of the nature of the psychical. We assume, as other natural sciences have led us to expect, that in mental life some kind of energy is at work; but we have nothing to go upon which will enable us to come nearer to a knowledge of it by analogies with other forms of energy. (Freud, 1940, p. 37)

In a fair assessment, we must acknowledge that Freud was trying in the late nineteenth century to understand in neurological detail the working of nature's most sophisticated computing and control mechanism: the human mind. For this, he could use only the neurology of his time. He had no access to the knowledge of cybernetics, information science, biology, and neuroscience that we have today. His initial project was overly ambitious and even today is far from complete. The research agenda outlined in the 1895 *Project for a Scientific Psychology* naturally had to be abandoned, but the initial energetic conception remained latent in all his later work.[15]

---

15   Pribam & Gill (1976) have a modern rereading of the *Project*, which, despite introducing some notions of control theory, does not entirely break free from the old notion of psychic energy. For more recent attempts at integrating neuroscience and psychoanalysis (or psychotherapy), see for example Corrigall & Wilkinson (2003) or Levin (1991, 2009).

Freud tried to explain the human mind as a psychic energy processor, but what kind of energy is that? Feynman (1989, p. 71) notes that not even physicists can say what energy is, strictly speaking. They only know it is something they can measure in different ways: for example, gravitational energy, kinetic energy, thermal energy, elastic energy, electrical energy, chemical energy, radiant energy, nuclear energy, mass-energy. Any form of energy can be transformed into any other form, according to the principle of energy conservation. Energy can be converted, but not destroyed.

Freud's psychic "energy" concept is different from the physicists' notion. Suppose an impulse to act resulting from an influx of psychic energy into the mind does not turn into actual action. This case would violate the principle of energy conservation. Suppose instead that there is a resulting action. In this case, the energy needed for the activity's mechanical task results from the nutrients ingested by the individual, not from psychic energy. For a person in a state of extreme starvation, lacking the strength to perform any physical activity, psychic energy can be of no help. It seems clear that Freud's psychic energy is not a form of energy as understood by physics, though it is related to the control of energy transformation. It looks more like information than energy.

Freud's energetic formulation is typical of the nineteenth century when, as noted by Norbert Wiener (1948), it was usual to understand living organisms as thermal machines burning nutrients to produce activity. Freud's generation saw the height of steam engines and locomotives and the beginning of electricity applications in the generation, transmission, and efficient use of energy. Concepts associated with energy economics, or what Wiener called power engineering, dominated scientific activity. In this intellectual environment, it was natural for Freud to use an analogous concept in his analysis of the mind.

The situation is now different. From the second half of the twentieth century, and benefiting from Wiener's pioneering contribution, the scientific study of living organisms' behavior shifted in part to communication and control processes, that is, to information engineering. The inspiration came from modern computers, where energy consumption is relatively insignificant, and the function that matters is not energy transformation but information transformation. Living things have come to be seen as relating to the outside world not only through the energy flows that condition their metabolic balance, but also through the flows of impressions and messages that can both enter and leave the organism. That is, living beings are seen now as information processors[16].

Neuroscientist Walter Freeman recently summarized this conceptual evolution in mind study:

> The core concept of brain theory in the nineteenth century was nerve energy, and the parent science was thermodynamics. The flow of nerve energy was conceived to follow hierarchies of reflexes along axonal pathways and through "contact barriers" between neurons that offered resistance. Giving due priority to the first law of thermodynamics, nerve energy was conceived to be conserved, so that if blocked by high resistance in one path, the energy would take another.

In the twentieth century, the core concept of nerve energy was replaced by "information," which was carried by action potential and processed in networks of neurons in accordance with the parent science of information theory. (Freeman, 2007, pp 16-17)

In today's twenty-first-century world, as I type this very phrase on a personal computer, it is simpler and more natural to understand the human

---

16 See Gleick (2001) for a broad and instructive discussion of the concept of information and its history.

mind as an information processor than as a neurological energy processor. When Freud speaks of psychic energy and its vicissitudes, he refers to a demand for action that originates in the organism's biological processes, is then processed by the mind, and ultimately produces commands from the mind to the body. That is, he is talking about an input of information from the body, followed by the mental processing of that information, and an output of information back to the body.

Imagine, for example, a primitive man in the African steppe who feels hungry and decides to hunt for something to eat. The hunter's body sends into to his mental process the information "I'm hungry," and this sets in motion the urge to eat. His mind begins processing this information along with an assessment of the outside world (where is it easier to find something to hunt?) and his memories of past hunting experiences. The result of the processing will be the communication of an action plan to the body, with the mind monitoring its execution for eventual corrections. The action plan could be: "grab your spear, run to the river to kill the boar, open the animal's body, extract the liver, and eat." Of course, hunting will require substantial physical energy consumption, but this has nothing to do with the mental process, which in contrast, is characterized by a relatively low need of energy. The mental process is just transforming the "I'm hungry" information input from the body into the "get your spear, run, etc." information output, sent back to the body.

To understand the mind's functioning as information processing, we do not need to know the brain's neurological functioning mechanism, just as we do not need to know anything about hardware to understand a computer's operation. The computer has evolved from the use of electrical relays to electronic valves, to transistors, to today's integrated circuits. Still, this knowledge is irrelevant to understanding its operation as an information processor. All that is required is to know the machine's interfaces with the outside world, such as the keyboard, mouse, video monitor, or printer, and understand how specific information inputs produce specific information outputs. Computer software is a set of programs that perform this kind of function of turning inputs into outputs. Yet, it is not necessary to know the internal logical structure of these programs. We only need to understand what each one does: what information outputs result from each information input, and how programs relate to each other in a software architecture[17].

Let me emphasize that the hypothesis of the mind as an information processor does not necessarily imply that one intends to use the "computer metaphor" to describe the brain's internal functioning mechanism, contrary to what Robert Epstein (2016) assumes. We are very far from understanding this mechanism, but as the modern digital computer is a well-known example of an information processor, we may sometimes refer to its operation to illustrate some argument. What we do know, as noted by Shimon Edelman (2008 and 2012), is that the brain produces a set of computations using its neurons through a process that we don't understand completely. In principle, different physical mechanisms can perform those same computations, suggesting the possibility of non-biological minds.

Incidentally, Edelman (2012) helps us clarify a common confusion about the concept of mind when he states that we can understand it as "the bundle of computations carried out collectively by brain neurons" (p. 34). It would be better to say that the mind is the set of resources that the brain has at its disposal to perform that computation package. It is like software for the brain.

We may understand a computer as a kind of non-biological mind. Indeed, the digital computer metaphor is not a proper explanation for the details of the human brain's functioning, but this does not mean that the mind is not an information processor. For example, my air conditioner is an information processor despite being very different from a digital computer.

---

17   For an accessible introduction to matters of hardware and software in modern computers see Petzold (1999).

It has a memory mechanism that stores information on which temperature to turn on or off. It also has a device to obtain an information input on room temperature and then a mechanism for turning the cooling system on or off according to the data on ambient temperature, and the information already stored in its memory on the desired temperature. It is not a digital computer, but it is, nonetheless, an information processor.

The information processing approach is a fundamental feature of the so-called cognitive sciences, including cognitive psychology (for example, Gardner, 1985, Eysenck and Keane, 2005, Eysenck 2012, Thagard 2005), but this should not prevent it from being also used by psychoanalysis. Only respect for the Freudian totem can explain why psychoanalysis has stayed so distant from the significant developments in the cognitive sciences from the mid-twentieth century, the only exception being perhaps Bowlby (1969) with his control theory concepts. In 1950, Rapaport wrote a review of Wiener's book on Cybernetics that already reveals the posture of isolation and even antagonism adopted by psychoanalysis towards the cognitive sciences in subsequent decades. Rapaport (1950, pp. 331–333) insists on the centrality of the "complex process of binding cathexes energies," which for him makes the dynamics of thought a combination of power- and communication-engineering. He does not think it possible to understand the dynamics of instinctive impulses with communication or information engineering concepts.

With respect to Chapter 7 of Wiener's book, entitled *Cybernetics and Psychopathology*, Rapaport states that "the less said, the better". Ironically in this chapter Wiener, perhaps uniquely among the greats of the exact sciences, reveals a rather good, if somewhat limited and simplistic, understanding of psychoanalysis:

The technique of the psychoanalyst consists in a series of means to discover and interpret these hidden memories, to make the patient accept them for what they are and by their acceptance modify, if not their content, at least the affective tone they carry, and thus make them less harmful. All this is perfectly consistent with the point of view of this book (Wiener, 1948, p. 149).

Wiener is perhaps suggesting that psychoanalysis could follow the example of the pioneers of cybernetics and computing, which was also the origin of the current cognitive sciences. But to participate in this journey, it would have to break free from Freud's classic energy formulation. Psychoanalysis chose not to enter this promising developmental path because it would require its totem's desecration.

A rare and noteworthy exception was Alexander (1958), who suggested a more constructive stance towards the nascent cognitive movement, a posture that resembles the one we want to adopt here:

Undoubtedly, we know little of the physiological basis of such phenomena as repression, substitution, sublimation, turning impulses against the self, etc., and our first task is to describe them in psychological terms as we observe them or conclude to their existence. What has to be kept in mind, however, is that these are but phenomena within a complex communication system as visualized by the cyberneticists, and eventually they will be expressed in general principles which prevail in all communication systems. We are not rivals, but collaborators with the representatives of this new branch of science. (Alexander, 1958, p. 186)

Our discussion of Freud's structural model will adopt a conception of the mind as an information processor. It bears some resemblance to the formulations of cognitive psychology, but the approach will be strictly psychoanalytic. In this sense, we differ from Bucci (1997), who also takes a cognitive approach, but rejects the Freudian theoretical basis[18]. By contrast, our goal is to reformulate this theory in terms of information processing that preserves as much as we can, and still has scientific value within the new conception[19]. We will undoubtedly violate the Freudian totem, but the revised theory will be free of obsolete nineteenth-century energy notions and much clearer and more intuitive.

---

18 For Bucci, "*the central concepts of the psychoanalytic theory... are all defined, explicitly or implicitly —within the energic framework of the metapsychology, or else undefined and without meaning*" (1997, p. 34).

19 Erdely (1985) is closer to what we intend when he tries to incorporate part of Freudian metapsychology into the scheme of analysis of cognitive psychology. However, our intention is the reverse, namely, to include a significant element of the cognitive approach into the Freudian structural model.

22. Pfunctions, Id and Ego

When Freud introduced the structural model to replace his topographic model in *The Ego and the Id* (1923), he presented a curious drawing to "illustrate" the new conception. He reproduced the same picture with slight modifications in the *New Introductory Lessons* of 1933. But what exactly is being shown there? What is the meaning of the "acoustic receptor" (the *Hörkappe* or "cap of hearing") hanging over the left side of the ego in the 1923 text, that Freud seems to attribute to a fact of brain anatomy? The marking of an area in the plane of the sheet of paper, which in principle defines a set of points in a two-dimensional mathematical space, suggests we are talking about a particular set of elements, but what elements are these? What exactly does Freud mean in the *New Introductory Lessons* when he notes that the drawing should be mentally corrected by the reader so that "the space occupied by the unconscious id is incomparably larger than that of the ego or the preconscious" (p. 98)?

Initially, one gets the impression that Freud's drawings could be caricatures of the human brain, confirming the energetic neurological model implicit in his first theoretical construction attempts. The 1923 text translator even suggested that the acoustic receiver of the drawing could be a reference to the Wernicke area, the brain region responsible for speech comprehension. From the 1895 *Project*, it would be possible to infer that the demarcated area elements are interconnected neuronal structures. A mental process would be a movement of psychic energy along some specific paths within that area.

It typically moves from the "depths" of the id towards the "surface" of the Pcpt-Cs (perceptual-conscious) system.

In *The Interpretation of Dreams*, however, we find Freud denying this physiological "spatial" conception of the mind when commenting on a passage by Fechner (1966) about the possibility of mental activities during a dream's having different "locations" than regular ones:

> We may, I think, dismiss the possibility of giving the phrase an anatomical interpretation and supposing it to refer to physiological cerebral localization or even to the histological layers of the cerebral cortex. It may be, however… applied to a mental apparatus built of a number of agencies arranged in a series one behind the other (Freud, 1900, ch. I-E, p. 113).

Freud suggests here that a spatial conception is still applicable if you conceive the mental apparatus as composed of "agencies" (*Instanzen*) or ψ-systems (psi-systems). To establish a sense of direction, all you need is to define an order in the set of ψ-systems with the assumption that "in a given psychical process the excitation passes through the systems in a particular temporal sequence" (1900, p. 685). A notion of spatial structure results from the way psychic energy is processed. We can measure the "distance" between any two components of the mental apparatus by the time required for psychic energy to move between them, and this metric is sufficient to define a structure.

In this conception, mental processing is associated with the neurological notion of the reflex arc. The typical component of mind and ψ-systems must be an apparatus that functions according to the classical principle of stimulation and response emphasized by behaviorists. Otto Fenichel masterfully summarized this central role of the reflex arc notion: "The basic pattern which is useful for the understanding of mental phenomena is the reflex arc. Stimuli from the outside world or from the body initiate a state of tension that seeks for motor or secretory discharge, bringing about relaxation." (Fenichel, 1995, p. 11)

Here's how Freud explains mental processing in *The Interpretation of Dreams*:

> The first thing that strikes us is that this apparatus, compounded of ψ-systems, has a sense of direction. All our psychical activity starts from stimuli (whether internal or external) and ends in innervations **[translator note: a highly ambiguous term...in the present case used by Freud to mean the transmission of energy into an efferent system]**. Accordingly, we shall ascribe a sensory and a motor end to the apparatus. At the sensory end there lies a system which receives perceptions; at the motor end there lies another, which opens the gateway to motor activity. Psychical processes advance in general from the perceptual end to the motor end. Thus...the psychical apparatus must be constructed like a reflex apparatus. Reflex processes remain the model of every psychical function (1900, p. 686).

It seems clear that here, as perhaps throughout his life, Freud was ultimately thinking about the energetic model of his 1895 *Project*, even as he stated otherwise. We know that he wrote this manuscript after his *Studies on Hysteria* in collaboration with Joseph Breuer, published in the same year. We only got to know the Project because he sent a manuscript to Wilhelm Fliess, who preserved it. We do not know if Freud kept a copy in his possession, as this was an era before the Xerox and the computer. We also do not know if he even showed the text to Breuer, with whom he was breaking relations. However, it is difficult to avoid the impression that Breuer was ultimately his target audience. It looks like the text was motivated by Breuer's brilliant theoretical chapter in *Studies on Hysteria*. Of course, we must understand this in the context of a complicated mentor-disciple relationship (Breger, 2000; 2009).

Freud shows that he was more advanced than Breuer as he introduced the idea of a structure of neurons, while Breuer still spoke of cerebral elements and cortical cells. He was undoubtedly aware of the recently published anatomical studies of Santiago Ramón y Cajal, with a relatively complete description of brain organization. At that time, however, the neuroscience achievements of Charles Sherrington, Edgar Adrian, and others did not yet exist. No one quite understood the chemical-electrical signaling mechanisms that allow communication between neurons without signal loss[20].

Breuer, in *Studies on Hysteria*, had already mentioned the notion, according to him old and previously anticipated by Pierre Janet, of an *"energy of the central nervous system as being a quantity distributed over the brain in changing and fluctuating manner"* (Breuer, 1895, p. 271, footnote 1). For Freud, this energy of non-specified nature (his *Quantität* Q) was sufficient to produce communication between the psi-systems and ultimately between the mental apparatus's sensory and motor terminations. His fundamental postulate, the principle of inertia, states that a neuron always aspires to free itself of Q by transmitting this energy charge to other neurons. In this way, the stimulus-response pattern characteristic of the reflex arc is generated even in a complex psi-system structure. The energy Q is a vehicle of communication between different components and regions of the brain.

This energetic conception of the mental apparatus was very complicated. It was never fully elaborated, and the *Project* was only published posthumously in 1950. True, it often seems implicit in Freud's theorizing but was gradually abandoned by psychoanalysis. There was a new understanding of id, ego, and superego concepts in terms of their functional characteristics with an implicit reference to information processing. That is already evident in Anna Freud (1937), who suggested that psychoanalysis' primary task was to gain as much knowledge as possible about "the three institutions of which we believe the

---

20   Kandel (2006) has an excellent, accessible history of these developments.

psychic personality to be constituted." Hartmann (1959, p. 331) refers to the mental apparatus' three components as "units of functions, or systems, or substructures of personality" that correspond to man's central conflicts. Arlow and Brenner (1964) state that structural theory divides the mind into the three groups of id, ego, and superego functions. Gedo and Goldberg (1973) note that the structural model "represents groupings of functions" (p. 36). That is, psychoanalysis seems to have evolved in practice from Freud's original energetic conception to a new structural conception of the mind as comprising a set of mental functions.

Rapaport and Gill (1959) attempted to formalize this understanding by proposing that "structures" can be inferred independently of their organic substrate, based on behavioral patterns. They are hierarchically ordered psychological configurations that change very slowly and somehow condition mental processes. Behavioral patterns seem to be the keywords here. However, Holt (1975) produced a scathing criticism by noting that the concept seems circular, defined in terms of the same phenomena it intends to explain.

Here, we see substantial amount of ambiguity and confusion with such terms as "function" and "structure." It is important to remember psychoanalysis was originally developed by physicians, and for a physician, the word *function* naturally refers to physiology and the notion of functionality. Thus Freud (1926) begins his discussion of inhibitions and symptoms by proposing to focus on ego functions related to sex, eating, locomotion, and professional work. For him, inhibition is "the expression of a restriction of an ego-function." Certain neurotic conditions will inhibit feeding and locomotion functions. When there is an inhibition in the work function, the individual feels a reduction in his pleasure in this activity or becomes less able to do it well. In every case, the notion of function seems to be associated with the idea of functionality or ability to perform a task. In this sense, a refrigerator's function is to keep food cold, and a car's function is to transport people.

But we can also find in Freud the term *function* associated with the notion of a control or regulation mechanism, that is, an information processing mechanism. For example, in the 1933 *New Essays*, he graphically describes the id as a "cauldron full of seething excitement" and the ego as a set of regulatory functions to control these impulses. Similarly, Arlow and Brenner (1964, pp 34-5) note that early in life, the ego consists of a limited set of sensory and motor functions that operate only as faithful servants of the id and as ambassadors to the outside world. With development, the ego becomes a "coherent organization of mental functions."

In all these instances of ego-regulatory functions, we are obviously thinking of information-processing mechanisms, rather than the ability to perform tasks, as in Freud's 1926 text. This possibility of ambiguity must have been what led some authors, such as Beres (1965) or Holt (1965), to propose the use of the term "*structure*" rather than "*function*"in the case of these regulatory functions. For example, for Sandler and Joffe (1987), the term "*function*" should be used only to talk about activities and processes, while the word "*structure*" would be reserved whenever we are talking about patterns of organization, schemata, agencies, apparatus, or mechanisms. In this case, besides macrostructures, defined by the three instances of id, ego, and superego, we could also think of substructures within these macrostructures.

The term "*structure*" seems indeed a natural choice when we are working with the Freudian conception that mental processing results from the displacement of psychic energy through specific brain circuits (as in the 1895 *Project*). The result of the processing at any given moment depends on the specific paths taken by the energy, and the set of all available alternative routes defines the mind structure. We can identify sub-sets defining substructures, and the mind can be enlarged, as in the process of ego-building, by creating new energy paths.

Here we have an essential point that is worth emphasizing. The idea of a structure only made sense within the conception of the mind as an energy processor. In this case, what characterizes any processing is the specific path that psychic energy uses to move within the mental apparatus. The set of these alternative pathways constructed throughout the individual's development defines his mind's structure and determines his state of mental health. However, this no longer makes sense when we understand the mind as an information processor.

How then, can the substitution of psychic energy for information allow us to solve the questions with which we begin this chapter? What exactly does it mean to say that the space occupied by the id is incomparably more extensive than that of the ego in Freud's classic drawing? In what sense is it possible to speak of a hierarchical organization between groups of mental functions?

The solution is to fully accept the notion that the mental apparatus is an information- processing system. When Freud refers to the reflex-arc principle, he is ultimately describing an information processor. There arises an internal or external stimulus (an information input) that is processed by the mental apparatus resulting in a motor or affective response (an information output). The reflex arc model is nothing more than an information processing model. It was undoubtedly in this sense that it continued to be used by Freud, Fenichel, and psychoanalysis in general even after discarding the obscure notion of psychic energy.

If the mental apparatus is primarily an information-processing system, nothing prevents us from thinking of it as a structure with several components, each an information-processing subsystem. Think of it as just a theoretical device, a useful analysis scheme, a kind of toy model like those used in physics or macroeconomics. The mental apparatus is made up of sets of processing functions that transform information inputs into information outputs. This notion bears some resemblance to the concept of "computational procedures" sometimes used in cognitive science (Thagard 2005). Or the idea of schema introduced by Piaget to indicate the "unit" of knowledge as a fundamental building block of intelligent behavior. Wadsworth (2004) suggests that schemata (plural of schema) can be thought of as index cards stored in the brain, each specifying how the individual should react to a stimulus or input of information. For example, a healthy baby has a sucking reflex activated by anything that touches his lips. It can suck on the nipple of a breast or a bottle or even a person's finger. For Piaget, we can say that the baby has a sucking schema.

It is useful to introduce a term that makes this notion of mental information processing more explicit. A natural choice I already introduced in Part II is 'processing function,' or just **'pfunction.'** My hypothesis is that the mental apparatus contains an arbitrarily defined set of pfunctions, each of which transforms information inputs into information outputs.

For example, consider a processing function to "add numbers." Suppose this pfunction is receiving as information inputs the numbers 2 and 3 to transform into the number 5. This information output can then be used as input for another processing function. For example, the pfunctions "write the result of the sum on a sheet of paper," or "say the result of the sum aloud," or "calculate the household budget," and so on. In a typical mental process, information is transformed by quantitative or logical operations along a chain of processing functions, successively transforming itself from input to output.

The notion of pfunction is analogous to the concepts of function, subroutine, or subprogram widely used in computer software programming. Any programming language allows you to write a set of instructions in code that defines a simple program that can operate as a function or subroutine, taking for example two numbers as inputs and producing the sum as output. A computer program is built on functions and subroutines used multiple times in its execution. A subroutine may also use other subroutines, and even a program may also use other subprograms. The set of functions, subroutines, and subprograms, and the complicated way they relate to one another define the software structure.

In the case of the mental apparatus, we can imagine a similar organization. We define an arbitrary set of pfunctions as the essential elements of mind and then identify mental structures as subsets of purpose-related pfunctions that can exchange inputs and outputs with each other. We can also identify sets of structures, which Freud called agencies or "regions" of the mind, as in the tripartite division of id, ego, and superego. But it is important to emphasize that any list of pfunctions we choose to describe the mental apparatus is merely arbitrary, one among infinite possibilities. It is just a theoretical construct, a toy model, as theoretical physicists like to say, not a biological explanation of how the brain works.

Let me add five relevant observations on the concept of pfunctions. First, we must distinguish between pfunctions and mental processes. This distinction is analogous to that done between computer software, a set of programs available for use at any given time, and the use of a computer when some of these programs are activated to perform specific computing tasks. Similarly, a mental process is information processing by the mind using some of its pfunctions.

Psychoanalytic literature does not always make a clear distinction between these concepts when it speaks of "contents" or "states" of the mind. Sometimes it is thinking of pfunctions structures that are available for use; in other cases, it refers to mental processes, or the use of a subset of these pfunctions to perform an information processing task. This conceptual distinction seems to be what Freud (1915b) had in mind when he identified mental life's topographical and dynamic points of view. The topographic point of view (as well as the later structural point of view) concerns the organization of structures and pfunctions, which we might call the mind's software. The dynamic point of view has to do with how information processing occurs using that software to perform specific tasks.

Freud also mentions an economic point of view dealing with the "vicissitudes of the amounts of arousal" moving through the psychic apparatus.

It concerns not the amount of information processed, in Shannon's (1940) sense, but specific characteristics of that information that can be altered by processing: e.g., the intensity of an instinctive impulse or the degree of anxiety produced by certain events.

The second observation concerns the difference between using the term pfunction to designate a mental processing function and the everyday use of the term "function" in the sense of utility or functionality. For example, a chair's function or its practical purpose is to allow you to sit on it. Likewise, the function of my ear is to allow me to hear. In principle, we can speak of "the function of a pfunction," meaning its usefulness or functionality. For example, the function of the pfunction that produces in our minds the sum of two numbers is to add numbers.

The third observation is that we must understand pfunctions as "black boxes," and psychoanalysis needs not to know their inner workings. It only needs to know which outputs are produced by which inputs. It is not necessary to understand either its internal logic or the neurological mechanisms activated in its execution. There is naturally some degree of arbitrariness in any hypothetical cataloguing of pfunctions. We can do this at different abstraction levels, much as theoretical physics can study a given phenomenon in terms of molecules, atoms, or subatomic particles. For example, we can treat the pfunction "driving a car" as a black box in a particular analysis context. But we can also understand this activity as a mental structure composed of various other pfunctions, for example, the pfunctions "control the steering wheel," "read the speedometer," "control the accelerator pedal," and "make gear changes." In turn, this last pfunction at a more detailed level of analysis breaks down into the pfunctions "controlling the clutch pedal" and "manipulating the gear lever."

The fourth observation is that we can identify a more natural relationship between some pfunctions than others, either because of their purposes and the types of processing they perform, or because they exchange inputs and outputs with each other. For example, the pfunction "adding numbers" seems more related to the pfunctions "multiplying numbers" or "working out the household budget" than the pfunctions "riding a bicycle" or "driving a car." In this sense, we can speak, with a reasonable margin of accuracy, of the "degree of proximity" between pfunctions, which allows us to rescue the structural model's traditional graphical representation. Apart from the exotic acoustic receptor, we can consider the points in Freud's figures as representing pfunctions organized graphically according to their degree of closeness and defining structures and regions of the mind.

Finally, the fifth, perhaps most important, observation is that several pfunctions can be used simultaneously; hence the mind is a parallel-information processor. This notion of parallel processing is no mystery for those using a modern computer, but often not adequately appreciated. You may be typing text on your computer while it plays your favorite music, downloads some files from the internet, and performs a routine scan for viruses. In this case, your machine is running at least four programs simultaneously, and I say "at least" because other operating system programs may also be running in the background without your knowledge. Von Neumann (1958), writing in the first valve-computer era, concluded that large and efficient natural processors (or automata), such as the human mind, should likely be parallel processors. Freud, at the end of the nineteenth century, had come to the same conclusion.

Stekel described this fact in an inspired way:

> ... the relation between what we want to express and what we are able to express originates mostly in the fact that we never have one thought but many thoughts, a whole polyphony of which the language express only the melody, while the middle voices and the counterpoints remain hidden ... I believe that thinking is a stream of which we see only the surface ... (1924, quoted by Rapaport, 1942, p. 152).

The parallel-processing capacity of the mind is evident when we notice that our nervous system may be performing a series of self-preservative control functions without our realizing it and even while we are busy with abstract thoughts or complex emotions. Besides, anyone can get direct confirmation of the phenomenon by reflecting on personal experiences. For example, a business employee drives her car from home to work while mentally reviewing the structure of a presentation she has to make as soon as arriving at the office. She wonders how good the performance will be, thinks about her boss' reaction, and gets angry at the thought that a particular colleague will probably try to ask problematic questions to hinder her performance. The image of her previous job and the sweet memory of her coworkers of that time come to mind. She once again is angry at that colleague who always seems willing to put her down. At this point, she feels a sense of fear, wondering who the boss will side with if there is an open confrontation with this uncomfortable colleague. While all these thoughts flow in her mind, she drives the car and performs intricate hand-and-foot operations to control the vehicle, while respecting traffic signs and regulations and keeping the right track. Often, if the absorption with her thoughts and emotions has been too intense, she will not even remember the facts and images observed along the way. This kind of typical experience undoubtedly demonstrates how multiple pfunctions can be performed simultaneously, in parallel.

Freud understood the mental apparatus as a psychic-energy processor whose bodily organ and scene of action is the brain or nervous system (1940, p.13). Of course, in order to function correctly, the brain must receive and send stimuli to the rest of the organism and the outside world. In psychological terms, this means that the mental apparatus must have interfaces or contact points with the body and the outside world. In Freud's energy conception, these interfaces must receive or transmit psychic energy, but they only need to receive or send information in our conception.

The mental apparatus has a set of pfunctions for information processing. Besides, just like a standard computer, it needs communication interfaces with the organism and the outside world. Moreover, it also needs a memory capability. I will discuss later the role of memory; our concern here is to examine how communication interfaces can affect the pfunction structure of the mind.

We have examples of the utilization of the communication interfaces between a computer and its user when he uses the keyboard or mouse to control and enter information into running programs, or when he uses the printer or video monitor to receive the information generated by those programs. Interfaces allow the user to communicate (*i.e.*, exchange information) with running programs. Similarly, we have communication interfaces that enable the exchange of information between the mental process and the organism or the outside world.

In the human mind, two interfaces are postulated, which we might call the perception interface and the somatic interface. The perception interface is a communication channel that uses the sensory organs of sight, hearing, touch, etc. The somatic interface is a channel of direct communication with the organism, through which inputs and outputs of information flow independently of sensory registers.

Freud (1933) defines the id as the part of the mind that is "closest" to the somatic interface: *i.e.*, the set of pfunctions that communicate directly with the non-sensory nervous system, receiving information about the general state of the organism and its homeostatic needs, and sending commands and instructions for its operation. The essential characteristic of the pfunctions that make up the id is the exchange of information with the biological world within the organism: *i.e.*, the ability to transform biological information into psychic information, and vice versa. For example, id pfunctions can turn biological information about the body's glucose level into psychic information that the body is in the mood to eat something sweet. Or they can turn the mind command "I want to stand" into the biological information necessary for the body to move the muscles to produce the desired result.

The other part of the mind that is "distant" from the somatic interface and "close" to the perception interface is called the ego (abstracting for the moment from the superegos). The pfunctions that constitute the ego have direct communication with the sensory organs. They receive inputs of information about the outside world and about the mental apparatus's conscious functioning. These pfunctions also control the sensory organs (for example, eye movement) and communicate with other ego pfunctions and id pfunctions.

The id is a set of pfunctions that are already present at birth. The ego is a set of pfunctions that do not exist at birth and are gradually acquired:

> Under the influence of the external world around us, one portion of the id has undergone a special development. From what was originally a cortical layer, equipped with the organs for receiving stimuli and with arrangements for acting as a protective shield against stimuli, a special organization has arisen which henceforward acts as an intermediary between the id and the external world. To this region of our mind we have given the name of ego (Freud, 1940, p. 14).

The roles played by the two regions in the mental process are well differentiated. The id, isolated from the outside world and in constant contact with the organism's biological activities, "detects with extraordinary acuteness certain changes in its interior, especially oscillations in the tension of its instinctual needs" (1940, p.85). It must communicate these oscillations to the ego, which happens in the form of a drive or instinctive impulse. Subsequently, if the ego reacts by devising an action plan to satisfy the impulse, the id must transfer to the organism the detailed instructions for carrying out the planned activities.

The ego's primary role, which is possible only because of its proximity to the interface of perception, is to match the demands of the id with external reality. It must take care of the organism's self-preservation from external events,

> by becoming aware of stimuli, by storing up experiences about them (in the memory), by avoiding excessively strong stimuli (through flight), by dealing with moderate stimuli (through adaptation) and finally by learning to bring about expedient changes in the external world to its own advantage (through activity) (Freud, 1940, p. 14).

Under normal conditions, these activities are possible because the ego has control over the id. Still, this control ceases to function adequately in certain severe conditions, or when the organism falls asleep. And, since only the ego can monitor the organism's spatial position in real-time, it also takes responsibility for controlling its mobility, permanently calibrating the instructions transmitted through the id to the somatic nervous system to obtain sufficient synchronization and adaptability, indispensable for active voluntary movement.

23. Drives and Homeostasis

We can now recap our understanding of the mental process, although we have not yet examined in detail the role of memory, which we will do later. The pleasure principle is the fundamental hypothesis: the mind always works to seek pleasure and to avoid displeasure. In *Beyond the Pleasure Principle* (1920), Freud notes that the idea already appeared in a short text by Gustav Fechner published in 1873. As pointed out by Franz Alexander, pleasure and displeasure are homeostatic concepts in the sense of Claude Bernard (1927) and Walter Cannon (1932):

> The basic function of the mental apparatus consists in sustaining the homeostatic equilibrium within the organism which is continuously disturbed by the very process of life and by changing environmental influences. This principle of stability has been formulated by Freud who attributed it to Fechner. (Alexander, 1951, p. 165)

The mind always works searching for homeostatic equilibrium (Alexander, 1963, p. 35). A state of homeostatic disequilibrium is experienced as discomfort, while the restoration of equilibrium is experienced as pleasure. Neuroscientist Jaak Panksepp (1998) notes this sensation of pleasure has a distinct "biological utility." It indicates that something is needed to restore homeostatic balance, which is fundamental for the individual's survival. Motivated by pleasure, animals consistently respond to changes in the environment in which they live and develop behavioral patterns that ensure homeostatic balance.

Our mind receives information inputs through the somatic interface and the perception interface. The somatic interface is the channel through which the body informs the id of its demands or needs. The id converts this information into a message that can be understood by the ego. For example, the information about low nutrient availability is transformed by the id into the instinctive impulse represented by the desire to eat. The drive to eat is the mental representation of the body's interest in nutrients. Likewise, all drives are mental representations of "somatic demands upon the mind" (Freud, 1940, p. 17). Drives result from homeostasis.

See how neuroscientist Antonio Damasio explains this relationship between homeostasis and instinctual impulses (drives, *die Triebe*) in his book *Self comes to Mind*. Homeostasis is the biological foundation of every animal:

> ... life requires that the body maintain a collection of parameter *ranges* at all costs for literally dozens of components in its dynamic interior. All the management operations to which I alluded earlier ... aim at maintaining the chemical parameters of a body's interior within the magic range compatible with life. The magic range is known as *homeostatic* and the process of achieving this balanced state is called *homeostasis*. (Damasio, 2010, p. 42)

Even in the simplest organisms, natural selection has perfected the mechanisms of homeostasis to ensure their healthy survival up to an age compatible with reproductive success:

> ... the minimal features that such simple organisms had to have so that they could succeed and let their genes travel on to the next generation were *sensing* of the organism's interior and exterior, *a*

response policy, and *movement*. Brains evolved as devices that could improve the business of sensing, deciding and moving, and run it in a more and more effective and differentiated manner. (Damasio, 2010, p. 50)

The hereditary transmission does not need to guarantee for each new organism all the instinctive mechanisms necessary for its survival and reproduction of the species. For this, the hereditary transmission of the organism's homeostatic design is sufficient:

For movement and sensing to work to the best advantage, the response policy must be something akin to an encompassing business plan... This is precisely what the *homeostatic design* that we find in creatures of all levels of complexity consists of: a collection of operation guidelines that must be followed for the organism to achieve its goals. The essence of the guidelines is quite simple: if this is present, then do that.

When one survey the spectacle of evolution, one is astounded by its many accomplishments.... The evolution of a response policy capable of leading organisms to a homeostatic state is no less spectacular. (Damasio, 2010, p. 51)

That is, homeostatic design produces operational guidelines that correspond to what we call instinctual impulse or drive:

As organisms evolved, the program underlying homeostasis became more complex, in terms of the conditions that prompted their engagement and the range of results. The more complex programs gradually became what we now know as drives, motivations, and emotions. In brief, homeostasis needs help from drives and motivations, which complex brains provide abundantly (Damasio, 2010, p. 55).

This concept of "homeostatic design" is fundamental to understanding how drives' repertoire can differ for different animal species. Within a given species, the drive repertoire available to any individual results from the hereditary transmission, and even in the case of self-preservative drives, we have significant differences between species. For example, a human being can hold his breath for just a few minutes before the instinctive urge to breathe mobilizes him wholly and drastically. But some types of sea elephant (such as the *Mirounga leonina*) may stay easily up to two hours without any breath because of the high concentration of myoglobin (an oxygen storage protein) in their muscles. Another example: a human being may stay without water for a few days before thirst, and the instinctual urge to drink something completely mobilizes him. But a camel can survive without water for more than a month. Nor is it necessary to speak of the differences of homeostatic design concerning sexual or ludic drives.

My conclusion is that drives are nothing more than "homeostatic impulses" to use Damasio's happy expression (2010, p. 292). These impulses can be the starting point for a mental process. Through a drive, the ego receives information from the id concerning a homeostatic disequilibrium. It begins a process of evaluating the feasibility of achieving it, given the outside world's objective conditions (still abstracting from the superego). This information on the actual reality external to the organism comes from the perception interface. Freud (1933) would say that the ego between a need and an action has interposed a postponement in the form of thought activity (p. 94). The result of this thought process may be an action plan for the realization of the impulse, which is transferred back to the body. For this last step, it is indispensable to have the id's participation, for only it can translate the ego's instructions into commands in the body's biological language. It is common in psychoanalysis to speak of drive discharge, but this only made sense in the traditional way of thinking in psychic energy charges. When we understand drive as information input to the ego relative to a body's demand, it seems more natural to speak of a drive's aim achievement than its discharge.

It is interesting to examine in more detail some crucial aspects of this process. One is the content of the conversation between body, id, and ego. The body sends demands to the id that it transforms into drives or instinctive impulses. It is interesting to know whether these demands are peremptory, to use a term introduced by Rapaport (1960), *i.e.,* whether their realization by the mind is obligatory or merely optional. Rapaport recalls that William James (1890) had already pointed to the distinction between imperative and optional motivations as an unresolved fundamental psychology problem. With his energetic model, Freud had to assume an imperative character, since, for him, a body's demand introduces a charge of psychic energy into the mind which, by the principle of energy conservation, must be discharged somehow. The mind does not have the option of ignoring this "quota of energy that presses in a particular direction" (Freud, 1933, p.120), moving in search of a discharge in the form of some specific action. The most it can do is to postpone the release or redirect the energy to later discharge through a different action. In the latter case, Freud would say that the drive was inhibited in its purpose or sublimated. In the energy model, the peremptory character of drives is an inevitable consequence of the energy-conservation principle.

The necessarily peremptory character of the body's demands in Freud's formulation is what led authors such as George Klein (1976b), Holt (1976), and Gill (1976) to a forceful critique of traditional metapsychology. They proposed the complete abandonment of the notion of drive and constructing a new clinical theory of psychoanalysis. In truth, this was a critique of the energetic model, not of the drive concept. When we put information in place of psychic energy, this criticism loses force, as we no longer need to attribute a peremptory character to the body's demands. If the mind receives an input of psychic energy from the body, the principle of conservation requires the

FREUD AND THE LUDIC MIND

discharge of the same amount of energy. However, suppose the mind receives an information input resulting from a specific demand from the body. In that case, the information output may just be: "*Sorry, but this won't be possible at this moment.*"

Indeed, it is not necessary to suppose that any message has a peremptory character in the conversation established between body, id, and ego. Consistent with the evidence reported by Holt (1976) and others, we can assume that most of the body's demands are appetitive, not impositions. The mind receives information that there are specific dispositions for certain satisfactions and that these body's interests have different intensities and urgencies. For example, the body (say of a small child) may be informing the mind that there is some willingness to eat, but it is neither too intense nor too urgent. At the same time, it reports strong immediate interest in an oral sexual impulse (*e.g.*, by sucking a pacifier). It also has a mild disposition for some age-syntonic ludic activity (*e.g.*, learning to walk).

The body's information on its dispositions and interests is the raw material with which the id works, creating the "psychic expression" of instinctive needs in the form of drives. Drives are simply translations for the ego, in a language it understands, of the body's biological information to the id. In the case mentioned above, the id would send the ego information on three impulses:

- a low-intensity drive to eat that is not very urgent,
- an intense and immediate sexual drive (relative to the oral component),
- a ludic drive of intermediate intensity and urgency.

From this point, the ego has to determine the objective viability of performing each of the three drives in order to choose one of them. One can imagine that its tendency will always be to select the most intense and urgent among the viable alternatives (or from the feasible and acceptable after the Freudian superego comes into play). But the most intense drive may be neglected because it is considered unfeasible. After this decision, the ego can keep up with its work, which is to "discover the most favorable and least perilous method of gaining satisfaction by taking the external world into account" (Freud, 1940, p. 17).

Note that in our example, only one of the three drives will be selected; the two others will be rejected and will disappear from the mind. Of course, any unrealized drive may later be once more proposed to the id. In the case of a self-preservative drive, this is inevitable, since the organic need behind it eventually must be met to ensure survival. The drive will keep on returning until attended, and each time will present itself with more intensity and urgency. In this sense, we can say that self-preservative demands tend to become peremptory after some time. But for non-self-preservative demands and drives, the ego response is unambiguously optional.

24. Memory and Repression

What is the role of memory in the mental process? Every computer has a memory device where information is stored to be used by its programs. This database is of fundamental importance for its functioning. Processing becomes faster and more efficient when the computer has a large memory with a higher capacity to write and read data. Similarly, pfunctions use memory to make the mental process more efficient. It is a tremendous evolutionary achievement of the higher animals, which has undoubtedly reached its most advanced stage in humans.

Freud had some difficulty in explaining the phenomenon of memory in his energetic model. If a mental process is a movement of psychic energy through a specific brain circuit, this sort of motion must be available for each new processing. How then to explain the creation of a permanent record of any processing that does not permanently block the circuits it has used? This difficulty was already made explicit in Breuer's theoretical analysis in *Studies in Hysteria*:

> For the basic essential function of the perceptual apparatus is that its status quo ante should be capable of being restored with the greatest possible rapidity; otherwise no proper further reception could take place. The essential of memory, on the other hand, is that no such restoration should occur but that every perception should create changes that are permanent. (Breuer, 1895, p. 263, footnote 1).

Freud's *The Interpretation of Dreams* attempts to solve this difficulty with the notion of two distinct but somewhat mysteriously articulated parallel systems that simultaneously perform both processing and recording activities. While being processed by one of the systems (having its psychic energy transferred forward in one mental circuit), any sensory stimulus creates a "memory-trace" in the other.

> ... memory-traces can only consist in permanent modifications of the elements of systems. But ...there are obvious difficulties involved in supposing that one and the same system can accurately retain modifications of its elements and yet remain perpetually open to the reception of fresh occasions for modification...We shall suppose that a system in the very front of the apparatus receives the perceptual stimuli but retains no traces of them and thus has no memory, while behind it there lies a second system which transforms the momentary excitations of the first system into permanent traces (Freud, 1900, p. 687).

This notion of parallelism, which is implicit in the idea of one system "in "front" of the mental apparatus and another "behind it" simultaneously and differently processing the same stimulus, has no reasonable explanation in the energy model. The most significant evidence for this is that twenty-four years later, Freud (1925c) was still concerned with drawing attention to an educational artifact for children, the mystic writing-pad, or "*wunderblock.*" He saw it as proof that it is possible to build a mechanism that provides not only a receptive surface, that can be used over and over again like a slate, but also retains permanent traces of what has been written, like an ordinary paper pad. The marvelous nature of this mental mechanism ("marvelous" seems to be a more accurate translation than Strachey's "mystic") never ceased to enchant Freud. But the apparent mystery of its operation results only from the energetic conception of mind.

When we understand the mind as an information processor, the mystery disappears. We know that in principle, any mechanism that has the property of assuming distinct, discrete states, such as on and off, can function as a memory device. It is not necessary to know precisely the mechanism used by the brain to create its memory; it is sufficient to note that it has some tools that allow a mental process to record and retrieve information. Unlike what is found in the energy model, there is no contradiction between processing a piece of data and its storage in memory. The sum of two numbers can be calculated, stored in memory, and then used in another calculation. Since information is not a form of energy, there is no conservation principle restricting its processing, contrary to what Freud believed to happen with his psychic energy.

How does memory work? Our knowledge of this is limited, even considering that many advances have been made by cognitive psychology since Miller's pioneering work (1956), and more recently by neuroscience, as reported by Kandel (2005 and 2006). In what follows, my intention is merely to speculate on some plausible hypotheses to try to update the traditional conception of psychoanalysis in a way consistent with more recent formulations.

Freud speaks of memory traces as permanent records, that is, as something that does not deteriorate spontaneously over time (see Damasio 2010, p. 132). It is as what happens on a computer: any information stored in memory remains there indefinitely if it is not changed or deleted. In this sense, we can say that our memory records have unlimited duration. The most significant evidence of this is that we often remember by associating ideas with ancient facts that we had previously imagined wholly forgotten. However, since the total memory storage capacity is necessarily limited, the mind must use some criteria to select the information to be stored. It needs pfunctions that evaluate existing records, selecting both those to delete to save memory capacity and those that still deserve preserving. Preservation possibly involves simplification and condensation, eliminating irrelevant details, and keeping only the essentials. This whole process of clearing and reorganizing memory is likely to occur continuously and unconsciously, even (and perhaps especially) during sleep. The choice of records to be preserved may be motivated by some utility criterion: *e.g.*, when we keep in mind a telephone number, we frequently use or consider important. It may also be motivated by the emotional charge associated with each record.

What we can say, by introspection, is that memory contains records of things, people, real experiences, and phantasies. It is interesting to note that in cognitive psychology, this conception of memory as an "information store" has been challenged by the so-called "constructivist theory" (Guenther, 1998). This theory argues that the mind does not collect the detailed record of each experience, even when it is affected, possibly permanently, by it. The process of remembering the past consists of reconstructing past experiences based on information available in the current situation.

My reaction to this is that the evidence that suggests a specific reconstruction element in the memory recall process does not invalidate the information repository's conception, but only indicates that it is a somewhat imperfect repository. Naturally, since memory has limited capacity, our records of facts and experiences can only be fragmentary. Unlike a modern computer, all we keep is what Freud called memory traces, that is, fragments of facts and experiences. Since gathering information must be selective, any memory necessarily involves a reconstruction process; this is precisely what results from the Freudian mechanism of association of ideas. The conception of memory as an information repository requires only an identification system for patterns in the collected experience records (Hall 1990).

Since memory is a large data set, its efficient operation will only be possible with a storage and organization logic that makes possible the quick retrieval of any information. In his *Two Principles*, Freud was probably thinking about this when he mentioned: "a system of notation . . . as part of what we call memory" (1911, p.38). *The Interpretation of Dreams* had already indicated how this memory organization could work:

> Our perceptions are linked with one another in our memory—first and foremost according to simultaneity of occurrence. We speak of this fact as association... We must... assume the basis of association lies in the mnemic systems. Association would thus consist in the fact that, as a result... of the laying down of facilitating paths, an excitation is transmitted from a given Mnem element more readily to one Mnem element than to another.
>
> Closer consideration will show the necessity for supposing the existence not of one but of several such Mnem elements, in which one and the same excitation, transmitted by the Pcpt elements, leaves a variety of different permanent records. The first of these Mnem systems will naturally contain the record of association in respect to simultaneity in time; while the same perceptual material will be arranged in the later systems in respect to other kinds of coincidence, so that one of these later systems, for instance, will record relations of similarity, and so on with the others. (Freud, 1900, p. 689)

In his energy model, Freud proposed that we imagine memory as organized into several overlapping categories, defined through associations. For example, suppose that I want to remember a former history teacher's forgotten name, when I only remember him as fat and blond. From my memory, I can select my history teachers' records and identify those that relate to fat men. Then, among the latter, those concerning fat and blond men. Thus, the research follows a logical sequence limited to a small memory segment, gaining speed and efficiency.

We only need some "associative keys" to be assigned to each memory fragment to have an efficient search engine through associations. Assume that these keys are like keywords or tags that can be "understood" by the mental process. With this organization of memory, the location of any information is much simpler, as it can result from searching through successive filters using these associative keys without the need for a direct search across the database. We may perhaps associate this notion of the associative key with the concept of "somatic markers," which Damasio (1994) describes as emotion-based signals.

Therefore, we can assume that our memory contains records of things, people, real experiences, or phantasies organized through associations. We can access any of these through an associative key mechanism. These keys identify characteristics and properties that are common to certain record sets. For example, a record with the four associative keys "man," "history teacher," "fat," and "blond" belongs to the intersection of four record sets: men, history teachers (men and women), fat people, and blond people.

Freud explains the association of ideas as consequence of this system of organizing memory records. For example, in free association of ideas in the psychoanalytic clinic, the mind, in a state of relaxation, reads unintended memory records. The associative keys then naturally indicate the most accessible paths to follow (Freud's "facilitative ways"). It is exactly like what happens when the mind is intentionally searching for important information. Of course, the exact way memory organizes itself into associations is a peculiar characteristic of each individual and reflects their life experience. Possibly it is also one of the determinants of his intelligence and creativity.

How is an associative key created? Palombo (1978) suggests an attractive model of the process of uploading information in memory through an associative tree such as that indicated by Newell, Shaw, and Simon (1958). The process occurs in stages that develop over time, possibly over several days. Information produced by the perception organs (external and internal) and thought processes (conscious or subconscious) initially goes to short-term memory (stage I). Then it is evaluated and reduced to a compact format that

218

corresponds to what Freud termed "residues of the day" (stage II). It is then analyzed through a matching process with material already in memory (in stage III). The final stage happens in long-term memory with the definition of an appropriate position in the associative tree, which is equivalent to creating an associative key. This process, which Palombo termed the "memory cycle," occurs in a continuous and parallel fashion in a healthy mind, possibly more intensely during sleep, when the limited brain resources are no longer used in the mental processing of the flow of consciousness.

Some types of associative keys are particularly important because they relate to fundamental concepts of psychoanalysis. Central to Freud's theoretical construction is the hypothesis that consciousness cannot access all memory records. In section II of *The Ego and the Id*, he notes that "only something which has once been a Cs perception can become conscious again" (Freud, 1923b, p. 358). Only the memory records created by a conscious mental process can be retrieved and used again by the stream of consciousness. In *The Unconscious*, he refers to the Cs system, which, still within the topographic model's logic, would include all psychic contents that, using Breuer's expression, have the property of *"being capable of becoming conscious"* (Freud, 1915b, p. 175).

These observations suggest that we may assume a unique associative key installed only when recording conscious information. We can also assume that the conscious mental process uses only memory records that contain such a key (a kind of consciousness key). It may happen that mental processing that occurred subconsciously in the reality-testing process (to be further discussed in Chapter 27) has never become conscious. In this case, it has not produced a memory record that can become conscious. There is an information subset in memory that has been created by conscious mental processes, and only it can be accessed by conscious mental processing.

This discussion naturally brings us to the theme of repression. Freud used the term with three distinct meanings:

- When the ego prevents the realization of an instinctive impulse produced by the id;
- When some memory record cannot become conscious;
- When a potentially conscious mental processing driven by the ego is excluded from conscious awareness.

We can examine the first two cases here, leaving the third for a further discussion of automatisms (Chapter 28 of Part VI).

The explanation of repression in the first sense of an ego restraint on id drives was not simple in the energetic model. It required the introduction of the curious notion of an *anticathexis*, a kind of psychic energy with an inverted polarity that can block the movement of a drive within the mental apparatus. Only through a permanent outlay of this transformed negative energy could the ego keep the repression barrier active as it appears in Freud's schematic representation of the mind in the *Ego and the Id* (1923b).

In a model of information-processing mind, the explanation of this phenomenon presents no difficulty, since drives are id demands without the peremptory character they inevitably assumed in the energetic model. Hence, they may or may not be met by the ego. In this sense, repression only occurs when the ego evaluates the circumstances and conditions of the moment (determined by the outside world or the superego) to be inadequate for realizing the drive.

In the second sense, repression blocks the access to a memory register by the conscious mental process. It is explained using the concept of associative key. Freud (1933, p. 35) notes that an example of this kind of repression happens with childhood sexual memories when a veil of amnesia about the early years of childhood conceals "painful impressions of anxiety, prohibition, disappointment, and punishment."

Each memory register carries a set of associative keys. Some of these keys are deleted with repression, making it difficult for search engines to access some registries and thus producing their apparent "forgetfulness." When a key is removed, some associative paths that could lead to the information are blocked. The higher the number of keys deleted, the stronger the lock and the more effective the search engines' restriction. Ultimately it is the amplitude of the blockade of associations that will determine the intensity of repression.

Imagine, for example, that five associative keys identify the record of a child sexual trauma. Suppose they are CA, CB, CC, CD, and CE, where CA indicates a sexual act, CB a traumatic situation, CC refers to the person who committed the abuse, CD the time of the fact, and CE the place where it occurred. In the process of repression, the mind erases some of these associative keys, making it difficult for search engines to access this register and producing its apparent "oblivion." In our example, if repression erases the first four keys, the child trauma can no longer be accessed through associations with the sexual act, trauma, of the person involved, or the time when it occurred. If repression had erased all five keys, the memory would have been irretrievably lost, but if a key remains, as in our example, this still allows its recovery. In this case, a process of association of ideas can locate the record through the CE key, relative to where the trauma occurred.

Repression does not eliminate the possibility of access to consciousness; it only removes access through specific associative sequences. Of course, if repression erases all associative keys relative to a record, it is hopelessly lost, becoming a broken fragment of memory. But this seldom happens, and if some keys are still active, it is still possible to retrieve the record through a complicated process of association of ideas. With this retrieval, the forgotten experience can be mentally "revived," and its original associative keys retrieved. In this way, the previously blocked memory register will again be available without conscious mental-processing restrictions.

25. Object and Self-Representation

Here I discuss two fundamental concepts of psychoanalysis: object and self-representation. Although widely used, the concept of object often lacks a precise definition. The *Three Essays on the Theory of Sexuality* (1905) already made a distinction between the sexual drive's aim, which is to obtain sensual pleasure, and its object, which is the person or thing that exerts sexual attraction. Freud (1915c) defines an object as "the thing in regard to which or through which the instinct is able to achieve its aim." Unfortunately, when using the term, Freud is not always concerned with distinguishing between the thing itself, which exists in the real world, and its mental representation, *i.e.*, its memory record (which may, of course, be a set of records). For psychoanalysis, the relevant concept is that of an object as mental representation, since only this can be affected by the mental process. When Freud speaks of a libido-invested (or cathected) person, he is talking about something that occurs in my mind with my mental representation of this person, not the real person. The same person can be a sexual object for me and not for you.

This lack of care with the use of the term has produced much inaccuracy in psychoanalytic literature. An example is Freud's (1915a) discussion of narcissism as an original libidinal investment in the ego from which a part later shifts to objects, like what happens to an amoeba when using its pseudopodia for locomotion and food. This thesis tends to induce the false-libido metaphor as a kind of instinctive discharge of energy that travels in space, like a laser beam, to locate and mark sexual objects, sometimes marking distant people, other times returning to the individual.

Arlow adequately summarizes the correct conception of the libidinal object:

> Freud . . . said that the object is the <u>mental</u> representation of something which is the source of intense libidinal gratification . . . The mental representation grows out of a mnemic image, a recollected set of sensory impressions accompanied by a pleasurable feeling tone (Arlow, 1986, pp. 129–130) . . . the memory traces of pleasurable sensory impressions connected with an external person become organized into a coherent memory structure, a mental representation of a person, which we call "object." (Arlow, 1986, p. 134)

In a precise definition, we may say that an object is any memory register (or set of registers) with an associative key linked to the realization of a drive. All memory records associated with impressions produced by a specific drive's successful realization receive the associative key characteristic of that drive. It is the modern translation for the Freudian concept of drive investment, or cathexization of mental representations. For Freud, a memory register gains object status when it receives a cathexis, that is, a charge of psychic energy. For me, this happens when it gets an associative-drive key. Naturally, for each type of drive, we will have a unique associative key. That means that in addition to sexual objects, we can also have, for example, objects associated with the ludic drive or associated with self-preservative drives, such as the impulse to eat.

Note that any memory record, be it of thing, person, or experience, real or imagined, can receive one or more drive-associative keys. Of course, nothing prevents the same memory register from receiving associative keys relating to different drives, in a phenomenon that Adler (1908) called "confluence of drives" (Freud, 1915c, p. 119). This confluence creates many exciting possibilities, such as an object that is sexual and ludic, or enjoyable to eat and ludic, or even enjoyable to eat and sexual.

An important issue in any discussion of memory is the concept of self-representation.

How does this concept articulate with the notion of associative keys as the primary mechanism of memory organization? To answer this question, imagine a hypothetical experiment in which a man closes his eyes and describes everything in his memory that seems naturally associated with himself. Suppose he has unrestricted access to conscious and unconscious memory records. The result will be a collection of facts, ideas, memories, images, and impressions that he considers in some way specific to himself. That is his personal facts and characteristics, memories and thoughts, talents and accomplishments, things, and material living conditions. These are the memory records that define one's identity for oneself. It may take some time for a full report, but at some point, it will cease. There will be nothing else in memory that the individual considers as naturally associated with himself. He did not mention other memory records because they are related to other people or with the outside world in general, not with his own person.

We can assume that all the memory records identified in this experiment belong to a single set of associations that certainly has something to do with the intuitive notion of self. If we postulate a specific associative key assigned to all these records, we begin to understand how the mental process can articulate a functional idea of self. For example, the notions of presence in space and continuity in time, so emphasized by Kohut and Winnicott as characteristics of the concept of self, are natural consequences of the linking through this associative key of memory records relating to different stages of life.

William James (1890, p. 991) had a similar conception, as he defined a man's self as the total of all he can call his own. It encompasses his body and psychic abilities and his clothes, his house, his wife, his children, his ancestors, his friends, his reputation, his achievements, his lands, his horses, his yacht, and even his bank account. The characteristic of all these things is that their idea produces in him the same kind of emotion, as they all have the same associative key.

One objection may be raised that a person's identity is not defined by just his memories, but also by his accustomed behavior. An individual is differentiated also by the structure of pfunctions that constitute his ego (and superegos). But strictly speaking, these pfunctions are not accessible to direct introspective examination, and we can only get an idea of them from memory records of our past behavior. Therefore, our knowledge of our mind's software can only be obtained indirectly by means of memories of past events. Hence our definition of ourselves can only include a perception of our behavior patterns built on our experience. In other words, the memories of our life's experiences are certainly part of our self and must be among those that receive an associative self-key.

Sandler and Rosenblatt have a similar formulation for the concept of self-representation [21]:

A "representation" can be considered to have a more or less enduring existence.... A child experiences many "images" of his mother... and on the basis of these, gradually creates a mother representation that encompasses a whole range of mother images, all of which bear the label "mother."

The notion of body representation can be extended to that of self-representation. Indeed, we can paraphrase Freud to say that the self-representation (one of the meanings of "ego" in Freud' writings) is first and foremost a body representation. The self-representation is, however, much more that a body representation. It includes all

---

21 See also Spiegel (1959) and Grossman (1982).

those aspects of the child's experience and activities that he later feels (consciously or unconsciously) to be his own. (Sandler & Rosenblatt, 1962, p. 62)

Of course, our perception of our life experience and our pfunctions can often be quite misleading. For example, a person may "forget" unpleasant experiences by the simple process of not assigning a self-key to them, so that it becomes easier to ignore that these unpleasant events ever happened in his or her life. Alternatively, some memories get distorted when receiving a self-associative key. Very often, people have quite misleading assessments of their way of being. These are just a few examples of the complexities we may encounter in the construction of the self-associative key system of different individuals.

This notion of a self-concept defined by an associative key is similar to the proposal of "somatic markers" by Antonio Damasio:

…what allows the mind to know that such dominions exist and belong to their mental owners—body, mind, past and present, and all the rest—is that the perception of any of these items generates emotions and feelings, and, in turn, the feelings accomplish the separation between the contents that belong to the self and those that do not. From my perspective, such feelings operate as markers. They are the emotion-based signals I designate as somatic markers. When contents that pertain to the self occur in the mind stream, they provoke the appearance of a marker, which joins the mind stream as an image, juxtaposed to the image that prompted it. (Damasio, 2010, p. 9)

Our main difference with Damasio is that he seems to understand the self as a feature of some mental processes. It seems more logical to understand it as a set of memory records with a specific associative key (or somatic marker). On account of this key, these records produce a characteristic emotion when retrieved by the mental process. Ultimately the perception of a self is created by the emotion associated with this set of memory records. The lack of care in distinguishing precisely between the notions of mental process, pfunctions structure, and memory record, which seems to occur with Damasio, is also endemic in both cognitive neuroscience and psychoanalysis itself.

The mental ability to articulate a self-concept is a distinct evolutionary advantage for any animal, even if its intelligence is limited to the sensorimotor level. The first prerequisite for survival is the ability to distinguish between what is part of one's organism and must be protected and preserved, and the rest of the world. Winnicott (1953) gave this the suggestive name of "limiting membrane." It corresponds to the perception of the notions of "inside" and "outside," fundamental for any organism's survival. In humans, with their long and fragile childhood, the associative key scheme defines the limiting membrane. The self evolves slowly and is subject to innumerable vicissitudes. This evolution results not only from the information acquired through the maturation of sensorimotor intelligence, but also from the memory records produced by the maturation of symbolic intelligence, cultural experiences, and relationships with other humans.

Freud (1915b) notes that at the beginning of mental life, the ego-subject (or self) comprises what is pleasurable and the external world what is indifferent, or possibly non-pleasurable. In a small child, all memory records associated with pleasant impressions receive an associative self-key. In the same text, Freud mentions Ferenzi (1909), suggesting the metaphor that the primitive self- introjects into itself anything that is a source of pleasure and expels whatever within itself becomes a source of displeasure. This inaccurate proposition, full of strange spatial allusions, comes down to a single idea related to associative keys. Freud and Ferenczi mean that the primitive ego assigns a self-key to any memory record associated with a pleasurable impression, even if it relates to something or someone from the outside world him (like the mother). On the other hand, it does not assign a self-key to any memory record associated with a sense of displeasure, even if it has to do with his person or an internal mental process. This primitive behavior, dominated by the pleasure principle, will have to be adjusted throughout life by the reality principle in order to construct an adult representation of the self.

PART VI. OTHER FREUDIAN THEMES

26. The Freudian Superego

We may think of ego development in the Freudian model as a process of experimentation and learning that incorporates new pfunctions into the mental apparatus. The human mind has the characteristic of being a kind of open software architecture that acquires new programs (*i.e.*, pfunctions) through use. In the case of a standard computer, the set of programs that make up the software must be coded and loaded on the machine before use. The analogous to the human mind would be a computer software that incorporates new programming routines as it is used. As explained at length by Piaget, this is the essence of the learning process that enables adaptation.[22]

What determines whether an interaction technique with the real world is added to the existing repertoire of ego pfunctions? Basically, a new pfunction will be added if it makes possible a gain in pleasure or a reduction in displeasure, in the present or future. Hence it may be helpful to define two classes of pfunctions: expansive pfunctions and defensive pfunctions.

An expansive pfunction enables the realization of an instinctive impulse in the face of reality principle's constraints. For example, the "eating a banana" pfunction allows the realization of the self-preservative drive to eat, or the "masturbating" pfunction allows the realization of the sexual drive. As regards the ludic drive, there are unlimited possibilities of expansive

---

22   See Piaget & Inhelder (1969). In the area of artificial intelligence, we find some attempts to produce something similar; for example, Kosa (1992) or Eiben & Smith (2003). Moravec (1998) and Kurzweil (1999) believe that very soon, intelligent computers (*i.e.*, robots) will outnumber humans.

pfunctions. For a toddler, a "walking" pfunction allows the exploration of his environment, while for grownups a "reading" pfunction gives access to all sorts of intellectual and cultural interests.

A defensive pfunction is built to avoid displeasure. Consider a small child who has just learned to manipulate some toys specifically designed for his age group (safe, non-toxic, etc.). He/she is now looking for new objects to handle, allowing him/her to derive ludic pleasure by extending his/her newly acquired handling ability. This way, the expansive pfunction "manipulate objects" is gradually consolidated into his/her mental apparatus. However, the child finds an electric iron turned on and burns his/her hands while trying to pick it up. The resulting displeasure causes the child to incorporate a *"never manipulate an electric iron"* pfunction. From then on, the child looking for objects to manipulate will retreat when she realizes that the next object within reach is an electric iron. Eventually, based on new experiences, the pfunction may evolve to a more sophisticated format such as *"never handle an electric iron unless it is not plugged and cold for sure."*

The acquisition of a defensive pfunction can result either from a traumatic event such as burning one's hand on an electric iron or a gradual learning process. Consider, for example, the case of a young man who managed to overcome the natural insecurities of his age and finally succeeded in his first sexual intercourse with his girlfriend. The sexual drive has motivated the acquisition of this expansive pfunction. Imagine, however, that the young man is exposed to reliable information on the risk of HIV contamination and has a colleague victimized by the disease. Hence, he may eventually incorporate the defensive pfunction *"when copulating, use a condom."*

A defensive pfunction often operates by inhibiting or modifying other ego pfunctions to avoid displeasure. This displeasure can result from a real threat from the outside world, as with the danger of an electric iron injury or the risk of AIDS. It may also result from within the mental apparatus itself, as emphasized by Freud (1926) and systematized by Anna Freud (1937) for different cases of defense mechanisms.

Among the defensive pfunctions, Freud noted the existence of a differentiated subset with specific characteristics, for which he adopted the suggestive term "superego" (or "over-I" in a more accurate translation for the German Über-*Ich*). He noted that some defensive superego pfunctions work as prolongations of "parental influence," that is, of behavioral patterns adopted, encouraged, recommended, or explicitly approved by relevant adults in the early stages of mental apparatus development. For example, the expansive pfunction "eating a banana" can be modified by the Freudian superego pfunction *"when eating a banana, remember to throw the peel into a trash can."* Or the expansive pfunction of masturbation may be inhibited by the Freudian superego pfunction *"it is forbidden to masturbate"*. Note that in this chapter I am dealing with Freud's original conception of the superego, while in Chapter 5 of Part II I have already discussed a different kind of superego, the support superego. To avoid confusion, I will always make an explicit distinction between Freudian superego pfunctions and support superego pfunctions.

There is something irrational in a Freudian superego pfunction, something imposed by culture and civilization that would not arise spontaneously. Why can't I throw the banana peel away without worrying where it will fall, as a monkey would surely do? Why prohibit such a natural manifestation of sexuality as the isolated act of masturbation, which poses no risk or nuisance to anyone else? For Freud, the superego's apparent irrationality is the price to be paid for the benefits of civilized life.

How to explain the emergence of the Freudian superego? We have seen that a defensive pfunction is incorporated into the ego when it reduces or eliminates the risk of displeasure, but of course not all defensive pfunctions belong to the Freudian superego. Remember, for example, the pfunction *"avoid a hot iron."* In the specific case of a Freudian superego pfunction, the explanation is that the displeasure being avoided results from the threat, real or imaginary, of rejection or loss of love from relevant adults.

In the *New Introductory Lessons* of 1933, Freud notes that the superego's formation occurs in a two-step process. The starting point is the primary relationship between the child and relevant adults, the most explicit expression of what Freud called the "infantile fixation of tenderness upon the mother" (Freud 1910). This fixation can also apply to the father and other adults experienced by the child as providers of basic needs. Initially parental authority (*i.e.*, from mother, father, or other relevant adults) governs the child by simultaneously offering evidence of love and punishment threats. The threats are perceived as real indications of a possible breakdown of the affective relationship. In extreme situations they can be dramatically amplified, as in fear of castration. Then, in a second step, the restrictions explicitly or implicitly imposed by adults as a condition for non-realization of threats go into the ego as defensive pfunctions.

Freud speaks of the superego as a precipitate or residue. Once consolidated, a Freudian superego pfunction can remain in operation indefinitely. The displeasure or trauma experienced or imagined in childhood, even though transitory, may be sufficient to keep the pfunction alive throughout life. However, we still have to explain how this defensive pfunction becomes consolidated as a Freudian superego pfunction.

In his 1940 *Outline* (p. 16), Freud raises the curious question of whether a Freudian superego exists in higher animals. He points out that they also have a long period of dependence in childhood. For him, this seems to be a necessary condition for the emergence of a superego. However, it is easy to show that a long period of dependence is not sufficient for an animal to have a Freudian superego. For that it is necessary that adult-approved behavior arises spontaneously in the individual, no longer dependent upon the vigilant presence of a "civilizing" agent.

Think about the case of the banana peel. The child realizes that by not throwing the banana peel in the garbage disposal as instructed by relevant adults, he becomes the target of possible punishment and, worse, feels the threat of a break in the primary affective relationship with these adults. Therefore, the child forces himself to throw the banana peel away whenever he notices an adult's vigilant presence. However, this behavior does not yet reveal that a Freudian superego pfunction is in place because, in the absence of nearby adults, the peel may not end up in the trash can. It is a behavior that results from what Beres (1958) called a "superego precursor."

An authentic Freudian superego pfunction appears when parental influence is effectively internalized, which can only happen when the child becomes capable of symbolic thinking. According to Piaget, this occurs after the second year of life. In this case, the child decides to throw the banana peel in the garbage can even when there is no risk of being watched by an adult. It does this because *it is the right thing to do*. The child incorporates the behavior patterns adopted, encouraged, recommended, or explicitly approved by the relevant adults.

Every component of both Freudian and support superegos results from a symbolic operation. A process of identification gives rise to a pfunction that may eventually be automated, making adult-transmitted civilized behavior a natural and spontaneous way of being, however irrational it may seem. This kind of symbolic internalization operation is something no animal can do, and that is why animals have no superego, contrary to what Freud came to suspect.

Domestic animals can quickly learn how to behave pleasantly to their civilized owners, but this is not a superego, just a result of conditioning. Gómez and Martín-Andrade's (2005) careful research on great apes demonstrated the absence of the symbolic even in acculturated or "linguistic" monkeys. Indeed, many pet owners may disagree, arguing that their "pets understand everything" and always behave very well. For example, when their cats always do their needs in the appropriate dirt tray or their dogs only do their needs when they stroll in certain places. These behaviors, however, have more to do with the inherent tendencies of each species or with conditioning. They are not the internalization of good behavior patterns endorsed by their loving owners.

This last observation brings us back to our initial question, of how to explain the emergence of a Freudian superego. It exists only when identification with relevant adults occurs so that their set of civilizing tenets effectively become second nature to the child. However, it is not clear that the threat of breaking the primary affective relationship with these adults is sufficient to produce this. The child may embody only a superego precursor, adopting civilized behavior when she perceives an adult's vigilant presence or when there is any risk that a relevant adult will receive information about this "inappropriate" behavior. Strictly speaking, then, what needs to be explained is how a superego precursor is transformed into a real superego. My somewhat surprising explanation, presented already in Part II, is that this results from processes of ludic identification and transmuting internalization that are consequences of a normal non-pathologic development of the ludic impulse.

27. Reality Testing and Fantasy

Freud suggested that the ego's initial response to a drive input is reality testing, "essentially an experimental kind of acting" (1911, p. 38) or "an experimental action, a motor palpating with small expenditure of discharge" (1925a, p. 440), or still "an experimental action carried out with small amounts of energy, in the same way as a general shifts small figures about a map before setting his large bodies of troops in motion" (1933, p. 111).

It is a subtle concept that Freud tries to elucidate in the context of a description of ego activity:

> [The ego] constructive function consists in interpolating, between the demand made by an instinct and the action that satisfies it, the activity of thought which, after taking its bearings in the present and assessing earlier experiences, endeavours by means of experimental actions to calculate the consequences of the course of action proposed. In this way the ego comes to a decision on whether the attempt to obtain satisfaction is to be carried out or postponed or whether it may not be necessary for the demand by the instinct to be suppressed altogether as being dangerous. (1940, p.86)

For Hartmann (1939, p. 59), this phenomenon was a fundamental evolutionary achievement that enabled man, whose somatic equipment is nothing exceptional, to achieve superiority over the environment. The human mind allows different alternatives to be "tested" in the abstract before deciding on a particular course of action. It is what Freud meant when he used the term "experimental action" to designate these mental simulations of actual activities. If the ego needs to assess the feasibility of satisfying a drive, and there are different ways to do it, each alternative can be subject to mental "experiment," possibly in parallel. It analyzes all the motor activities required for execution and the possible consequences and reactions from the outside world.

The parallel-processing capacity of the mind makes mental experimentation highly efficient, allowing for the simultaneous testing of many alternatives. In practice, however, the process is likely to be significantly simplified using memory. It allows for the storage of information about past experiences with the same drive and the advantages or constraints offered by different external conditions. With this information, the mind can reduce the number of alternatives to test, if it shifts from the goal of seeking the optimal solution within the universe of possibilities to the more limited purpose of finding a satisfactory one, though not necessarily the best. This simplification corresponds to what an economist calls bounded or limited rationality.[23] In this case, ego decisions will inevitably be strongly influenced by past experiences, with the thought process giving great importance to routines and procedures that produced good outcomes in the past.

Even with bounded rationality, the mind must continually perform enormous numbers of logical operations, which must happen at high speed without our even realizing it. Freud suggests that this occurs in two successive steps. In the first step, which takes place exclusively in imagination,

---

23　This concept was introduced by Herbert Simon (1979, 1982) as an alternative to the traditional hypothesis that economic agents (such as consumers or companies) seek to maximize their material well-being or profitability from a thorough assessment of all their options. The limited rationality hypothesis recognizes that decision-makers have limited ability to formulate and solve complex problems and to process information. The result is a limited search for new information and a preference for pocket rules and routines developed from experience.

experimentation uses only the available memory registers of the same drive's previous experiences. This first step must be complemented, in a second step, by a "reality test" to determine if the information recorded in memory is still relevant to current reality. Freud (1925) highlighted the importance of the second stage:

> ...thinking possesses the capacity to bring before the mind once more something that has once been perceived, by reproducing it as a presentation without the external object having still to be there. The first and immediate aim, therefore, of reality-testing is, not to find an object in real perception which corresponds to the one presented, but to refind such an object, to convince oneself that it is still there. (p. 440)

Because memory registers are typically condensed and possibly distorted, reality testing must be concerned with that as well. A perception's memory register is not always reliable and may have been modified by omissions or by confusion with other records. An essential part of reality testing is determining the extent of these distortions.

The processing of a drive impulse does not always consist of the sum of imagination and reality test. We have in fantasy an activity that is characterized by the absence of reality check. In this case, only the first experimental step occurs, using just memory registers. For Freud, fantasy is a product of imagination that can produce the pleasurable illusion of satisfaction of some desire:

> A general tendency of our mental apparatus...seems to find expression in the tenacity with which we hold on to the sources of pleasure at our disposal, and in the difficulty with which we renounce them. With the introduction of the reality principle one species of

thought-activity was split off; it was kept free from reality-testing and remained subordinated to the pleasure principle alone. This activity is phantasying, which begins already in children's play, and later, continued as daydreaming, abandons dependence on real objects. (1911, p. 39)

Fantasy is characterized not only by the absence of reality testing but also by its producing pleasure or displeasure. Sometimes, a kind of pleasure can be generated in mind by the perception of a drive's future fulfillment, even if the impression is false. It seems clear that in this case, there is both a pleasure of anticipation, produced by the expectation of satisfaction, and a pleasure of fulfillment, experienced when it occurs.

Given what this book has already discussed, there is no escaping the conclusion that we have a ludic-drive manifestation when this anticipatory pleasure occurs. This was implicitly recognized by Freud (1908) when he pointed out that fantasy is a substitute for playfulness. Growing up, people stop playing and seem to give up the pleasure they got from playing. However, anyone who understands the human mind knows that nothing is harder for a man than giving up a joy he has already experienced. We never renounce anything; we trade one thing for another. What appears to be a resignation is the formation of a substitute or subrogation. Similarly, when she stops playing, the growing child only abdicates the link with real objects; instead of playing, she now fantasizes.

Stern (1990, p. 14) seemed to confirm this when he noted that several decades of childhood research have revealed the presence and importance of a form of pleasure different from classical instinctual satisfaction. It is a form of pleasure that does not result from self-preservative needs or sexual and aggressive impulses. We now know, of course, that it does result from the ludic impulse. Children typically spend a lot of time and energy to create and maintain anticipatory states experienced as delight and joy. This is pleasure resulting from a ludic activity. Similarly, for an adult, the anticipation of a sexual encounter can be seen as a ludic activity that produces joy, the differentiated kind of pleasure resulting from the ludic drive. When sexual activity finally occurs, a sensual pleasure arises that is characteristic of the sexual drive.

We must also recognize that fantasy may not be pleasurable when it involves anticipating a traumatic experience or the possibility of internal or external danger. In this case, it can produce displeasure and anxiety. For example, imagine that an individual is about to speak in public and is anxious that his speech may be a significant failure, generating unpleasant manifestations of disapproval. The initiative to commit to making the address may have resulted from a ludic impulse, but the fantasy of imminent failure produces not pleasure but displeasure. If he overcomes the anxiety and the speech is successful, he will attain the joy of the ludic impulse's satisfaction despite the transitory displeasure of anticipation. On the other hand, if the individual cancels the speech, his fantasy of failure (as a ludic frustration object) will have nullified the ludic pleasure entirely.

The ability to construct fantasies develops either as a compensation for the frustrations imposed by the reality principle or as a defense mechanism for unpleasant experiences. It never, however, implies a total loss of contact with reality. The mind continues to use ego-developed pfunctions in the process of adapting to reality. In other words, the reality remains present in the memory records used and in the logical constraints resulting from the ego's pfunctions. But as the actual test does not occur, the real world is dealt with in thought, not as it is but as it could be. It is as if there were a kind of imaginary world that separated from the real world when the reality principle emerged. In this fantasy world, one can gain satisfaction or displeasure through illusions.

But note that the individual *de facto* recognizes these illusions as out of reality. Only in the psychotic are illusions confused with reality. In psychosis, there is hallucination, a mental process resembling fantasy but with significant differences. This process, unlike fantasy, develops without any intrinsic commitment to reality and without any notion of space, time, or logic.

28. Automatisms and Neurotic Symptoms

Psychoanalysis has never shown considerable interest in automatism, although it is mentioned a few times by Freud. For example, we find the following definition in his book on jokes: "...such processes which run their course in the preconscious but lack the cathexis of attention with which consciousness is linked, may aptly be given the name of 'automatic'." (Freud 1905b, p. 273)

In the second of his *Introductory Lessons*, he also mentions the phenomenon:

> There are a large number of procedures that one carries out purely automatically, with very little attention, but nevertheless performs with complete security. A walker, who scarcely knows where he is going, keeps to the right path for all that, and stops at his destination without having gone astray...An expert pianist strikes the right keys without thinking. He may, of course, make an occasional mistake; but if automatic playing increases the danger of bungling, that danger would be at its greatest for a virtuoso, whose playing, as a result of prolonged practice, has become entirely automatic. We know, on the contrary, that many procedures are carried out with quite particular certainty if they are not the object of a specially high degree of attention. (Freud, 1916, p. 35)

Why did psychoanalysis, later on, ignore the theme of automatism? Why, in all the vast psychoanalytic literature, do we hardly find references to the subject? We may offer only an entirely speculative explanation. As it is known, Pierre Janet was a French psychologist who also went to the Salpêtrière of Charcot. In an embryonic and imprecise way, he formulated some of the fundamental ideas later developed by Freud, such as the association of ideas, the hysterical conversion, and the unconscious (or subconscious). Janet had already stood out with his first book of 1889, *L'Automatisme Psychologique*, which consolidated research material he had published since 1886 in the *Revue Philosophique*. It gave him worldwide fame that even led to a cycle of lectures at the Harvard Medical School (Janet, 2010). Though only part of his extensive and ambitious work, that first book was sufficient for the notion of automatism to be strongly associated with his name.

Many citations to Janet in the 1895 *Studies on Hysteria* show that Breuer and Freud highly respected him. In a footnote in the first chapter of the book, the authors give Janet priority in developing the cathartic method of therapy. Freud still quotes Janet at the beginning of his "Formulations on the Two Principles of Mental Functioning" of 1911, recognizing that he had correctly identified the phenomenon of loss of "reality function" in neurotics, even though he had not established the correct connection between this disorder and the fundamental determinants of neurosis, the repressions.

Janet, however, did not develop equal respect for Freud's work and the emerging psychoanalysis movement. In August 1913, an International Medical Congress took place in London, where the psychiatric section intended to evaluate psychoanalysis. Janet was put face to face with young Jung, and we can imagine the intensity of the resulting conflict (Ellenberger, 1970). Janet claimed his priority in discovering the cathartic method and argued that psychoanalysis was simply a development of his fundamental idea. On the other hand, he sharply criticized the technique of dream interpretation and the thesis of neuroses' sexual origin. This, of course, meant an irreconcilable breach.

Ernest Jones (1914–1915) immediately published an outraged official response, and Freud himself could not hide his anger and irritation in the 1925 *Autobiographical Study*:

> As I write these lines, a number of papers and newspaper articles have reached me from France, which give evidence of a violent objection to the acceptance of psychoanalysis... I read, for instance, that I made use of my visit to Paris to familiarize myself with the theories of Pierre Janet and then made off with my booty, I should therefore like to say explicitly that during the whole of my visit to the Salpêtrière Janet's name was never so much as mentioned (p. 11).
>
> I always treated Janet himself with respect, since his discoveries coincided to a considerable extent with those of Breuer, which had been made earlier but were published later than his. But when in the course of time psychoanalysis became a subject of discussion in France, Janet behaved ill, showed ignorance of the facts and used ugly arguments. And finally he revealed himself to my eyes and destroyed the value of his own work by declaring that when he had spoken of 'unconscious' mental acts he had meant nothing by the phrase—it had been no more than a *façon de parler* (p. 33)

This way, Pierre Janet, the famous French theorist, who had undeniably been a precursor of psychoanalysis, became a despicable traitor by turning violently against it. The reaction was to run down his name. The concept of automatism, his trademark, was virtually banned from politically correct speech within the movement.[24]

---

24   Some references to Janet have reappeared recently in works on dissociation by Van der Hart & Friedman (1989), Bromberg (2001), and Howel (2005).

Among famous psychoanalysts, only Hartmann and Alexander have relevant discussions on automatism. Still, it is interesting to see the care with which Hartmann seeks to dissociate himself from Janet in Chapter 8 of his *Ego Psychology and the Adaptation Problem*, in a rather cryptic phrase: "Janet frequently uses the term automatism, but his usage is ambiguous, since he subsumes under it a variety of processes including most of those which we consider unconscious in the strict sense, particularly the mechanisms of the unconscious." (1939, p. 89)

Hartmann points that the ego can use somatic resources to perform motor actions. These actions get organized into procedures for specific purposes, and they work automatically in the case of procedures already consolidated in the mind. With increasing exercise of the action, its intermediate steps disappear from consciousness (p. 88). Not only motor behavior, but perception and thinking, too, can be automatized. Exercise automatizes methods of problem-solving, just as much as it does with walking, speaking, or writing (p. 88). The benefit of automatization is evident. By using it we apply means which already exist, that we need not create anew for every occasion (p. 91).

Alexander also discusses the phenomenon of automatism. The mental apparatus tends to substitute automatisms for the tentative, experimental examination of reality, therefore preserving in tonic form the achievements of exhausting "reality testing" (1961, p. 211). The phenomenon is like a "conditioned reflex," so that through repetition useful behavior patterns become automatic and effortless (1963, pp. 36–38).

Hartmann and Alexander taught that mental processes' automation consists of empowering the ego for specific complex sequences of thought to be used routinely. Some intermediate steps disappear from consciousness, become mechanical, and no longer require attention investment. It means replacing some steps in a thought sequence with somatic mechanisms (or conditioned reflexes), resulting in a substantial gain in mental processing efficiency.

However, it is important to note that when the ego incorporates a new pfunction into its repertoire, it will at first necessarily be flexible, that is, non-automated. The mind is trying to accomplish a processing task it has never done before. Once the pfunction is consolidated and available for use at any time, the mind can take care of its automation. A child who learns to walk needs flexible pfunctions to keep his balance while moving, which requires a great deal of conscious attention. Automation occurs when the pfunction is effectively mastered, and the monitoring of walking becomes unnecessary as it disappears from consciousness. Even an adult in particular conditions, such as when walking over rough terrain with the risk of an accident, may need to re-monitor his balance with an investment of attention: *i.e.*, walking may again require the use of flexible pfunctions.

Alexander (1963, pp 38-39) points out that an automated pfunction, while allowing for improved mental-processing efficiency, also has the disadvantage that it sometimes makes it difficult to adapt when external conditions change. Hartmann (1939, p. 92) agrees that a well-adjusted ego must be capable of both automatic and flexible behaviors. Of course, the ability to tailor the degree of behavioral flexibility to each real situation is not simple at all and can even be considered an indication of mental health. Part of the problem is that reversing an automatism is not always a trivial process. Not all automatisms can be altered immediately, and without transition, by a mere decision of the will. This statement's empirical proof is quite simple: try, for example, to "unlearn" riding a bicycle!

A healthy adult should be able to migrate from an automatic behavior pattern to a flexible behavior pattern or *vice versa* whenever necessary. One way to ensure this, which indeed happens in some cases, is to have an alternative flexible version for the automated pfunction. In practice, however, it would be very inefficient to maintain duplicate versions of all automatic ego pfunctions. A better alternative is to create memory registers at the time of automation with instructions on using the flexible version of the pfunction. For example, these records may contain a set of remembrances on the experience of learning the flexible pfunction. They may also include a set of tips and instructions, a kind of user manual that would, for example, be sufficient to teach the pfunction to a beginner. The important thing is to have these records stored and available in memory to be retrieved when you want to rebuild the flexible pfunction. In this way, the flexible pfunction can be eliminated and replaced by the automatic pfunction, with the guarantee of its reactivation at any time.

The secret of repression in the case of pre-conscious mental processes and neurotic symptoms is a consequence of this fact that, in many cases, an automated ego pfunction has a set of memory records associated with it, which make it possible to revert to a flexible form (*i.e.*, by its "de-automatization"). Repression merely eliminates the associative keys that link those memory registers to the automated pfunction, in a process similar to what we have seen in our earlier discussion on repression of memory registers. Unpleasant memories, possibly of traumatic experiences or fantasies, which would allow understanding how the automated pfunction was initially constructed and took the form of a neurotic symptom, become inaccessible to any process of association of ideas that has today's reality of the symptom as its starting point. Memory records that contain the memories and "instructions for use" that would allow de-automatization and consequent elimination of the symptom are not erased from memory, but are no longer accessible to most associative sequences.

In his *Introductory Lessons* of 1916, Freud notes that repression does not exclude the neurotic mental process from conscious awareness, as it remains as an automated symptom. It excludes only the associative connections with the psychic pre-determinants of the neurosis. These are registers related to internal conflicts that were converted into neurotic symptoms at the origin of the pathology. "Their psychical pre-determinants which we infer by means of analysis are unconscious, at least until we have made them conscious to the patient." (Freud, 1916, p. 345)

So far, we have seen how a conditioning process constructs automatic functions from the frequent repetition of certain behaviors. It seems to suggest that symptom building always involves a lengthy process of repetition and training, which is undoubtedly true in many cases. However, clinical evidence indicates that the rapid construction of neurotic symptoms may also occur in the case of trauma. In these cases, the tremendous affect charge involved produces a fast and intense process of repetitions, which happens primarily at the fantasy level and in dreams. Here too, constructing the symptom via conditioning requires many repetitions, but these are somewhat compressed in a short period. Freud (1916, p. 340) identified this process in the experience of war neuroses.

In many neuroses, something else may happen beyond eliminating associative keys related to the forbidden content. A "false" associative connection may arise between the symptom and an anxiety-generating memory record. This record may be a memory fragment of an experience, real or imagined, that produces the diffuse anticipation of some extremely unpleasant calamity. It is a way of strengthening the defense system to prevent access to the inappropriate content's memory at the neurosis' origin. In *Obsessive Actions and Religious Practices* of 1907, Freud identifies this false associative connection with an unconscious sense of guilt. The fake associative relationship with fuzzy anxiety-generating memories explains the minimal tolerance shown by many neurotics with any deviation from their ceremonial automatisms. It even led Freud to associate them with religious practices. The individual recognizes that these activities are meaningless formalities, yet any departure from formal routine produces extreme anxiety. Great care in their execution seems to give the ceremonial a sacred character.

This may be a good point to discuss the notion of an unconscious Freudian superego. In an Oedipal relationship, the child automates a particular behavior. It may be a defense against the anxiety of losing the primary affective contact with his or her relevant adults, or, in the most extreme case, against the fear of castration. For example, the child eats a banana and throws the peel on the floor, and as the father scolds him, he realizes that he must throw it into the trash can to avoid the risk of losing his father's love or, in an extreme case, of being castrated by him. Repetition of the scene, or variants of it, results in the automation of behavior that we might define as *"being careful with garbage."* Initially, the child is aware that he or she is learning to be "well educated" about garbage *"so that my parents are happy with me."* At least initially, the memory records associated with the automatic behavior can still be accessible to consciousness.

Eventually, however, with the heightened feelings of conflict and ambivalence toward parents, access to these records is blocked. The automatic behavior of taking care of garbage remains, but now as a sort of second nature. The memories of the educational process that built it, and the childhood fantasies about parents that were undoubtedly produced by it, disappear in childhood amnesia. The result is that Freudian superego incorporated the automated pfunction, but its motivation became unconscious. It is in this sense that Freud speaks of an unconscious superego.

Freud identifies the superego as a precipitate in ego formation through which the strong parental influence exerted in childhood extends throughout life. Alexander (1963) further notes that the superego is a "deposit" of automatisms, comparable to a "complex set of conditioned reflexes." This fact was recently "rediscovered" by Marianne Goldberger (1996), who suggests that people, in general, cannot remember the circumstances under which they have assimilated the moral rules that govern their behavior. Automatisms can, of course, be perceived by consciousness, as happens, for example, in the case of neurotic symptoms; what remains hidden is the original motivation of these behaviors, which Alexander (1925) compares to an introjected legal code of bygone days. Only in this sense can one think, as illustrated by Freud in the curious figure of his *New Introductory Lessons* of 1932, of a Freudian superego that seems partly submerged in the unconscious region of the mind. A similar analysis applies to the support superego. The parental influence exerted in childhood also extends throughout life as a set of automated pfunctions that support the full realization of ludic impulses.

29. Repeating and Working Through

This chapter aims to understand the need for working through in neurosis therapy, and for that we must first discuss the Freudian notion of the compulsion to repeat. In his paper "Remembering, Repeating, and Working-Through" of 1914, Freud had already noted the clinical phenomenon of a tendency to repeat unpleasant or even painful childhood experiences automatically. He concluded that in psychoanalytic treatment, a patient tends to reproduce what has been repressed not as a remembrance, but as an action automatically repeated. The patient always seems to prefer repeating instead of recalling. He usually repeats his symptoms during the treatment process even after the analyst achieves precise interpretations of his neurosis' origin. In his *Beyond the Pleasure Principle* of 1920, Freud noted that the phenomenon seems to have the characteristics of a drive impulse. It justified introducing the hypothesis of a death instinct into his theoretical framework, but this, as we have seen, is hard to accept when the mind is an information processor.

Freud (1920, p. 293) argued it is possible to identify three manifestations of this drive:

- .Children's impulse to play.
- Recurrent dreams in traumatic neuroses.
- The tendency to repeat symptoms in the psychoanalytic treatment of neuroses.

Yet these manifestations can be considered independent phenomena. In the first case of the playing child, we have already seen in Hendrick's discussion how children's sensorimotor play typically involves an almost compulsive practice and training effort. It is nothing more than the process of adaptation and incorporation of new pfunctions into the ego. Hence, in this case, the compulsion to repeat just results from the ludic impulse.

The second manifestation of that compulsion, as pointed out by Freud, is in the recurring dreams of traumatic neuroses, which he even considered as the strongest evidence for the need of a new and mysterious death instinct. He argued that since these dreams are deeply unpleasant, they are not compatible with the idea that every dream is the fulfillment of a wish, albeit in hallucinatory form. In that sense, they could not be consistent with the pleasure principle.

However, as Freud himself has shown, dealing with conflict through symptom or ceremonial formation can be considered a defensive measure. In the case of traumatic neuroses, recurring dreams are part of the process of forming a protective neurotic ceremonial. They occur at an early stage of neurosis and tend to disappear when symptoms become automatic. Dreams are just evidence that the individual is still trying to deal with an unresolved traumatic situation. The eventual resolution will block the memory records of the original experience and convert them into neurotic symptoms. This argument has recently been confirmed by Ernest Hartmann (2001), who notes that the dream is essentially a replay of the experience shortly after the trauma. In a matter of days or weeks, however, new material is added to the dream making connections with previous experiences, and making the trauma "contextualized," that is, placing this emotionally disturbing new material into a context of adequate memories. Recurring dreams only allow quick conversion of trauma into symptoms. This behavior is not inconsistent with the pleasure principle. The organism is just trying to maintain its homeostatic balance in a situation of internal conflict between the reenactment of a traumatic experience and a repressive superego.

We still have a third manifestation of the compulsion to repeat, as a ubiquitous phenomenon in psychoanalytic therapy. In *Beyond the Pleasure Principle*, Freud explains how the evolution of psychoanalytic technique uncovered this phenomenon:

> Twenty-five years of intensive work have meant that the immediate aims of psychoanalytic practice are completely different today from what they were at the beginning. At first...psychoanalysis was above all an art of interpretation. As the therapeutic need was not met by this process, the next task that immediately arose was to compel the patient to confirm the analyst's interpretation on the basis of his own memory.
>
> It then became increasingly clear, however, that...the patient is unable to remember all that is repressed within him, especially perhaps its most essential elements, and thus fails to be convinced that the interpretation presented to him is the correct one. Instead, he is driven to repeat the repressed matter as an experience in the present, instead of remembering it as something belonging to the past, which is what the physician would much rather see happen (Freud, 1920, p. 56, underlined in the original).

The conclusion was that the compulsion to repeat symptoms during therapy results from the patient's unconscious resistance to accepting the analyst's interpretation to explain his neurosis' origin. Because neurosis results from the difficulty in dealing with an internal conflict produced by a traumatic experience, this same difficulty precludes acceptance of interpretation in therapy. In a successful treatment, the transfer mechanism replaces the original neurosis by a new transfer neurosis, so that the same trauma can be remembered and worked out in the relationship with the analyst. When this happens, the battle is over: the patient accepts the validity of the interpretation, and the therapy—which wholly depends on this acceptance—can be successfully concluded.

However, it seems quite evident that this understanding presented by Freud in *"Beyond the Pleasure Principle"* of the compulsion to repeat symptoms and of the healing process of neuroses was very simplistic, since it assumed that the acceptance of the correct interpretation is sufficient by itself to disable neurotic symptoms. We know that there is a tautological element in this statement. It is always possible to say that when symptoms persist despite therapy, the patient's resistance has prevented the recovery of the repressed content and the interpretation's actual acceptance. In this case, it is not possible to test whether the interpretation is correct or not. The possibility arises of a disturbing element of suggestion by the analyst on the patient.

Freud himself acknowledged this difficulty in his 1937 essay "Constructions in Analysis." He suggested that we should not think of analysis as a process in which the therapist submits interpretations for patient evaluation. It would be more appropriate to think of it as a process in which he offers constructions. These constructions are presented only as provisional conjectures, which can be confirmed or rejected. The analyst should not claim authority for them, or demand direct agreement from the patient, let alone argue with him if at first, he denies them. Only further development of treatment can indicate whether the constructs are correct or useless. The idea is that if the construction is correct, or at least an approximation of the truth, the patient's behavior in the transference will produce subtle and unconscious communication of this fact. Sometimes the patient will respond to a correct construction with an unmistakable aggravation of his symptoms and general condition. It will be up to the analyst to interpret this indirect communication from the patient. Then he may introduce a new construct to be confirmed or rejected again, and so on. If the treatment is successful, this process will converge to gradual consolidation in the transfer of mutual conviction, for patient and analyst, about the validity of the explanation for the neurosis' origin. However, what is missing is a plausible explanation of the process by which the emergence of this sure conviction in the analyst's construction can produce in the patient the elimination of neurotic symptoms.

When we consider the phenomenon of automatism, our understanding of the compulsion to repeat symptoms is significantly improved. As we have seen in the typical neurotic situation, there is a conversion of internal conflict or traumatic experience into symptoms. Simultaneously, there is a blockage of access to those memory registers related to those events that gave rise to the pathology. The process of memory retrieval through the association of ideas, which was the essence of Breuer and Freud's original cathartic method, remains a fundamental part of neurosis therapy, aimed precisely at unlocking access to these memory records in order to understand the original meaning of the pathology. Moreover, the interpretation of the transference in the therapeutic relationship, which is the technique later suggested by Freud, is mainly concerned with disabling the automatisms that resulted from neurosis. The goal of elaboration is to disable the compulsive repetition of neurotic symptoms.

This understanding seems compatible with Freud's more sophisticated formulation in his 1937 *Analysis Terminable and Interminable*, which demonstrates an accurate understanding of the mechanics of the psychoanalytic therapy of neuroses. The book points to the role of automatisms, termed "regular modes of reaction," even though without a more in-depth discussion of the concept:

The mechanisms of defense serve the purpose of keeping off dangers. It cannot be disputed that they are successful in this; and it is doubtful whether the ego could do without them altogether during its development. But it is also certain that they may become dangers themselves ... Each person uses no more than a selection of them, but these become fixated in his ego. They become *regular modes of reaction* of his character, which are repeated throughout his life whenever a situation occurs that is similar to the original one. This turns them into infantilisms, and they share the fate of so many institutions which attempt to keep themselves in existence after the time of their usefulness has passed.... The adult's ego, with its increased strength, continues to defend itself against dangers which no longer exist in reality ... Thus, we can easily understand how the defensive mechanisms, by bringing about an ever more extensive alienation from the external world and a permanent weakening of the ego, pave the way for, and encourage, the outbreak of neurosis (Freud, 1937, pp. 29–30, *my italics*).

The book also rightly highlights the importance of the de-automatization stage in the healing process, which is called "ego-analysis":

What we are trying to discover is what influence the alteration of the ego which corresponds to [the defensive mechanisms] has upon our therapeutic efforts. The material for an answer to this question is given in the volume by Anna Freud to which I have already referred. The essential point is that the patient repeats these modes of reaction during the work of analysis as well, that he produces them before our eyes, as it were. In fact, it is only in this way that we get to know them. This does not mean that they make analysis impossible. On the contrary, they constitute half of our analytic task. The other half, the one which was first tackled by analysis in its early days, is the uncovering of what is hidden in the id. During the treatment our therapeutic work is constantly swinging backwards and forwards like a pendulum between a piece of id-analysis and a piece of ego-analysis. In the one case we want to make something from the id conscious, in the other we want to correct something in the ego (Freud, 1937, p. 30).

In this text, Freud defines ego analysis as "the correction of something in the ego," but I would describe it as the deactivation of an automatism. On the other hand, what he calls id analysis, defined as "the revelation of something hidden in the id," I would describe as the unlocking of memory records concerning the origin of neurosis. The expression "hidden in the id" is somewhat inaccurate, because we are not talking about a pfunction of the id, but a repressed memory register. The only thing in common in these concepts is that both concern unconscious mental elements, the first by definition, and the second owing to repression. Unfortunately, this kind of inaccuracy, of not distinguishing between a pfunction and a memory record, was quite common in Freud's work and remains endemic in much of psychoanalytic literature.

The exact way ego analysis produces the deactivation of neurotic automatisms is something not well understood by psychoanalysis. However, the extensive clinical experience accumulated over a century demonstrates that the de-automatization of symptoms is possible only in a long therapy process. But why is this working-through process necessary and time-consuming? Why do neurotic symptoms not simply disappear once the patient hears the correct interpretation? In 1920, Freud argued that this is so because resistance precludes the patient's full acceptance of the interpretation. But later, Freud (1937a) achieved a deeper understanding of the need to "correct something in the ego," that is, eliminating automatisms.

One explanation for the need for lengthy elaboration is that to eliminate a symptom, you must also deactivate its "false" associative connections with anxiety-producing memory registers. These act as resistances to de-automatization. The difficulty created by them is that the ego comes to regard healing as a new threat. The de-automatization intended in the ego requires the unlocking of these connections through analysis of the id. In other words, it requires the neutralization of anxiety-generating memories through the association of ideas and interpretation. That is the meaning of Freud's pendulous swinging movement, a necessarily lengthy process in which therapy gradually evolves. Its focus shifts between id analysis and ego analysis, between the recovery of unconscious memory records and the deactivation of automatisms.

Another factor that explains why elaboration is necessary and time-consuming is the very nature of the de-automatization intended by ego analysis. As Hartmann (1939) recalled, not all automatisms can be changed easily. In practice, automatism's deactivation is never a simple process; on the contrary, it is usually complex and challenging. It may even be impossible. Imagine, for example, that you want to unlearn riding a bicycle. It seems impossible: after all, everyone knows that this is one thing that once learned, one never forgets. The same goes for unlearning how to play the piano, unlearning how to drive a car with a manual transmission, unlearning how to read, etc. It is what happens in most automatism cases and can undoubtedly occur more often than we would like in the case of neurotic symptoms.

However, a little thought shows that even unlearning to ride a bicycle may still be possible under certain conditions. Imagine that we could condition the individual (using chemicals, for example) to feel bad whenever riding a bike. Then he would become incapable of doing it. That is, the automatism would be neutralized by a new automatism, "feeling bad when riding a bicycle." In many cases, perhaps most, de-automatization is such a process. A new compensating automatism neutralizes a neurotic automatism. The problem is that any automatism, as Alexander said, is similar to a conditioned reflex, which means that building a new automatism will always require a necessarily lengthy conditioning process.

Based on what we have discussed so far about the relationship between repression, automatism, and neuroses, we can summarize what appears to be the correct conception of the psychoanalytic treatment of neuroses. When the neurosis sets in, we know that some experience of internal conflict or trauma gave rise to an automatic symptom. Simultaneously, repression has blocked access to the memory records of the pathology's triggering experience. Moreover, a false associative connection between the symptom and an anxiety-generating memory record arises, which is a way of reinforcing the defense of the neurosis.

The process of psychoanalytic therapy of neuroses thus consists of eliminating this false connection and, if possible, in re-establishing access to memory records relating to the triggering experience of the neurosis. The restoration of this latter access can be the starting point for gradual symptom deactivation, which is ultimately quite similar to what behaviorists call the extinction of conditioning. When it is impossible to re-establish access to memory registers, the only solution is to build a new automatism through transference to neutralize the neurotic symptom. In this case, the symptom does not disappear, but the new compensating automatism minimizes its pathological effects. The patient regains the ability to live comfortably managing his neurosis.

PART VII. FINAL REMARKS

30. The Practical Task

In his seminal 1966 article on "Forms and Transformations of Narcissism," Kohut wrote that "the interplay between the narcissistic self, the ego, and the superego determines the characteristic flavor of the personality" (p. 109). It is a phrase that still puzzles many experts, as it seems to be mixing concepts of self psychology with notions of the old Freudian metapsychology. The correct statement could be that the interplay between the support superego, the ego, the Freudian superego, and the reflex of impulsive aggression determines the characteristic flavor of the personality. This conclusion results from four changes in classical Freudian metapsychology:

1) The replacement of energy by information.
2) Understanding drives as homeostatic impulses
3) The introduction of a new ludic drive
4) A new understanding of impulsive aggression as a reflex conditioned by life experience

These four innovations allow for the construction of a new psychoanalytic theory of the mind that incorporates ideas from many of the discipline's greatest thinkers. It is relevant for mental pathologies of different origins, whether associated with the sexual drive, the ludic drive, or resulting from an excessively restraining inner world configuration. We can see it as a three-dimensional framework, encompassing classic Freudian disorders, Kohut-Winnicott personality disorders, and Melanie Klein's anxious inhibitions. It also allows the possibility of complex interactions of these three dimensions.

Examining in detail the therapeutic follow-up of this new theoretical construct is far beyond this book's scope. I can only add a few suggestions for future research. I begin using the succinct definition of "good analysis" from Kohut's *How Does Analysis Cure?*:

> A good analysis will have explained to the patient how the short-comings of the selfobject milieu brought about the deficits in his self structure... Self psychology is at one with the technical principle that interpretation in general, and the interpretation of transferences in particular, is the major instrumentality of therapeutic psychoanalysis... Only if the analyst is able to grasp accurately the experiences of this analysand, present and past, will he, via interpretations, set up a working-through process that re-creates in the analysis a situation that provides protracted, development-enhancing exposure to optimal frustrations. It is this opportunity, insufficiently provided to the analysand in childhood, that is offered once more in analysis (Kohut, 1984, p. 209).

This definition assumes that the essence of the problem is the absence of a reasonably well-developed support superego that should have resulted from the internalization of an adequate number of support objects and identifications. It translates for Kohut as the absence of a cohesive and well-structured adult self, and for Winnicott as the absence of a sufficiently supportive potential space resulting from a good-enough mother. In all these conceptions, the problem has nothing to do with memory content, but only with the absence of those specific pfunctions that make healthy and creative living possible. The therapy's objective should be to internalize these pfunctions into the support superego through narcissistic transference.

The reader can imagine how this definition of a "good analysis" would be reformulated by Melanie Klein. For her, the essence of the problem lies precisely in the content of memory. A memory loaded with bad and persecutory objects makes healthy living impossible. Consequently, the main goal of therapy should be to "clean up" memory, excluding or in some way neutralizing these bad objects accumulated, possibly through phantasies, since early childhood. This goal is achieved by identifying the frustration objects and their manifestations of ambivalence, anxiety, and aggression in the transference.

Adherents of these two distinct dimensions of metapsychology certainly agree that the goal of therapy is to allow for creative and satisfying living, characterized by personal initiatives and projects, a high level of self-confidence, and the absence of severe episodes of anxiety and depression. The problem is to determine which of the two dimensions applies to any specific case, with the possibility of both being equally relevant.

And we have not even said anything about Freudian disorders. They typically result either from a sexual phantasy or trauma, real or imaginary, that has been converted into a neurotic symptom or from an excessively repressive Freudian superego that hinders the healthy functioning of the adult ego. Neurotic disorders are easy to diagnose but difficult to cure, because they tend to change into automatisms. Freud himself, in his *Analysis Terminable and Interminable* (1937), noted that war traumas appear to be the only easily treatable automatisms. Disorders resulting from a repressive superego are equally challenging to deal with because superegos are like "deposits of automatisms," as pointed out by Franz Alexander (1925). James Strachey (1934) suggested that transference may allow the internalization of new pfunctions that compensate or partially neutralize the more perversely repressive aspects of the Freudian superego. I remember, though, that to modify, offset or cancel an automatism can be as tricky as unlearning to ride a bicycle.

When we consider the Kleinian and ludic dimensions of metapsychology, there arises one observation that is more sociological than psychological, but may have some relevance for the clinic. In the ludic dimension, pathology typically results from failures and deficiencies (whether intentional or not) in the care of parents or guardians during childhood, in what Winnicott brilliantly summed up with the notion of absence of a sufficiently good mother. Hence the pathology results from some "fault" or omission of parents or adults responsible for the child. In the Kleinian dimension, however, since pathology results primarily from unconscious childhood fantasies, it makes no sense to attribute responsibility to parents. For Klein, we can have an individual with a good-enough mother and severe personality disorders. These observations, moreover, suggest that information on the personalities of parents and on family life experiences in childhood may be useful for an accurate diagnosis of the nature of the pathology, even when it does not result directly from psychoanalytic investigation.

A comparison of different therapeutic approaches may suggest useful points of contact between these different metapsychology dimensions. For example, does the complex Kleinian dynamics of paranoid-schizoid and depressive positions affects the early acquisition of support objects? Is there an impact of the inner world's bad or persecutory objects on the identifications and transmuting internalizations that give rise to the support superego? How do good support objects interact with bad frustration objects in building the inner world? How can this be affected by the presence or absence of a well-structured support superego? Can the existence of a repressive Freudian superego affect the Kleinian assembly of bad and good objects? What are the implications for therapy of the internalization of perverse and false-self identifications?

Another important question is whether a specific treatment is appropriate for each of the pathological dimensions. Is it possible that the same therapeutic approach will produce curative effects in different dimensions?

More specifically, can a wrong interpretation cure? What is the relevance of our new ideas on metapsychology for modern relational approaches, both in theory and clinic? How could the clinical phenomena of intersubjective unconscious communication, early mentioned by Bollas (1987; 2009) and recently discussed by Stern (2005) and Spezzano (2012), fit into this new three-dimensional approach to the theory of mind? These are just some of the instigating questions arising from the new ideas of this book.

Appendix A: Dreams

Since Freud's remarkable breakthrough with his 1900 book, dream interpretation has become a hallmark of psychoanalysis. Dream analysis was "the royal way of knowing the unconscious activities of the mind" (Freud 1900, ch. 7, E) in the early years. Later, as the psychoanalytic clinic evolved, leaving behind its initial goal of making the unconscious conscious, the emphasis on dreams disappeared. The elaborate technique of interpretation developed by the pioneers became increasingly relegated to the background, almost as something of historical interest only, as pointed out by Gedo (2005, ch. 10).

However, it turns out that dreams constitute a phenomenon that naturally lends itself to scientific investigation. This has sparked a great deal of research interest in cognitive psychology and neuroscience. Barcaro (2010) has a review of relevant literature. So far, however, the results have been disappointing, as is evident from Levin's (2009, p. 191) conclusion that the short answer to the question of why we dream is that we do not know for sure.

The Freudian dream model, accurately formulated and purged of some exaggeration (such as attempts to identify typical symbolisms), is still the most exciting and compelling explanation for the phenomenon. Freud developed the theory primarily using the topographic model, assuming the mind as an energy processor. Still, it holds fast, without significant problems, in the context of a reformulated structural model that takes the mind as an information processor.

We may begin by noting that the concept of the dream itself is a source of inaccuracy throughout the literature. What is a dream? Freud (1940a, ch.

V) speaks of "psychic activity during sleep that we perceive as dreams." A dream is a memory record generated by psychic activity during sleep, basically a memory trace or the memory of a hallucinating experience while sleeping. Freud began the tradition that permeates the literature of using the term "dream" with little care to indicate both the memory record and the psychic activity that produced the record. A few times, he carefully distinguished between the "latent dream-thoughts" and the memory record produced by them through the "dream-work." The first became known as the *latent* dream, the second as the *manifest* dream. In the dream work, thoughts get distorted so that after waking, we remember not the actual dream process, but only a facade behind which the detailed account of the process remains hidden.

If the mind is a parallel-information processor, dream-thoughts are simple to explain. When I am awake, my brain processes thoughts simultaneously consciously and unconsciously. The stream of consciousness is only a small part of psychic activity since the process of mental experimentation and the test of reality (Stekel's polyphony of thoughts) occur primarily outside this stream (pre-consciously or unconsciously, Freud would say). When I go to sleep, there is a drastic reduction in psychic activity, and activity in the perceptual-conscious apparatus (Pcpt-Cs) in particular, so that the stream of consciousness almost disappears. However, the unconscious mental process is not fully affected and continues to occur in the form of dreamlike thoughts. Possibly this parallel processing is less intense during sleep. Still, we know that it happens with enough intensity and frequency to generate the memory records that we perceive as dreams (manifest dreams).

Here, however, a significant conceptual difficulty naturally arises. A fundamental hypothesis of the Freudian model is that only memory records created by a conscious mental process can be retrieved and utilized again by the stream of consciousness. Section II of "The Ego and the Id" (1923), notes that "only something which has once been a Cs perception can become conscious," where Cs means conscious. The manifest dream is a memory record that can be consciously retrieved. How is this possible if it was created by a dream-thinking process (the latent dream) that developed outside the flow of consciousness?

To eliminate this difficulty, Freud postulates that the conscious-perceptual apparatus (Pcpt-Cs) is inaccessible to thought processes during sleep, but not to perceptions of external and internal origin. Consciousness is not entirely dormant, because the organism must have the ability to react to potentially threatening changes in the outside world or somatic balance. Here is how he formulates this hypothesis in *The Interpretation of Dreams*:

> I must assume that the state of sleep makes the sensory surface of consciousness which is directed towards the Pcs far more unsusceptible to excitation than the surface directed towards the Pcpt systems. Moreover, this abandonment of interest in thought-processes during the night has a purpose: thinking is to come to a standstill, for the Pcs requires sleep (Freud, 1900, ch. 7, D, p. 730).

In this text, the topographic concept of Pcs is roughly equivalent to the structural concept of ego. The biological purpose of sleep is the recovery of the organism, and this requires the disengagement of any interest in the outside world. All monitoring and control activities of the ego must stop. We must be unable to experience our conscious relationships with the outside world. Sleep is indispensable for the ego to recover from the stress of its continuous rational activity during the day.

In the Freudian model, a typical thought process will be either the construction of a drive (*e.g.*, "*I want to have sex with a particular person*," "*I want to play*") or a reality test (*e.g.*, "*can this wish be fulfilled without unpleasant consequences to me*"). It always aims to have access to consciousness, which is a precondition for realizing the instinctive impulse through motor activities. In Freud's original conception, this was a movement of energy within the mental apparatus toward discharge and action. If the mind is an information processor this just results from the pleasure principle's operation, in which the body manages somatic demands to maintain its homeostatic balance.

In dreams, due to the blocking of thought process access to the conscious-perceptual apparatus (Pcpt-Cs), a latent dream process can only reach consciousness if it becomes either an external perception or an internal perception. What is needed is either a piece of information from external reality or an internal somatic demand sufficiently urgent to require a reaction from the organism (as would happen, for example, with severe stomach pain or a loud noise). Here is how *The Interpretation of Dreams* puts it:

> Once, however, a dream has become a <u>perception</u>, it is in a position to excite consciousness, by means of the qualities it has now acquired. This sensory excitation proceeds to perform what is its essential function: it directs a part of the available cathectic energy in the Pcs into attention to what is causing the excitation. It must therefore be admitted that every dream has an arousing effect, that it sets a part of the quiescent force of the Pcs in action (Freud, 1900, cap 7, D, p. 731, underlined in the original).

This transformation of a preconscious thought process (the latent dream) into something that is admitted by the perceptual-conscious apparatus (Pcpt-Cs) as a perception (and no longer as a thought process) is what results from the dream work. Understanding of exactly how this transformation occurs is not straightforward. The final result is to translate a processing of information that uses a typical ego language into another that uses a typical id language.

It may also happen that the dream-thinking process, now transformed into an information product of the id, is reinforced by repressed instinctual impulses, which increases its capacity to press the ego for satisfaction. This opportunistic participation of repressed instinctive impulses in dreamwork is almost inevitable and is present in nearly every dream.

Freud suggests that, in the end, this dream-transforming activity will have produced distortions that transformed the original sequence of thought into a set of images, a kind of pictographic puzzle composed as a "rebus" or a figurative puzzle (ch. 6, p. 382). A rebus is a charade that uses a pictogram to designate, not the object it represents, but another object whose name is phonetically similar. It consists of using a pictogram to represent a phonogram. For example, a rebus may represent the English word "before" by the image of a bee along with the number four. Here's how Freud sums it up:

> It [the dream-work] consists of a peculiar way of treating the preconscious material of thought, so that its component parts become *condensed*, its mental emphasis becomes *displaced*, and the whole of it is translated into visual images or *dramatized* and filled out by a deceptive *secondary elaboration*. The dream work is an excellent example of the processes occurring in the deeper, unconscious layers of the mind, which differ considerably from the familiar normal process of thought (Freud, 1925b, p. 50, italics in the original).

The transformation of latent dreamlike thinking into a perception of sufficient intensity can disturb sleep, requiring a momentary reactivation of the consciousness stream. Usually, this reactivation is only partial, but it may also occur that a disturbance is of sufficient intensity to awaken the individual entirely. In any case, it is at this moment of momentary interruption of sleep and partial or total reactivation of consciousness that the mind stores in memory what we know as the manifest dream. *The Interpretation of Dreams* accurately describes these "near-awakening" moments:

Experience shows that dreaming is compatible with sleeping, even if it interrupts sleep several times during the night. One wakes up for an instant and then falls asleep again at once (Freud, 1900, ch. 7, D, p. 733).

Freud, in *The Interpretation of Dreams*, evaluates a "very attractive" conjecture suggested by Goblot that dream work (the latent dream) would occupy no more than the transitional period between sleep and waking. Kleitman (1963), one of the so-called REM sleep state discoverers, seems to have a modern formulation of the same thesis. Awakening usually requires a certain amount of time, and only during that period would the latent dream occur. Freud's opinion, however, was that dream work probably evolves over a long period, even though the emergence of the dream in consciousness can be rapid and explosive:

Certain personal experiences of my own lead me to suspect that the dream-work often requires more than a day and a night in order to achieve its result...In my opinion even the demand for the dream to be made intelligible as a perceptual event may be put into effect before the dream attracts consciousness to itself. From then onwards, however, the pace is accelerated, for at that point a dream is treated in the same fashion as anything else that is perceived. It is like a firework, which takes hours to prepare but goes off in a moment (Freud, 1900, ch. 7, D, p. 732).

The conclusion is that some dreams can be registered at any near--waking moment during sleep, although possibly most only do so at the actual awakening.

The dream process has by now either acquired sufficient intensity through the dream-work to attract consciousness to itself and arouse the preconscious, irrespectively of the time and depth of sleep; or its intensity is insufficient to achieve this and it must remain in a state of readiness until, just before waking, attention becomes more mobile and comes to meet it. The majority of dreams appear to operate with comparatively low psychical intensities, for they mostly wait until the moment of waking. But this also explains the fact that, if we are suddenly woken from deep sleep, we usually perceive something that we have dreamt (Freud, 1900, ch. 7, D, p. 732).

What is important is to understand that only when the dream work can access consciousness in the form of perception of hallucinated experience does the manifest dream's memory register occur. It is a memory-trace that the consciousness stream can later recover. Of course, as suggested by Palombo (1978), this memory record immediately begins to be processed in a typical memory cycle, during which it goes through a secondary overhaul and a superego censorship screen. Freud sometimes considered this secondary revision as part of the dream work, but other times did not. It seems more logical to regard it as something that happens as part of the memory cycle that comes into operation after the dream work has accomplished its purpose of creating the conscious memory record of the manifest dream.

The memory cycle is already in operation during the rest of the sleep, so that the manifest dream remembered in the morning or later may have already undergone considerable modification. Secondary elaboration is an attempt to give intelligibility to the first recorded version of the manifest dream, but its result is usually the opposite of the intended one:

As a result of its efforts, the dream loses its appearance of absurdity and disconnectedness and approximates to the model of an intelligible experience. But its efforts are not always crowned with success. Dreams occur which, at a superficial view, may seem faultlessly logical and reasonable...Dreams which are of such a kind have been subjected to a far-reaching revision by this psychical function [*i.e.* by secondary elaboration] that is akin to waking thought: they appear to have meaning, but that meaning is as far removed as possible from their true significance. If we analyze them, we can convince ourselves that it is in these dreams that the secondary revision has played about with the material the most freely... In other dreams this tendentious revision has only partly succeed; coherence seems to rule for a certain distance, but the dream then becomes senseless or confused... In yet other dreams the revision has failed altogether: we find ourselves helplessly face to face with a meaningless heap of fragmentary material (Freud, 1900, ch. 6, I, pp. 630–631).

I have failed to mention the role of the "wish-fulfillment" mechanism in dream theory. Note that at the time of *The Interpretation of Dreams*, Freud had not yet developed his drive theory. Based on this theory, the term "wish fulfillment" must logically be translated as "drive fulfillment." Since much of the thought process is motivated by id's drive demands, we can conclude that wish-fulfillment, in this sense, is a common feature of most mental activity. It holds for both waking and dreamlike activity. However, in the case of dreams, when Freud speaks of "wish fulfillment," he is thinking on the fulfillment of a repressed drive.

Let us see how this happens. The near awakening produced by the attack of dream work on consciousness is experienced as an undesirable night's rest disturbance. The mental apparatus that wishes to remain asleep has a way of avoiding or at least postponing such disruption. It can ensure that the sequence of latent dream-thinking extends into the harmless hallucinatory experience of a repressed instinctive impulse. Hence, it prevents the dream work from proceeding in its attempt to get the conscience's attention using the expedient of a false perception of experience. The result is that in virtually every dream, we can identify a component of the fulfillment of a repressed instinctual impulse. Here's how Freud sums this up in the *New Introductory Lessons*:

> In every dream an instinctual wish has to be represented as fulfilled. The shutting-off of mental life from reality at night and the regression to primitive mechanisms which this makes possible enable this wished-for instinctual satisfaction to be experienced in a hallucinatory manner as occurring in the present. As a result of this same regression, ideas are transformed in the dream into visual pictures; the latent dream-thoughts, that is to say, are dramatized and illustrated (Freud, 1933, p. 23).

Freud's dream theory is a construction of striking ingenuity that, despite some inaccuracies and exaggerations, still seems to be the best explanation for a phenomenon that occurs in the deepest, most unconscious layers of the mind. We have seen that it easily fits into the reformulated structural model developed in this book. Its clinical use as a basis for dream interpretation has become somewhat controversial, with criticisms for having a large subjectivity component. However, it still is one of the most thought-provoking ideas for the psychoanalytic clinic.

Appendix B: Psychoanalysis as Non-Experimental Science

This appendix addresses methodological issues in a scientific approach to the psychoanalytic theory of mind. Every science uses models, from which predictions are derived and tested empirically. First, it has an activity of constructing logically consistent models. Then a testing activity confronts the model with data. It can be validated (as a provisional truth of science), or rejected entirely, or returned to the theory-building activity with suggestions for improvement. The result is a simplified representation of reality using the fewest possible hypotheses, allowing the logical derivation of propositions that can be verified empirically. For Hawking, "a good theory... must accurately describe a wide range of observations based on a model that contains only a few arbitrary elements, and it must make well-defined predictions about the results of future observations" (1988, p. 9).

This definition also applies to psychoanalysis, but in this case, it is essential to understand that we are dealing with a non-experimental science. Its primary testing tool is the analytical process, which is obviously not a controlled experiment and always involves a good deal of imprecision and subjectivity. The theory of mind constructed by psychoanalysis can, in principle, be "verified" empirically by the study of human behavior inside the clinic and outside it. Freud and many others have shown this in applied psychoanalytic work, but it is not the same thing as an experimental test. As a matter of fact, what happens with psychoanalysis is not different from what happens, for example, with economic science. An economic model can only really be "tested" through economic history, that is, by careful observation of human behavior in the real world of business, consumption, and production. In this respect, it has even less experimental resources than psychoanalysis. In economics, there is nothing comparable to the relatively controlled and repetitive observation environment of the clinic throughout an intense and prolonged analysis process. The so-called "experimental economics," developed from the pioneering work of Vernon Smith (2003), winner of the 2002 Nobel Prize, was built mostly from straightforward and artificial experiments with university students that are far from allowing a valid test of relevant economic theories.

Failure to understand the non-experimental nature of psychoanalysis has given rise to many negative assessments. Consider, for example, the curious ambiguity of Eric Kandel, the distinguished neuroscientist, and Nobel Prize winner. On the one hand, he says that "psychoanalysis still represents the most coherent and intellectually satisfying view of the mind" (2005, p. 64). On the other hand, he says that by 1960, sixty years after its introduction, psychoanalysis had wholly exhausted its original investigative power, leaving little to be learned just by listening carefully to individual patients (2006, p. 365). This last observation's mistake is evident when we remember that Winnicott's *Playing and Reality* appeared in 1971, and Kohut's *The Restoration of the Self* in 1977, to name just two notable examples.

However, Kandel's most serious criticism is that psychoanalysis, despite its initial promise, has not evolved scientifically and has not developed objective methods to test its conclusions. For him, psychoanalysis was introduced by Freud with a scientific motivation. Still, it rarely used scientific methods in practice, failing in the following years to submit its proposals to experimental tests. The emphasis of modern behavioral science on controlling the experimenter's bias through blind experiments, in which the investigator does not know which participants have been affected by the intervention under test, has practically never been present among psychoanalysts.

The problem with this criticism is that it implicitly assumes that experimentation is the only defining characteristic of any science. From Karl Popper, however, we learned that what defines any discipline's scientific status is not the possibility of experimentation, but the refutability of its propositions. A non-experimental science is possible if its conclusions can, at least in principle, be shown false by observing reality even without experiments. Astronomy, economics, and meteorology are examples of non-experimental sciences.

A non-experimental science has no controlled experiments, but these can be partly replaced by "natural experiments," resulting from careful observation of the behavior of the system's variables under study. In a natural experiment, an independent variable is not artificially manipulated, as in a controlled trial, but results from a change in the real world (a natural intervention). Scientists assume that this change occurred at random, affecting only a few variables in the system while the other variables remained constant. This hypothesis is equivalent to supposing that the treatment and control groups created by the natural experiment are similar in terms of all the observed and unobserved factors that can affect the result of interest, except for the independent variable.

For example, astronomy claims that a star is just a cloud of hydrogen that has collapsed. This proposition's experimental refutation is impossible since no one can imagine how to collect a giant cloud of hydrogen and wait a few billion years for a star to appear. Nevertheless, a natural experiment results when we observe several hydrogen clouds at different stages of the collapse process.

Popper (1963, pp 156-7) explains the importance of refutability by noting that if we do not know how to test a theory, either by experiment or empirical observation, we may doubt whether the type of explanation proposed by it makes any sense. If there is a certainty that we cannot test the theory, then our doubt increases, and we may suspect that it is just a myth or fairy tale. On the other hand, if we can test a theory empirically, it implies that a specific type of event cannot happen, and so it is effectively saying something about the real world.

Is it possible to say that psychoanalysis is, in fact, a non-experimental science within this criterion? Unfortunately, Popper himself started a very unfavorable tradition within the philosophy of science when he chose psychoanalysis as one of his favorite examples of a non-scientific discipline (along with Marxism!). Yet his argument, in this case, demonstrates a superficial and quite mistaken understanding.

For example, Popper (1963, p. 46) illustrates the non-refutability, which he considers endemic in psychoanalysis, by considering two extreme cases of human behavior: the case of a man "who pushes a child into the water with the intention of drowning it" and the case of another man "who sacrifices his life in an attempt to save the child." For him, psychoanalysis would claim that the first man suffered from repression (possibly from "some component of his Oedipus complex"), while the second man had achieved the sublimation but suffered from feelings of inferiority and needed to prove to himself that he dared to rescue the child. So, there would be explanations in psychoanalytic theory for the two contradictory behaviors, and the empirical observation of how a certain man behaved would be useless to establish refutability. Popper says he cannot think of any human behavior that this theory is unable to interpret.

This argument is so silly that we would not even take it seriously had it not been presented by Popper. Of course, psychoanalysis can explain different types of human personalities and behaviors. In this, it does not differ, for example, from astronomy, which has complex stellar classification schemes admitting the existence of different types of stars with varying patterns of evolution. A psychoanalyst identifies the behavior of the man who drowns the child as typical of a psychopathic personality, characterized by self-centeredness, coldness, insensitivity to others' feelings, and the ability to commit cruel acts without any remorse or guilt. For the psychoanalyst, this behavior pattern results from a very deficient formation of his Freudian superego, which is the part of the mental apparatus that guarantees the individual's adherence to the rules of behavior and the moral standards of society.

The behavior of the man who sacrifices his life to save a child, on the other hand, could be considered as typical of a particular case of manic personality that we could call heroic. It shows the presence of a support superego that produces a lot of self-confidence, or, as Kohut would say, of a self with a very intense idealization of the parental *imago*. Besides, one can perceive the presence of a manic dimension to explain why the individual may end up getting involved in a fatal accident. However, these two behavior patterns are very atypical, since most reasonable people would neither push the child into a drowning situation nor take excessive risks to save her.

The theoretical analysis of this case by psychoanalysis allows for some perfectly refutable propositions, contrary to Popper's claims. Imagine, for example, that we put a group of individuals in psychoanalytic evaluation for a time sufficient to identify three distinct subsets: one with individuals with a psychopathic personality, another with individuals with a heroic manic personality, and the third subset with individuals who fit neither of the previous cases. Naturally, most individuals assessed will be in this last category. Nevertheless, if the number of individuals is large enough, we can expect to have unequivocally identified some psychopaths and some heroic maniacs. So, we can propose two perfectly refutable propositions: 1) no heroic maniac will be responsible for a child's drowning, and 2) no psychopath will lose his life trying to avoid it.

As Popper (1963, p. 48) pointed out, the essence of a good scientific theory is its prohibition of some things to happen. The real test of a theory is always an attempt to refute it. In the example above, we have shown how it is possible to start from the psychoanalytic understanding of the human mind to formulate two refutable and empirically testable propositions. It can be difficult to do in practice, but what matters for a theory's scientific status is that it is possible to design a precisely specified test.

It is interesting to note how the psychoanalytic explanation of those two extreme behavior patterns used the superego concept intensively. Compare with Popper's assessment of the Freudian model of the mental apparatus:

> ...for Freud's epic of the Ego, the Superego, and the Id, no substantially stronger claim to scientific status can be made... than for Homer's collected stories from Olympus. These theories describe some facts, but in the manner of myths. They contain most interesting psychological suggestions, but not in testable form. (Popper, 1963, p. 50).

However, Freudian concepts are much more than mere myths. Together with the qualitative notions of conscious and unconscious, they constitute a logically formulated theoretical model that allows for a sophisticated and detailed explanation of human motivations and mental processes. Naturally, any theory involves an arbitrary classification scheme. What matters is whether it can organize and logically structure our thinking on specific issues, and whether it produces empirically refutable propositions.

A theoretical model should only be evaluated by the explanatory power of its predictions, never by the realism of its hypotheses. In the case of physics, for example, the so-called standard model postulates that all matter is composed of quarks and leptons of different types, "flavors" and "colors" and their respective anti-particles (Lederman, 1993). It would certainly seem as "epic" to Homer as Freud's structural model! Of course, we cannot directly test the "realism" of particle physics hypotheses, as it is impossible to observe a quark. Yet the standard model can be tested indirectly by the result of experiments on large particle accelerators. As these results have so far been compatible with the theory's predictions, physicists consider that the model has been corroborated (that is, successfully confirmed) by empirical tests.

In psychoanalysis, as in economics, controlled experimentation is not possible, but refutable scientific propositions can still be formulated and tested by empirical observation in natural experiments. In both cases, however, we can only corroborate what Popper called "statistical propositions," that is, propositions with a reasonable probability of being right. For example, the refutable statements presented above about psychopathic and heroic personalities and the drowning of the child may have only probabilistic validity, in the sense of being confirmed with a certain degree of statistical confidence. A more precise formulation could be that: 1) there is a small probability that some heroic maniac will drown a child, and 2) there is a small probability of some psychopath's losing his life trying to prevent a child from drowning.

In economic science, all refutable propositions are statistical. They are probabilistic statements. Consider, for example, the law of demand, one of the pillars of economic theory. This law states that the quantity demanded of a commodity must increase when its price decreases or, in other words, that when the price of a commodity decreases, consumers will be willing to buy a larger quantity of it. It turns out that this statement may not be correct if market conditions also change, for example, if consumers income and purchasing power decrease, or if consumers interest in that specific commodity is negatively affected by the emergence of a more attractive alternative. The law of demand may also not be valid for certain goods in which it is possible to interpret a price reduction as signaling worsening product quality. It is a relatively rare phenomenon that economists call *adverse selection*. In that case, a price reduction can scare consumers away. A typical example is the used car market, where a very cheap bargain may indicate low quality.

Economists deal with this degree of imprecision in their statements by introducing the qualifier "*ceteris paribus*," a Latin phrase meaning "everything else constant." So, the law of demand is understood to state that the quantity demanded of a commodity will increase, *ceteris paribus*, when its price decreases. In other words, a price reduction will effectively increase the quantity consumers are willing to buy if their income and preferences do not change, and if it is not a rare case of adverse selection.

In Hawking's definition, already mentioned, a good theory should make precise predictions about the results of future observations. In the case of a non-experimental science, such as economics, these predictions can only be probabilistic. Strictly speaking, this makes a precise refutation impossible, since one can always circumvent an unfavorable observation for the theory, claiming *a posteriori* the occurrence of an improbable event. However, the solution implicit in the use of the condition of *ceteris paribus* is that facts considered mathematically improbable rarely happen. Through the study of economic history and direct observation of the real world of business and material wealth production, the economist develops an "educated judgment," an ability to assess the plausibility of any theory from accumulated professional experience. It is the only way to corroborate refutable propositions in this type of science. If most observations of relevant phenomena do not refute a proposition that includes the condition of *ceteris paribus*, we may consider it as corroborated even if it has been refuted in a few cases. In such refutation cases, it is in the economist's interest to determine why the condition of *ceteris paribus* did not hold. Nevertheless, corroboration can still be assumed even though these outliers are not well understood.

Science advances through the improvement of its models. Still, when empirical testing methods are fragile or deficient, as in both psychoanalysis and economics, it can be difficult to unambiguously identify a given model as superior to other alternative models. In this case, several models can be considered equally plausible in the light of empirical evidence. Hence, choosing the appropriate model for a given situation can only result from an informed judgment. John Maynard Keynes, one of the greatest economists of the twentieth century, stated that economics is, above all, a particular branch of logic. It is a way of thinking in terms of specific models coupled with the art of choosing the model relevant for each moment in the real world. Good economists are scarce, said Keynes, "because the gift for using vigilant observation to choose good models, although it does not require a highly specialized intellectual technique, appears to be a very rare one" (Keynes, 1973, p. 297).

Interestingly, Popper seems far more optimistic about the scientific status of economics than Keynes himself or, for that matter, most economists. They do not usually spend much time on methodological discussions. Blaug, one of the rare exceptions, correctly recognizes the ceteris paribus qualifier's role in economic theory but follows Popper in a negative assessment of psychoanalysis. For him, it is just an attempt to understand neurotic symptoms as a disguised form of communication or some sort of hermeneutics. He concludes that "the status of the refutability criterion in economics is approximately halfway between its status in psychoanalysis and its status in physics." (Blaug, 1968, p. 675)

Popper presents the following example of what a precisely refutable economic proposition would be:

> Just as we can learn from a physicist that under certain physical conditions a boiler will explode, so we can learn from the economist that under certain social conditions, such as shortage of commodities, controlled prices, and, say, the absence of an effective punitive system, a black market will develop. (Popper, 1963, p. 456)

The example, however, is fallacious. By defining the situation as a scarcity of goods at controlled prices, Popper assumes markets where demand law would work as predicted by theory, without price controls. If prices want to rise, but administrative authorities do not permit it, and there is no active punishment for black market transactions, these transactions will be the natural solution to produce the necessary price increase. But the proposition is merely stating that prices with a tendency to go up will do so through black markets when the government does not allow it in legal markets.

Hutchison (1976) argues Popper is too optimistic about economics' scientific status but unduly pessimistic about psychoanalysis. In psychoanalysis, as well as in economics, controlled experiments are not possible. Nevertheless, a vigilant observation during a continuous process of analysis, which always offers many possibilities for repetition of similar situations, can produce an informed judgment sufficient to corroborate many probabilistic statements with a high degree of confidence.

Kandel is indeed right when he argues that psychoanalysis should not regress to a non-scientific way of thinking. It would deny the understanding of Freud himself (1940b) who recorded, in his posthumously published "Some Elementary Lessons," that since psychoanalysis is part of psychology, it obviously cannot be anything other than natural science. Patrizia Giampieri-Deutsch (2005) notes that Freud only followed the custom of his philosophy professor Franz Brentano by using the term "natural science" in the sense of knowledge based on direct experience, although not necessarily on controlled experiments. Brentano (1973, p. 1) wrote: "my place in psychology is the empirical point of view and my only teacher is experience."

Freud also clearly stated his position on the scientific nature of psychoanalysis in his *An Outline of Psychoanalysis*:

The hypothesis we have adopted of a psychical apparatus extended in space, expediently put together, developed by the exigencies of life ... has put us in a position to establish psychology on foundations similar to those of any other science, such, for instance, as physics (Freud, 1940a, p. 82).

We have discovered technical methods of filling up the gaps in the phenomena of our consciousness, and we make use of these methods just as a physicist makes use of experiment. In this manner we infer a number of processes which are in themselves 'unknowable' and interpolate them in those that are conscious to us (Freud, 1940a, p. 83).

As in any science, psychoanalysis must advance through the empirical confirmation of propositions derived from theoretical models. As we have seen, these empirical confirmations result from vigilant observation in clinical activity, which is undoubtedly the most natural and productive path for psychoanalysis. However, it is not necessary to exclude the contribution of other forms of empirical testing as well, even if controlled experiments are not possible. The hypothetical natural test discussed above, about heroic psychopathic and maniac personalities and child drowning, could be considered an example of this. As suggested by Angrist and Pischke (2009), the detailed description of an ideal experiment, even if practically unviable, can be instrumental in helping us to formulate the questions we want to elucidate accurately. Besides, we can always use an experimental spirit to analyze non-experimental data.

Trygve Haavelmo, one of the pioneers in the application of statistical methods to economics, lucidly summed up the interaction between theoretical formulation, natural experiments, and vigilant observation that may also be relevant to psychoanalysis:

... we usually have some such experiment in mind when we construct theories, although -unfortunately- most economists do not describe their design of experiments explicitly. If they did, they would see that the experiments they have in mind may be grouped into two different classes, namely, (1) experiments that we would like to make to see if certain real economic phenomena—when artificially isolated from "other influences"—would verify certain hypothesis, and (2) the stream of experiments that Nature is steadily turning out from her own enormous laboratory, and which we merely watch as passive observers. (Haavelmo, 1944, p. 14)

It is interesting to note that in a way, Freud himself (1918) did not resist the temptation to carry out a natural experiment when in the famous case of the Wolfman, he decided to impose a deadline for the end of the analysis to find out how this would affect the patient. Alexander (1963, p. 284) reports similar natural experiments with temporary interruptions of analyzes performed by Max Eitingon in the 1920s at the outpatient clinic of the Psychoanalytic Institute in Berlin. The technique was also systematically tested by Alexander at the Psychoanalytic Institute in Chicago.

These natural experiments remind us of the controversial Stanley Milgram (1974) study at Yale University on how people respond to authority. There was a fictitious situation in which volunteers received energetic orders from those responsible for the experiment to deliver progressively stronger painful shocks to victims who complained a lot, with some even warning of severe heart problems. The volunteers did not know that the shocks were deceptive with actors posing as victims, but many people considered the experiment unethical and psychologically abusive. It certainly does not look like the right path for the development of empirical tests in psychoanalysis.

In the case of a scientific theory that underlies a therapeutic technique, one can, in principle, consider the therapy itself as a natural experiment. It does happen in psychoanalysis, where vigilant observation in the clinic gives the analyst a high degree of conviction concerning the theory's various probabilistic statements. This conviction is the basis for the gradual formation of an informed judgment that gives him the conditions to accept or reject the theory's different formulations, aspects, and details. This way, he progressively consolidates in his mind a personal understanding of the human mental process.

Something quite different is trying to transform the psychoanalytic clinic into a controlled experiment, to produce what Kandel calls evidence-based psychotherapy. It is surprising to see Kandel (2006), who has some psychoanalysis knowledge, pointing to Aaron Beck's cognitive behavioral therapy as a model to follow. Beck and his associates (1979) produced controlled clinical tests to assess the effectiveness of a new form of brief therapy to treat mild or moderate depression cases. His technique assumes that individuals suffer from a distorted pattern of thinking. Short-term treatment (five to fifteen sessions) produces results superior to placebo cases and comparable to cases that used antidepressant medication. For Kandel, Beck's main merit was to have empirically tested his psychotherapy proposal, showing how the discipline can move towards evidence-based effectiveness studies.

However, Beck and associates' empirical tests are of minimal relevance for a scientific evaluation of his theory. Psychoanalysis has always recognized that short-term treatments can have some therapeutic effect, albeit limited and possibly transitory. Several authors, such as Stone (1954), Gill (1954), Ticho (1970), and Kohut (1980), recognized this. Freud himself (1937) noted that even in the Wolfman case, in which he failed to eliminate the main neurotic symptoms, the initial phase of treatment produced some positive effects. As the patient regained some of his independence and interest in life, in addition to being able to adjust his relationships with the people most important to him, it probably would have been considered a success case in Beck's type of assessment.

Alexander explains in a simple way why brief therapies can have therapeutic value:

Neurosis implies an inadequate substitution of symptoms for realistic gratifications, and frustration is one of its inevitable results. In therapy [the patient] hopes for relief and finds opportunity to gratify some of his regressive needs for dependence. This may reduce the need for gratification through symptoms. This explains why all forms of treatment in which the physician offers help and gives emotional support may have a therapeutic effect… Emotional and intellectual support is to some degree present in all forms of treatment. It results from the therapeutic situation itself, independently of the special techniques employed, provided the therapist instills confidence in this patient. (Alexander, 1963, p. 274).

Empirical evaluation of the effectiveness of psychoanalytic treatments has been the subject of several significant research efforts, as shown by Bucci (2005), Giampieri-Deutsch (2005), Wallerstein (2005), or Weinberger e Levy (2005). A central problem in this type of assessment, particularly in the case of outcome evaluation, is that psychoanalysis does not always have an explicit and consensual specification about the therapy's purpose. Freud spoked about eliminating neurotic symptoms by making the repressed unconscious conscious, ego psychology about improving the ego's ability to deal with internal and external conflicts, Melanie Klein about the ability to deal with aggression, Kohut about self-cohesion, and Winnicott about creative living. It is not easy to imagine how to produce scales and coded manuals for a type of evaluation that, as demanded by Kandel, effectively captures the diversity and possible nuances in defining a precise mental-health concept.

Cooper (2005) wrote an insightful introduction to Kandel's (2005) essay on "Biology and the Future of Psychoanalysis." He notes the current situation of "theoretical pluralism" and the intense and permanent debate about whether psychoanalysis should adopt some scientific methodology or limit itself to being a hermeneutic discipline. For Cooper, the latter option will not allow the discipline to advance significantly, and the adoption of a scientific approach is necessary and inevitable, including an increasing interaction with neuroscience. He seems to agree with Kandel's observations that psychoanalysis isolation from the academic-university environment has hampered its development.

One cannot object to an effort to expand the use of a scientific methodology in psychoanalysis, not least because, as noted above, it is always possible to analyze non-experimental data with an experimental approach. The dialogue with neuroscience and cognitive psychology can undoubtedly be beneficial because, in the final analysis, the three disciplines are parallel developments of the same single effort to unravel the human mind's secrets. However, they are disciplines with different focuses and approaches, a condition that naturally implies the use of different methodologies.

In psychoanalysis, the fundamental thing to remember is that it is an essentially non-experimental science. Theoretical elaboration must seek the formulation of conjectures that can be statistically refuted by the vigilant observation of human behavior. As noted by Bucci (2005, p. 320), the clinical experience with the basic rule of free association produces a "naturalistic context for the systematic study of the inner life" of human beings. As pointed out by the economist Haavelmo (1944), the "laboratory" of human nature is continually bringing out many natural experiments that we can observe passively. They allow us to build the internal conviction necessary and sufficient to corroborate or refute our conjectures.

But the fact of dispensing with controlled experiments does not free psychoanalysis from the need to have good models. Quite the opposite! For a vigilant observation to gain respectability as an empirical test methodology, its theoretical basis must use well-defined concepts. It must produce conjectures that are, in principle, empirically refutable, with reasonable security, in the context of natural experiments. The problem with the apparent scientific stagnation of psychoanalysis and its low reputation in academic circles is not the absence of controlled trials, as Kandel suggested. If that were the case, economic science would be in the same situation!

The problem is mainly in the theoretical pluralism pointed out by Cooper. It is also in the way psychoanalysis often works with merely impressionistic conceptions of mental phenomena. The loss of scientific respectability stems not from the absence of controlled experiments, but in psychoanalysis' lacking exact definitions for many of the concepts it uses. For fragile sciences on the experimental side, such as psychoanalysis and economics, it is essential to have a solid theoretical basis with precise propositions defined in logically consistent structures.

References

Adler, A. (1908). Der Agressionstrieb im Lebem und in der Neurose [The aggression drive in life and in the neurosis]. *Fortschritte der Medizin, 26*, 577.

Alexander, F, 1925. A metapsychological description of the process of cure. *International Journal of Psychoanalysis, 6*, 13–34.

—— (1951). Three fundamental dynamic principles of the mental apparatus and of the behavior of living organisms. In F. Alexander (1961). *The scope of psychoanalysis: selected papers of Franz Alexander 1921–1961*. New York: Basic Books.

—— (1958). A contribution to the theory of play. *Psychoanalytic Quarterly, 27*, 175–193.

—— (1958). Unexplored areas in psychoanalytic theory and treatment–part I. In F. Alexander (1961). *The scope of psychoanalysis: selected papers of Franz Alexander 1921–1961*. New York: Basic Books.

—— (1961). *The scope of psychoanalysis: selected papers of Franz Alexander 1921-1961*. New York: Basic Books.

—— (1963). *Fundamentals of psychoanalysis*. 2nd ed. New York: W.W. Norton & Co.

Angrist, J.D. & Pischke J. (2005). *Mostly Harmless Econometrics: An empiricist's companion*. Princeton, NJ: Princeton University Press.

Ariès, P. (1962). *Centuries of childhood*. New York: A. A. Knopf.

Arlow, J.A. (1986). Object Concept and Object Choice. In P. Buckley (Ed.). (1986). *Essential papers on object relations*. New York: New York University Press.

—— & Brenner, C. (1964). *Psychoanalytic concepts and the structural theory.* Madison, CT: International Universities Press.

Auchincloss, E.L. (Ed.). (2005). *The quiet revolution in American psychoanalysis: selected papers of Arnold Cooper.* New York: Brunner-Routledge.

Baldwin, J.M. (1902). *Dictionary of Philosophy and Psychology.* London: Macmillan.

Barbosa, R. (2004). *Schiller e a cultura estética [Schiller and the aesthetic culture].* Brazil: Jorge Zahar.

Barcaro, U. (2010). *The interwoven sources of dreams.* London: Karnac.

Beck, A.T.; Rush, A.J.; Shaw, B.F. & Emery, G. (1979). *Cognitive therapy of depression.* New York: The Guilford Press.

Bekoff, M. (2007). *The emotional life of animals.* Novato, California: New World Library.

—— & Byers, J.A. (1998). *Animal play: evolutionary, comparative, and ecological perspectives.* Cambridge: Cambridge University Press.

Beres, D. (1958). Vicissitudes of Superego Functions and Superego Precursors in Childhood. *Psychoanalytic Study of the Child, 13*, 324–351.

—— (1965). Structure and function in psycho-analysis. *International Journal of Psychoanalysis, 46*, 53–63.

Bernard, C. (1927). *An introduction to the study of experimental medicine.* London: Macmillan. (Original work published 1865)

Bernfeld, S. (1929). *The psychology of the infant.* New York: Brentano's.

Blatz, W.E. & Millichamp, D.A. (1935). *The development of emotion in the infant.* Canada: University of Toronto Studies, Child Development Series.

Blaug, M. (1968). *Economic theory in retrospect.* Homewood, Illinois: Richard D, Irwin Inc.

Bollas, C. (1987). *The shadow of the object.* New York: Columbia University Press.

—— (2009). *The evocative object world.* London: Routledge.

Bowlby, J. (1958). The Nature of the Child's Tie to his mother. *International Journal of Psychoanalysis, 39*, 350–373.

—— (1969/1982). *Attachment.* 2nd ed. New York: Basic Books.

—— (1979). *The making and breaking of affectional bonds.* London: Tavistock Publications.

—— (1988). *A secure base.* London: Routledge.

—— (1980). *Loss, sadness, and depression.* New York: Basic Books.

Breger, L. (2000). *Freud darkness in the midst of vision.* New York: John Wiley & Sons.

—— (2009). *A dream of undying fame: how Freud betrayed his mentor and invented psychoanalysis.* New York: Basic Books.

Brenner, C. (1973). *An elementary textbook of psychoanalysis.* 2nd ed. New York: Random House.

—— (1990). On pleasurable affects. In R.A. Glick & S. Bone (1990). *Pleasure beyond the pleasure principle.* New Haven, CT: Yale University Press.

—— (2002). Conflict, compromise formation, and structural theory. *The Psychoanalytic Quarterly, 71,* 397–417. Also in A.C. Cooper (Ed.). (2006). *Contemporary psychoanalysis in America.* Arlington, VA: American Psychiatric Publishing Inc.

Brentano, F. (1973). *Psychology from an empirical standpoint.* London: Routledge. (Original work published 1874)

Breuer, J. & Freud, S. (1974). *Studies on hysteria. Standard Edition,* 2. The Pelican Freud Library, 3. London: Penguin Books. (Original work published 1895)

Bromberg, P.M. (2001). Treating patients with symptoms—and symptoms with patience. *Psychoanalytic Dialogues, 11,* 891–912.

Bronowski, J. (1973). *The ascent of man.* Boston: Little, Brown and Company.

Brown, S. (1998). Play as an organizing principle: clinical evidence and personal observations. In M. Bekoff & J.A. Byers (1998). *Animal play: evolutionary, comparative and ecological perspectives.* Cambridge, MA: Cambridge University Press.

—— (2009). *Play: how it shapes the brain, opens the imagination, and invigorates the soul.* New York: Avery Penguin Group.

Bryson, B. (2011). *At home: a short history of private life*. London: Black Swan Penguin.

Bucci, W. (1985). Dual coding: a cognitive model for psychoanalytic research. *Journal of the American Psychoanalytic Association, 33*, 571-607.

—— (1997). *Psychoanalysis & cognitive science: a multiple code theory*. New York: The Guilford Press.

—— (2005). Process research. In E.S. Person; A.M. Cooper & G.O. Gabbard. (Eds.) (2005). *Textbook of Psychoanalysis*. Arlington, VA: American Psychiatric Publishing.

Buckley, P. (Ed.). (1986). *Essential papers on object relations*. New York: New York University Press.

Bühler, K. (1930). *The mental development of the child*. New York: Harcourt Brace.

Burghardt, G.M. (1998). The evolutionary origins of play revisited: lessons from turtles. In M. Bekoff & J.A. Byers (1998). *Animal play: evolutionary, comparative, and ecological perspectives*. Cambridge, UK: Cambridge University Press.

—— (2005). *The genesis of animal play: testing the limits*. Cambridge, MA: The MIT Press.

Byers, J.A. (1998). Biological effects of locomotor play. In M. Bekoff & J.A. Byers (1998). *Animal play: evolutionary, comparative, and ecological perspectives*. Cambridge, UK: Cambridge University Press.

Cannon, W.B. (1932). *The wisdom of the body*. New York: W.W. Norton & Co.

Caper, R. (1988). *Immaterial facts: Freud's discovery of psychic reality and Klein's development of his work*. London: Routledge.

Cooper, A.M. (2005a). Psychoanalysis at one hundred: beginnings of maturity. In E.L. Auchincloss (Ed.). (2005). *The quiet revolution in American psychoanalysis: selected papers of Arnold Cooper*. New York: Brunner-Routledge.

—— (2005b). Psychoanalysis today: new wine in old bottles or the hidden revolution in psychoanalysis. In E.L. Auchincloss (Ed.). (2005). *The quiet revolution in American psychoanalysis: selected papers of Arnold Cooper.* New York: Brunner-Routledge.

—— (2005c). Commentary on Biology and the Future of Psychoanalysis. In Kandel 2005, 59–62.

—— (2005d). Psychoanalytic inquiry and new knowledge. In E.L. Auchincloss (Ed.). (2005). *The quiet revolution in American psychoanalysis: selected papers of Arnold Cooper.* New York: Brunner-Routledge.

—— (Ed.). (2006). *Contemporary psychoanalysis in America.* Arlington, VA: American Psychiatric Publishing Inc.

Corrigall, J. & Wilkinson, H. (2003). *Revolutionary connections: psychotherapy and neuroscience.* London: Karnac.

Csikszentmihalyi, M. (1975). *Beyond boredom and anxiety: experiencing flow in work and play.* San Francisco: Jossey Bass.

Damasio, A. (1994). *Descartes' error.* New York: Putnam.

—— (2010). *Self comes to mind: constructing the conscious brain.* New York: Pantheon Books.

—— (2018). *The strange order of things: life, feeling and the making of cultures.* New York: Pantheon Books.

Darwin, C. (1872). *The expression of emotions in man and animals.* Minneapolis, MN: Filiquarian Publishing.

—— (1877). A biographical sketch of an infant. *Mind, 2,* 285–294.

Detrick, D.W. & Detrick, S.P. (1989). *Self-psychology: comparisons and contrasts.* Hillsdale, NJ: The Analytic Press.

Eastwood, J.D.; Frischen, A; Fenske M.J. & Smilek, D. (2012). The unengaged mind: defining boredom in terms of attention. *Perspectives on Psychological Science, 7,* 482–495.

Edelman, S. (2008). *Computing the mind: how the mind really works.* Oxford: Oxford University Press.

—— (2012). *The happiness of pursuit.* New York: Basic Books.

Eiben, A.E. & Smith, J. E. (2003). *Introduction to evolutionary computing*. New York: Springer.

Ellenberger, H.F. (1970). *The discovery of the unconscious*. New York: Basic Books.

Epstein, R. (2016). The empty brain: your brain does not process information, retrieve knowledge, or store memories. In short: your brain is not a computer. In *Aeon*, 18 May 2016. Retrieved from: https://aeon.co/essays/your-brain-does-not-process-information-and-it-is-not-a-computer

Erdely, M.H. (1985). *Psychoanalysis: Freud's cognitive psychology*. New York: W. H. Freeman and Co.

Erikson, E.H. (1950). *Childhood and society*. New York: W. W. Norton and Co.

Etchegoyen, R. (1985). Identification and its vicissitudes. *International Journal of Psychoanalysis, 6*, 3–18.

Ethel S.P.; Cooper, A.M. & Gabbard G.O. (Eds.). (2005). *Textbook in psychoanalysis*. Arlington, VA: The American Psychiatric Publishing.

Eysenck, M.W. (2012). *Fundamentals of cognition*. New York: Psychology Press.

—— & Keane, M.T. (2005). *Cognitive psychology: a student's handbook*. New York: Psychology Press.

Fairbairn, W.R.D. (1943). The repression and the return of bad objects (with special reference to the war neuroses). *The British Journal of Medical Psychology, XIX*. Also in W.R.D. Fairbairn, *Psychoanalytic studies of the personality*. III. London: Brunner-Routledge 1952.

Fagen, R. (1981). *Animal play behavior*. Oxford: Oxford University Press.

—— (1995). Animal play, games of angels, biology, and Brian. In A.D. Pellegrini (Ed.). (1995). *The future of play theory*. New York: State University of New York Press.

Fass, P.S. (2013) (Ed.). *The Routledge history of childhood in the Western World*. London: Routledge.

Fechner, G.T. (1873). *Einige Ideen zur Schöpfungs und Entwickelungsgeschichte der Organismen [Some Ideas on the History of Organism Creation and Development]*. Wiesbaden, Germany: Breitkopf und Härtel.

—— (1966). *Elements of psychophysics*. New York: Holt, Rinehart, and Winston. (Original work published 1889)

Fenichel, O. (1934). On the Psychology of Boredom. *Imago, 20,* 270-281.

—— (1935). A Critique of the Death Instinct. *Imago, 21,* 458-466.

—— (1995). *The psychoanalytic theory of neurosis*. New York: W. W. Norton. 50th anniversary ed. (Original work published 1945)

Feynman, R. (1989). *Six easy pieces*. New York: Perseus Books.

Fosshage, J.L. (1989). On aggression: its forms and functions. In R. Galler; D. Gould & J. Levy (1998). *Aggression Contemporary Controversies: Psychoanalytic Inquiry, 18,* 1. Hillsdale, NJ: Analytic Press.

Freeman, W. (2000). *How brains make up their minds*. New York: Columbia University Press.

—— (2007). A biological theory of brain function and its relevance to psychoanalysis. In C. Piers; J.P. Muller & J. Brent (2007). *Self-organizing complexity in psychological systems*. Lanham, MD: Jason Aronson Inc.

Freud, A. (1937). *The ego and the mechanisms of defense*. Madison, CT: International Universities Press.

Freud, S. (1895). *Project for a scientific psychology. Standard Edition, 1*. New York: W.W. Norton & Co., 1966.

—— (1899). *Screen memories. Standard Edition, 3*. New York: W.W. Norton & Co., 1962.

—— (1900). *The interpretation of dreams. Standard Edition, 4*. The Pelican Freud Library, 4. London: Penguin Books, 1976.

—— (1901). *The psychopathology of everyday life. Standard Edition, 7*. New York: W.W. Norton & Co., 1960.

—— (1905a). *Three essays on the theory of sexuality. Standard Edition, 7*. New York: W.W. Norton & Co., 1955.

—— (1905b). *Jokes and their relation to the unconscious. Standard Edition, 8*. New York: W.W. Norton & Co., 1960.

—— (1907). *Obsessive actions and religious practices. Standard Edition*, 9. New York: W.W. Norton & Co., 1962.

—— (1908). *Creative writers and daydreaming. Standard Edition.* 9. New York: W.W. Norton & Co., 1962.

—— (1909). *Analysis of a phobia in a five-year-old boy. Standard Edition*, 10. New York: W.W. Norton & Co.,1955.

—— (1910). *A special type of object-choice made by men. Standard Edition*, 11. New York: W.W. Norton & Co.,1958.

—— (1911). Formulations on the two principles of mental functioning. *On Metapsychology. Standard Edition, 12.* The Pelican Freud Library, 11. London: Penguin Books.,1984.

—— (1912). Concerning the most universal debasement in the erotic life. *The Psychology of Love. Standard Edition, 11.* London: Penguin Books.

—— (1914). Remembering, repeating, and working through. In *Beyond the Pleasure Principle and Other Writings.* Translation: J. Reddick. London: Penguin Books, 2003.

—— (1915a). On narcissism: an introduction. *On Metapsychology, Standard Edition, 11.* The Pelican Freud Library, 11. London: Penguin Books, 1984.

—— (1915b). The Unconscious. *On Metapsychology, Standard Edition, 11.* The Pelican Freud Library, 11. London: Penguin Books, 1984.

—— (1915c). Instincts and Their Vicissitudes. *On Metapsychology, Standard Edition, 14.* The Pelican Freud Library, 11. London: Penguin Books,1984.

—— (1916). *Introductory lectures on psychoanalysis. Standard Edition, 15–16.* New York: W.W. Norton & Co, 1966.

—— (1918). *From the history of an infantile neurosis. Standard Edition, 17.* New York: W.W. Norton & Co.

—— (1919). *Lines of advance in psycho-analytic therapy. Standard Edition, 17.* New York: W.W. Norton & Co.

—— (1920). Beyond the pleasure principle. *Beyond the Pleasure Principle and Other Writings. Standard Edition, 18.* Translation J. Reddick, London: Penguin Books, 2003.

—— (1921). *Group psychology and the analysis of the ego. Standard Edition, 18.* The Pelican Freud Library: Civilization, Society and Religion, 12, London: Penguin Books, 1985.

—— (1923b). The ego and the id. *On Metapsychology. Standard Edition, 19.* The Pelican Freud Library, 11, London: Penguin Books, 1984.

—— (1925b). An autobiographical study. *Standard Edition, 20.* New York: W.W. Norton & Co., 1952.

—— (1925c). A note upon the mystic writing-pad. *On Metapsychology. Standard Edition 19.* The Pelican Freud Library, 11. London: Penguin Books, 1984.

—— (1926). *Inhibitions, symptoms, and anxiety. Standard Edition, 19.* New York: W.W. Norton & Co., 1959

—— (1927). Fetishism. *Standard Edition, 21.* New York: W.W. Norton & Co., 1959.

—— (1930). *Civilization and its discontents. Standard Edition, 21.* New York: W.W. Norton & Co., 1959.

—— (1933). New introductory lectures on psychoanalysis. *Standard Edition, 22.* New York: W.W. Norton & Co., 1965.

—— (1937a). *Analysis terminable and interminable. Standard Edition, 22.* In J. Sandler (Ed.). *On Freud's Analysis Terminable and Interminable.* London: The International Psychoanalytical Association, 1987.

—— (1937b). *Constructions in analysis. Standard Edition, 23.* New York: W.W. Norton & Co.,1964.

—— (1940a). *An outline of psychoanalysis. Standard Edition, 23.* New York: W.W. Norton & Co., 1949.

—— (1940b). *Some elementary lessons in psychoanalysis.* New York: *Standard Edition, 23,* 1949.

—— & Andreas-Salome, L. *Freud and Lou Andreas-Salome: Letters.* E. Pfeiffer (Ed.). New York: W. W. Norton & Co.

Gabbard, G.O.; Litowitz, B.E. & Williams, P. (Eds.). (2012). *Textbook of Psychoanalysis: Second Edition.* Arlington, VA: American Psychiatric Publishing.

Gallese, V. (2001). The shared manifold hypothesis: from mirror neurons to empathy. *Journal of Consciousness Studies, 8,* 33–50.

Galler, R.; Gould, D. & Levy, J. (1998). *Aggression Contemporary Controversies: Psychoanalytic Inquiry, 18,* 1. Hillsdale, NJ: Analytic Press.

Gardner, H. (1985). *The mind's new science: a history of the cognitive revolution.* New York: Basic Books.

Gedo, J.E. (1989). Self-psychology: a post-Kohutian view. In D.W. Detrick & S.P. Detrick. (1989). *Self-psychology: comparisons and contrasts.* Hillsdale, NJ: The Analytic Press.

—— (2005). *Psychoanalysis as biological science: a comprehensive theory.* Baltimore, MD: The John Hopkins University Press.

Gedo, J.E., & Goldberg, A. (1973). *Models of the mind: a psychoanalytic theory.* Chicago: The University of Chicago Press.

Gill, M.M. (1954). Psychoanalysis and exploratory psychotherapy. *Journal of the American Psychoanalytic Association, 2,* 771–777.

—— (1963). *Topography and systems in psychoanalytic theory.* Madison, CT: International Universities Press.

—— (1976). Metapsychology is not psychology. In M.M. Gill. & P.S. Holzman (1976). *Psychology versus metapsychology: psychoanalytic essays in memory of George S. Klein.* Madison, CT: International Universities Press.

—— & Holzman, P.S. (1976). *Psychology versus metapsychology: psychoanalytic essays in memory of George S. Klein.* Madison, CT: International Universities Press.

Gleick, J. (2001). *The information: a theory, a flood.* New York: Pantheon Books.

Gleitman, H., Reisberg, D. & Gross, J. (2007). *Psychology.* 7th ed. New York: W.W. Norton & Co.

Glick, R.A. & Bone, S. (1990). *Pleasure beyond the pleasure principle*. New Haven, CT: Yale University Press.

Goldberger, M. (1996). Daydreams: even more secret than dreams. *Symposium: the secret of dreams*. Western New England Psychoanalytic Society. New Haven, CT: Yale University Press.

Gómez, J. (2004). *Apes, monkeys, children and the growth of mind*. Cambridge, MA: Harvard University Press.

—— & Martín-Andrade, B. (2005). Fantasy play in apes. In A.D. Pellegrini & P.K Smith. (2005). *The nature of play: great apes and humans*. New York: The Guilford Press.

Grassian, S. (1983). Psychopathological effects of solitary confinement. *American Journal of Psychiatry, 140*, 1,450–1,454.

—— (2006). Psychiatric effects of solitary confinement. *Journal of Law and Policy, 22*, 325–383.

Greenberg, J. (2012). Psychoanalysis in North America after Freud. In G.O. Gabbard; B.E. Litowitz & P. Williams (Eds.). (2012). *Textbook of Psychoanalysis: Second Edition*. Arlington, VA: American Psychiatric Publishing.

Groos, K. (1896). *The play of animals*. New York: D. Appleton and Company (Kessinger Reprints).

—— (1901). *The play of man*. New York: D. Appleton and Company (Kessinger Reprints).

—— (1904). *Das Seelenleben des Kindes*. Berlin: Verlag von Reuther & Reichard.

Grossman, W.I. (1982). The self as fantasy: fantasy as theory. *The Journal of the American Psychoanalytic Association, 30*, 919–937. Also in *Contemporary psychoanalysis in America*. Arlington, VA: American Psychiatric Publishing Inc.

Haavelmo, T. (1944). The probability approach in econometrics. *Econometrica, 12*, 91–115.

Hall, J.F. (1990). Reconstructive and reproductive models of memory. *Bulletins of the Psychonomic Society, 28,* 191-194.

Hall, S.L. (1998). Object play by adult animals. In M. Bekoff, & J.A. Byers (1998). *Animal play: evolutionary, comparative, and ecological perspectives.* Cambridge: Cambridge University Press.

Halliwell-Phillipps, J.O. (1849). *Popular rhymes and nursery tales.* Retrieved from: www. gutenberg.org.

Harcourt, R. (1991). Survivorship costs of play in the South American Fur Seal. *Animal Behavior, 42,* 509-511.

Hartmann, E. (2001). *Dreams and nightmares: the origin and meaning of dreams,* New York: Perseus.

Hartmann, H. (1939). *Ego psychology and the problem of adaptation.* New York: International University Press.

—— (1948). Comments on the psychoanalytic theory of instinctual drives. *Essays on Ego Psychology.* (1964). New York: International University Press.

—— (1950). Comments on the psychoanalytic theory of the ego. In *Essays on ego psychology.* (1964). New York: International University Press.

—— (1955). On the theory of sublimation. In *Essays on ego psychology.* (1964). New York: International University Press.

—— (1959). Psychoanalysis as a scientific theory. In *Essays on ego psychology.* (1964). New York: International University Press.

——, Kris, E. & Loewenstein, R.M. (1949). Notes on the theory of aggression. *Psychoanalytic Study of the Child, 3/4,* 9-36.

Hawking, S. (1988). *A brief history of time.* New York: Bantam Books.

Heimlich, S. & Boran, J. (2001). *Killer whales.* Florida: Voyageur Press.

Hendrick, I. (1934). *Facts and theories of psychoanalysis.* London: Kegan Paul.

—— (1936). Ego development and certain character problems. *Psychoanalytic Quarterly, 5,* 320-346.

—— (1942). Instinct and the ego during infancy. *Psychoanalytic Quarterly, 11,* 33-57.

—— (1943a). Work and the pleasure principle. *Psychoanalytic Quarterly, 12*, 311–329.

—— (1943b). The discussion of the 'instinct to master': a letter to the editors. *Psychoanalytic Quarterly, 12*, 561–565.

—— (1951). Early development of the ego: identification in infancy. *Psychoanalytic Quarterly, 20*, 44–61.

—— (1964). Narcissism and the pre-puberty ego ideal. *Journal of the American Psychoanalytic Association, 7*, 522–528.

—— (1966). *Facts and Theories of Psychoanalysis*, Third Edition, New York: Dell Publishing.

Henricks, T. (2006). *Play reconsidered: sociological perspectives on human expression.* Champaign, Il: The University of Illinois Press.

—— (2015). Play as a basic pathway to the self. *American Journal of Play, 7*, 271–297.

Hiruki, L.H. et al. (1999). Hunting and social behavior of leopard seals. *Journal of Zoology, 249*, 97–109.

Holt, R.R. (Ed.) (1967). *Motives and thoughts: psychoanalytic essays in honor of David Rapaport.* New York: International University Press.

—— (1965). Ego autonomy re-evaluated. *International Journal of Psychoanalysis, 46*, 151–167.

—— (1975). The past and future of ego psychology. *Psychoanalytic Quarterly, 44*, 550–576.

—— (1976). Drive or wish? A reconsideration of the psychoanalytic theory of motivation. In M.M. Gill & P.S. Holzman (1976). *Psychology versus metapsychology: psychoanalytic essays in memory of George S. Klein.* Madison, CT: International Universities Press.

Hrdy, S.B. (1979). Infanticide among animals: a review, classification, and examination of the implications for the reproductive strategies of females. *Ethology and Sociobiology, 1*, 1, 13–40.

—— (2009) *Mothers and others: the revolutionary origins of mutual understanding.* Cambridge, MA: Harvard University Press.

Huizinga, J. (1955). *Homo Ludens: a study of the play element in culture.* Boston: Beacon Press.

Hunt, M. (2007). *The story of psychology.* New York: Anchor Books.

Hutchison, T.W. (1976). On the History and Philosophy of Science and Economics. In S. Latsis (1976). *Method and Appraisal in Economics.* Cambridge: Cambridge University Press.

James, W. (1950). *The principles of psychology.* V.1. Mineola, NY: Dover Publications. (Original work published 1890)

Janet, P. (2020). *L'Automatisme Psychologique: Essai de Psychologie Expérimentale sur les Formes Inferieure de l'Activité Humaine.* Paris: L'Harmattan. (Original work published 1889)

—— (2010). *The major symptoms of hysteria: fifteen lectures given in the Medical School of Harvard University.* London: Nabu Press (Original work published 1907)

Jeannerod, M. & Frak, V. (1999). Mental imaging of motor activity in humans. *Current Opinion in Neurobiology, 9,* 735–739.

Johnson. A.A. (2019). *Introduction to key concepts and evolutions in psychoanalysis,* London: Routledge.

Jones, E. (1914–1915). Professor Janet on psychoanalysis: a rejoinder. *Journal of Abnormal Psychology, 9,* 400–410.

—— (1958). *Sigmund Freud: life and work.* London: The Hogarth Press.

Kandel, E. (2005). *Psychiatry, psychoanalysis, and the new biology of mind.* Arlington, VA: American Psychiatric Publishing, Inc.

—— (2006). *In search of memory: the emergence of a new science of mind.* New York: W.W. Norton & Co.

—— (2012). *The age of insight: the quest to understand the unconscious in art, mind, and brain, from Vienna, 1900 to the present.* New York: Random House.

Kernberg, O. (1984). *Severe personality disorders: psychotherapeutic strategies*. New Haven, CT: Yale University Press.

—— (2001). Recent developments in the technical approaches of English-language psychoanalytic schools. *The Psychoanalytic Quarterly*, 70, 3, 519–547. Also in A.C. Cooper (Ed.). (2006). *Contemporary psychoanalysis in America*. Arlington, VA: American Psychiatric Publishing Inc.

Keynes, J.M. (1973). *The collected writings of John Maynard Keynes*. v. XIV. In Moggridge, D. (Ed.), London: Macmillan.

Kierkegaard, S. (1938). *Purity of heart*. New York: Harper and Row. (Original work published 1846)

Klein, G.S. (1967). Peremptory ideation: structure and force in motivated ideas. In Holt, R.R. (Ed.) (1967). *Motives and thought psychoanalytic essays in honor of David Rapaport*. Madison, CT: International University Press.

—— (1976a). Freud's two theories of sexuality. In M.M. Gill. & P.S. Holzman (1976). *Psychology versus metapsychology: psychoanalytic essays in memory of George S. Klein*. Madison, CT: International Universities Press.

—— (1976b). *Psychoanalytic Theory: An Exploration of Essentials*. Madison, CT: International Universities Press.

Klein, M. (1928). Early stages of the Oedipus conflict. In Mitchell, J. (Ed.) (1986). *The selected Melanie Klein*. New York: The Free Press.

—— (1937). Love, guilt, and reparation. In M. Klein & J. Riviere. (1937/1964). *Love, hate and reparation*. New York: W.W. Norton & Co.

—— (1940). Mourning and its relation to manic-depressive states. In J. Mitchell (Ed.). (1986). *The selected Melanie Klein*. New York: The Free Press.

—— (1952). On observing the behavior of young infants. In *Envy and gratitude: a study of unconscious sources*. (1957). London: Tavistock Publications.

Kleitman, N. (1963). *Sleep and wakefulness*. 2nd ed. Chicago: University of Chicago Press.

Kohut, H. (1959). Introspection, empathy, and psychoanalysis. *Journal of the American Psychoanalytic Association*, 7, 459–483. Also in P.H. Ornstein

(1978). *The search for the self: selected writings of Heinz Kohut,* 1950–1978. (v.4). Madison, CT: International Universities Press.

—— (1966). Forms and transformations of narcissism. *Journal of the American Psychoanalytic Association, 14,* 243–272. Also in Kohut (1985). *Self psychology and the humanities.* (1985) New York: W.W. Norton & Co.

—— (1970). Narcissism as a resistance and as a driving force in psychoanalysis. In P. H. Ornstein (Ed.). (1978). *The search for the self: selected writings of Heinz Kohut,* 1950-1978. (v.2). Madison, CT: International Universities Press.

—— (1971). *The analysis of the self.* Madison, CT: International Universities Press.

—— (1972). Thoughts on narcissism and narcissistic rage. In *Self psychology and the humanities.* (1985) New York: W.W. Norton & Co.

—— (1976). Creativeness, charisma, group psychology: reflections on the self-analysis of Freud. In *Self psychology and the humanities.* (1985) New York: W.W. Norton & Co.

—— (1977). *The restoration of the self.* Madison, CT: International Universities Press.

—— (1980). Reflections. In A. Goldberg (Ed.). *Advances in self psychology* (pp. 473–554). Madison, CT: International Universities Press.

—— (1981). Idealization and cultural selfobjects. In *Self psychology and the humanities.* (1985) New York: W.W. Norton & Co.

—— (1981b). On empathy. In P. H. Ornstein (Ed.). (1978). *The search for the self: selected writings of Heinz Kohut,* 1950–1978. (v.4). Madison, CT: International Universities Press.

—— (1981c). Introspection, empathy, and the semicircle of mental health. In In P. H. Ornstein (Ed.). (1978). *The search for the self: selected writings of Heinz Kohut,* 1950–1978. (v.4). Madison, CT: International Universities Press.

—— (1984). *How Does Analysis Cure?* Chicago: The University of Chicago Press.

—— (1985). *Self psychology and the humanities.* New York: W.W. Norton & Co.

—— (1994). *The curve of life: Correspondence of Heinz Kohut, 1923–1981*. Chicago: The University of Chicago Press.

—— & Seitz, P. (1963). Concepts and theories of psychoanalysis. In P. F. D. Rubovits-Seitz (1999). *Kohut's Freudian vision*. Hillsdale, NJ: The Analytic Press.

—— & Wolf, E.S. (1978). The disorders of the self and their treatment: an outline. *International Journal of Psychoanalysis, 59*, 413–425.

Konner, M. (2010). *The evolution of childhood*. Cambridge, MA: Belknap Harvard University Press.

Kosa, J.R. (1992). *Genetic programming*. Cambridge, MA: The MIT Press.

Lamb, M. (1981). *The role of the father in child development*. 2nd ed. Hoboken, NJ: John Wiley and Sons.

Lederman, L. (1993). *The God particle*. New York: Delta Book.

Leider, R.J. (1998). In the belly of the beast: the vicissitudes of aggression. In R. Galler; D. Gould & J. Levy (1998). *Aggression Contemporary Controversies: Psychoanalytic Inquiry, 18*, 1. Hillsdale, NJ: Analytic Press.

Levin, F. (1991). *Mapping the mind*. Hillsdale, NJ: The Analytic Press.

—— (2009). *Emotion and the psychodynamics of the cerebellum*. London: Karnac.

Lewis, K. P (2005). *Social play in the great apes*. In A.D. Pellegrini & P.K. Smith (2005). *The nature of play: great apes and humans*. New York: The Guilford Press.

Lichtenberg, J.D. (1983). *Psychoanalysis and infant research*. Hillsdale, NJ: The Analytic Press.

—— (1989). *Psychoanalysis and motivation*. Hillsdale, NJ: The Analytic Press.

Lorenz, K. (1963). *On aggression*. San Diego, CA: Harcourt and Brace Co.

Lutz, T. (1999). *Crying: the natural & cultural history of tears*. New York: W.W. Norton and Co.

Lynch, V.J. (1981). Basic Concepts. In H. Jackson. *Using self psychology in psychotherapy*, Lanham, MD: Jason Aronson Inc.

315

MacCord, K. (2014). Johann Friedrich Blumenbach (1752–1840). In *Embryo Project Encyclopedia*. Tempe, AZ: Arizona State University Center for Biology and Society.

Mahler, M.S.; Pine, F. & Bergman, A. (1975). *The psychological birth of the human infant: symbiosis and individuation*. New York: Basic Books.

Makari, G. (2015). *Soul machine: the invention of the modern mind*. New York: W.W. Norton and Co.

Mielicka-Pawowska, H. (2016). *Contemporary Homo Ludens*. New Castle upon Tyne, UK: Cambridge Scholars Publishing.

Middlemore, M.P. (1941) *The nursing couple*. London: Hamish Hamilton.

Milgram, S. (1974). *Obedience to authority: an experimental view*. New York: HarperCollins.

Miller, G.A. (1956). The magic number seven, plus or minus two: some limits to our capacity for processing information. *Psychological Review, 63*, 81–93.

Mitchell, J. (Ed.) (1986). *The selected Melanie Klein*. New York: The Free Press.

Mitchell, S. (1988). *Relational concepts in psychoanalysis: an integration*. Cambridge, MA: Harvard University Press.

—— (1997). *Influence and autonomy in psychoanalysis*. Hillsdale, NJ: Analytic Press.

—— (1998). Aggression and the endangered self. In R. Galler; D. Gould & J. Levy (1998). *Aggression Contemporary Controversies: Psychoanalytic Inquiry, 18*, 1. Hillsdale, NJ: Analytic Press.

Mitchell, S. & Black, M. J. (1995). *Freud and beyond*. New York: Basic Books.

Moravec, H. (1998). *Robot: mere machine to transcend mind*. Oxford: Oxford University Press.

Morrison, A.P. (Ed.). (1986). *Essential papers on narcissism*. New York: New York University Press.

Nelson, J. (2005). *Seeing through tears: crying and attachment*. London: Routledge.

Newell, A.; Shaw, J.C. & Simon, H.A. (1958). Elements of a theory of human problem solving. *Psychological Review, 65*, 151–166.

Newell, A. & Simon, H.A. (1972). *Human problem solving*. Hoboken, NJ: Prentice-Hall.

Nurse, P. (2020). *What is Life*. New York: W.W. Norton & Co.

Ornstein, A. (1998). The fate of narcissistic rage in psychotherapy. In R. Galler, D. Gould & J. Levy (1998). *Aggression Contemporary Controversies: Psychoanalytic Inquiry, 18*, 1. Hillsdale, NJ: Analytic Press.

Ornstein, P.H. (Ed.). (1978). *The search for the self: selected writings of Heinz Kohut, 1950–1978*. vols. 1–4. Madison, CT: International Universities Press.

Paccioni, J.P. (2002). Le terme "Trieb" et l'homme comme fin dernière et ultime. *Revue Germanique Internationale*. Retrieved from: http://rgi.revues.org/904

Packer, C. (2001). Infanticide Is No Fantasy. *American Anthropologist, 102*, 829-831.

———— & Pusey, A.E. (1984). Infanticide in carnivores. In Hausfaster & Hrdy, Eds, *Infanticide: Comparative and Evolutionary Perspectives*. New York: Aldine, 31–42

Parens, H. (1973). Aggression: a reconsideration. *Journal of the American Psychoanalytic Association, 21*, 34-60.

—— (1979). *The development of aggression in early childhood*. Lanham, MD: Jason Aronson.

Pfaff, D.W. (1999). *Drive: neurobiological and molecular mechanisms of sexual motivation*. Cambridge, MA: MIT Press.

—— (2006). *Brain arousal and information theory*. Cambridge, MA: Harvard University Press.

Palombo, S.R. (1978). *Dreaming and memory: a new information processing model*. New York: Basic Books.

Panksepp, J. (1998). *Affective neuroscience: the foundations of human and animal emotions*. Oxford: Oxford University Press.

Panksepp, J. & Biven, L. (2012). *The archaeology of mind: neuroevolutionary origins of human emotions*. New York: W.W. Norton and Co.

Pascal, B. (1954). *Pensées, oeuvres complètes.* Paris: Librairie Gallimard.

Pellegrini, A.D. (Ed.). (1995). *The future of play theory.* New York: State University of New York Press.

Pellegrini, A.D. & Smith, P.K. (2005). *The nature of play: great apes and humans.* New York: The Guilford Press.

Pellis, S.M. & Iwaniuk, A.N. (1999). The problem of adult play fighting: a comparative analysis of play and courtship in primates. *Ethology, 105,* 783–806.

—— (2000). Adult-adult play in primates: comparative analysis of its origin, distribution, and evolution. *Ethology, 106,* 1,083–1,104.

Person, E.S.; Cooper, A.M. & Gabbard, G.O. (Eds.) (2005). *Textbook of Psychoanalysis.* Arlington, VA: American Psychiatric Publishing.

Petzold, C. (1999). *Code: the hidden language of computer hardware and software.* Redmond, WA: Microsoft Press.

Pfaff, D.A. (1999). *Drive: neurobiological and molecular mechanisms of sexual motivation.* Cambridge, MA: The MIT Press.

—— (2006). *Brain arousal and information theory: neural and genetic mechanisms.* Cambridge, MA: Harvard University Press.

Phillips, A. (1993). *On kissing, tickling and being bored.* Cambridge, MA: Harvard University Press.

Piaget, J. (1962). *Plays, dreams, and imitation in childhood.* New York: W.W. Norton & Co. (Original work published 1951)

—— (1971). *Biology and knowledge.* Chicago: University of Chicago Press.

Piaget, J. & Cook, M.T. (1952). *The origins of intelligence in children.* New York: Basic Books.

Piaget, J. & Inhelder, B. (1969). *The psychology of the child.* New York: Basic Books.

Pine, F. (2005). Theories of motivation in psychoanalysis. In E.S. Person; A.M. Cooper. & G.O. Gabbard, (Eds.) (2005). *Textbook of Psychoanalysis.* Arlington, VA: American Psychiatric Publishing.

Popper, K. (1959). *The logic of scientific discoveries.* London: Routledge. (Original work published 1934)

—— (1957). *The poverty of historicism.* London: Routledge.

—— (1963). *Conjectures and refutations.* London: Routledge.

Power, T.G. (2000). *Play and exploration in children and animals.* Mahwah, NJ: Lawrence Erlbaum Associates.

Pribram, K.H. & Gill, M. (1976). *Freud's project re-assessed.* New York: Basic Books.

Rank, O. (1993). *The trauma of birth.* New York: Dover. (Original work published 1924)

—— (1935). *Truth and reality.* New York: W.W. Norton & Co. (Original work published 1929)

—— (1932). *Art and the artist: creative urge and personality development.* New York: W.W. Norton & Co.

Rapaport, D. (1942). *Emotions and memory.* The Menninger Clinic Monograph Series, 2. Baltimore, MD: Williams and Wilkins Co.

—— (1967). Book Review of Norbert Wiener Cybernetics. In M. Gill (Ed.) *The collected papers of David Rapaport.* New York: Basic Books. (Original work published 1950)

—— (1960). On the Psychoanalytic Theory of Motivation. In M. Gill (Ed.) *The collected papers of David Rapaport.* New York: Basic Books.

Rapaport, D. & Gill, M. (1959). The Points of View and Assumptions of Metapsychology. *International Journal of Psycho-Analysis, 40,* 153–162.

Rendell L. & H. Whitehead (2001). Culture in whales and dolphins. *Behavioral and Brain Sciences, 24,* 309–382.

Richards R.J. (2000). Kant and Blumenbach on the Bildungstrieb: a historical misunderstanding. *Studies in History and Philosophy of Biological and Biomedical Sciences, 31*(1), 11–32.

Rizzolatti, G.; Fogassi, L. & Gallese, V. (2001). Neurophysiological mechanisms underlying the understanding and imitation of action. *National Review of Neuroscience, 2,* 661–670.

Rizzolatti, G. & Graighero, L. (2004). The mirror-neuron system. *Annual Review of Neuroscience, 27,* 169–192.

Rubovits-Seitz, P. F. D. (1999). *Kohut's Freudian vision.* Hillsdale, NJ: The Analytic Press.

Sandler, J. (1960). The concept of superego. *Psychoanalytic Study of the Child, 15,* 128–162. Also in J. Sandler (1987). *From safety to superego: selected papers of Joseph Sandler.* London: Karnac Books.

—— (1981). Unconscious wishes and human relationships. *Contemporary Psychoanalysis, 17,* 180–195.

—— (1987). *From safety to superego: selected papers of Joseph Sandler.* London: Karnac Books.

—— (Ed.). (1987) *On Freud's Analysis Terminable and Interminable.* London: The International Psychoanalytical Association.

Sandler, J. & Joffe, W. (1965). The tendency to persistence in psychological function and development. In J. Sandler (1987). *From safety to superego: selected papers of Joseph Sandler.* London: Karnac Books.

Sandler, J. & Rosenblatt, B. (1962). The Representational World. *Psychoanalytic Study of the Child, 17,* 128–145. Also in J. Sandler (1987). *From safety to superego: selected papers of Joseph Sandler.* London: Karnac Books.

Schafer, R. (1960). The loving and beloved superego. *Psychoanalytic Study of the Child, 15,* 163–188.

Schiller, F. (2004). *On the aesthetic education of man.* Mineola, NY: Dover Publications. (Original work published 1795)

Seabright, P. (2004). *The company of strangers: a natural history of economic life.* Princeton, NJ: Princeton University Press.

Segal, H. (1974). *Introduction to the work of Melanie Klein.* New York: Basic Books.

Shannon, C. (1949). *The mathematical theory of communication.* Champaign, Illinois: University of Illinois Press.

Siegel, A.M. (1996). *Heinz Kohut and the psychology of the self.* London: Routledge.

Simon, H.A (1979). *Models of thought*. New Haven, CT: Yale University Press.

—— (1982). *Models of bounded rationality*. Cambridge, MA: The MIT Press.

Sinkewicz, R.E. (2003). *Evagrius of Pontus: The Greek Ascetic Corpus*. Oxford: Oxford University Press.

Smith, P.K. (2005). Social and pretend play in children. In A.D. Pellegrini & P.K. Smith (2005). *The nature of play: great apes and humans*. New York: The Guilford Press.

Smith, V. (2003). Constructivist and ecological rationality in economics. In T. Frängsmyr (Ed.). *The Nobel Prizes 2002*. Stockholm: Nobel Foundation. Retrieved from: www.nobelprize.org

Snell, R. (2004). Introduction. In F. Schiller (1795/2004). *On the aesthetic education of man*. Mineola, NY: Dover Publications.

Spencer, H. (1872). *Principles of psychology*. London: Williams and Norgate.

Spiegel, L.A. (1959). The self, the sense of self, and perception. *Psychoanalytic Study of the Child, 14*, 81–109.

Stechler, G.; Halton A. (1987). Emergence of assertion, aggression in infancy: systems approach. *Journal of the American Psychoanalytic Association, 35*, 821–838.

Stekel, W. (1924). Polyphonie des Denskens. *Fortschritte der Sexualwissenschaft und Psychanalyse, 1*, 1–16.

Stern, D.N. (1990). Joy and satisfaction in infancy. In R.A. Glick & A. Bone (1990). *Pleasure beyond the pleasure principle*. New Haven, CT: Yale University Press.

—— (2005). Intersubjectivity. In E.S. Person; A.M. Cooper. & G.O. Gabbard, (Eds.) (2005). *Textbook of psychoanalysis*. Arlington, VA: American Psychiatric Publishing.

—— (2010). *Forms of vitality*. Oxford: Oxford University Press.

Stolorow, R.D. (1975). Toward a functional definition of narcissism. *International Journal of Psychoanalysis, 56*, 179–185. Also in Morrison,

A.P. (Ed.). (1986). *Essential papers on narcissism*. New York: New York University Press.

—— (1976). Psychoanalytic reflections on client-centered therapy in the light of modern conception of narcissism. *Psychotherapy: Theory, Research and Practice, 13*, 26–29.

—— (1988). Integrating self psychology and classical psychoanalysis: an experience-near approach. In Goldberg, A. (Ed.). *Learning from Kohut: progress in self psychology*. New York: Routledge.

—— (2011). From mind to world, from drive to affectivity: a phenomenological-contextualist psychoanalytic perspective. In *Attachment: New Directions in Psychotherapy and Relational Psychoanalysis, 5*, 1–14.

Stolorow, R.D. & Atwood, G.E. (1976). An ego-psychological analysis of the work and life of Otto Rank in the light of modern conceptions of narcissism. *International Review of Psychoanalysis, 3*, 441–459.

Stone, L. (1951). Psychoanalysis and brief psychotherapy. *The Psychoanalytic Quarterly, 20*, 215–236.

Strachey, J. (1934). The nature of the therapeutic action of psycho-analysis, *International Journal of Psycho-Analysis, 15*, 127–159.

Strozier, C.B. (2001). *Heinz Kohut: the making of a psychoanalyst*. New York: Other Press.

Svendsen, L. (2005). *A philosophy of boredom*. Clerkenwell, UK: Reaktion Books.

Thagard, P. (2005). *Mind: introduction to cognitive science*. Cambridge, MA: The MIT Press.

Ticho, E. (1970). Differences between Psychoanalysis and Psychotherapy. *Bulletin of Menninger Clinic, 34*, 128–138.

Tomkins, S. (1963). *Affect, imagery, consciousness: the negative affect*. New York: Springer Publishing.

Toohey, P. (2011). *Boredom: a lively history*. New Haven, CT: Yale University Press.

Treurniet, N. (1980). On the self. *International Journal of Psychoanalysis, 61*, 325–333.

Van der Hart, O.; Friedman, B. (1989). A Readers Guide to Pierre Janet on Dissociation: A Neglected Intellectual Heritage. *Dissociation*, 2, p. 3-15.

Veblen, T. (1914). *The instinct of workmanship and the state of industrial arts. Whitefish*, Montana: Kessinger Publishing.

Von Neumann, J. (1958). *The computer and the brain*. New Haven, CT: Yale University Press.

Wadsworth, B.J. (2004). *Piaget's theory of cognitive and affective development: foundations of constructivism.* London: Longman Publishing.

Wälder, R. (1933). The psychoanalytic theory of play. *Psychoanalytic Quarterly*, 2, 208-224.

Wallerstein, R.S. (1988). One psychoanalysis or many? *International Journal of Psychoanalysis*, 69, 5-21. Also in A.C. Cooper (Ed.). (2006). *Contemporary psychoanalysis in America.* Arlington, VA: American Psychiatric Publishing Inc.

—— (2005). Outcome Research. In E.S. Person; A. M. Cooper & G.O. Gabbard (Eds.). (2005). *Textbook of Psychoanalysis.* Arlington, VA: American Psychiatric Publishing.

Walter, C. (2007). *Thumbs, toes, and tears.* New York: Walker & Company.

Weinberger, J.; Levy, K.N. (2005). Psychology. E.S. Person; A.M. Cooper & G.O. Gabbard (Eds.). (2005). *Textbook of Psychoanalysis.* Arlington, VA: American Psychiatric Publishing.

Wemelsfelder, F. (2005). Animal Boredom: Understanding the Tedium of their Lives. In *Mental Health and Well-being in Animals*, Arlington, VA: Blackwell Publishing.

Wenzel, S. (2003). *The sin of sloth: 'acedia' in medieval thought and literature.* Chapel Hill. NC: University of North Carolina Press.

Widlocker, D. (1985). The Wish for Identification and Structural Effects in the Work of Freud. *International Journal of Psychoanalysis*, 6, 31-46.

Wiener, N. (1948). *Cybernetics: or control and communication in the animal and the machine.* Cambridge, MA: The MIT Press.

Winnicott, D.W. (1949). Mind and its relation to the psyche-soma. *Through pediatrics to psychoanalysis: collected papers.* London: Routledge.

—— (1953). Transitional objects and transitional phenomena. *International Journal of Psychoanalysis, 34,* 89–97. Also in D.W. Winnicott. (1971). *Playing and reality,* London: Brunner-Routledge.

—— (1958). The capacity to be alone. *International Journal of Psychoanalysis, 39,* 416–420. Also in D.W. Winnicott. (1965). *The maturational process and the facilitating environment.* Madison, CT: International Universities Press.

—— (1959). Classification: is there a psychoanalytic contribution to psychiatric classification? In D.W. Winnicott. (1965). *The maturational process and the facilitating environment.* Madison, CT: International Universities Press.

—— (1960). Ego distortions in terms of true and false self. In D.W. Winnicott (1965). *The maturational process and the facilitating environment.* Madison, CT: International Universities Press.

—— (1971). *Playing and reality. London:* New York: Brunner-Routledge.

—— (1986). *Home is where we start from: essays by a psychoanalyst.* New York: W. W. Norton.

—— (1988). *Human nature.* New York: Schocken Books.

Wolff, P.H. (1969). The natural history of crying and other vocalizations in early infancy. In B. Foss (Ed.) (1969). *Determinants of Infant Behavior.* New York: Barnes and Noble, 81–109.